Privacy

Privacy

Concealing the Eighteenth-Century Self

PATRICIA MEYER SPACKS

The University of Chicago Press
Chicago and London

Patricia Meyer Spacks is the Edgar F. Shannon Professor of English at the University of Virginia. She is the author of eleven books, including *Desire and Truth: Functions of Plot in Eighteenth-Century English Novels* and *Boredom: The Literary History of a State of Mind*, both published by the University of Chicago Press.

The University of Chicago Press, Chicago 60637
The University of Chicago Press, Ltd., London
© 2003 by The University of Chicago
All rights reserved. Published 2003
Printed in the United States of America

12 11 10 09 08 07 06 05 04 03   1 2 3 4 5

ISBN: 0–226–76860–0 (cloth)

Library of Congress Cataloging-in-Publication Data
Spacks, Patricia Ann Meyer.
  Privacy : concealing the eighteenth-century self / Patricia Meyer Spacks.
    p. cm.
  Includes bibliographical references (p.) and index.
  ISBN: 0–226–76860–0 (cloth : alk. paper)
    1. English fiction—18th century—History and criticism. 2. Privacy in literature. 3. Secrecy in literature. 4. Self in literature. I. Title.
  PR858.P72 S67 2003
  823'.509353—dc21

                                        2002152993

♾ The paper used in this publication meets the minimum requirements of the American National Standard for Information Sciences—Permanence of Paper for Printed Library Materials, ANSI Z39.48–1992.

Contents

Acknowledgments   vii

1 | *Privacies*   1
2 | *Privacies of Reading*   27
3 | *The Performance of Sensibility*   55
4 | *Privacy, Dissimulation, and Propriety*   87
5 | *Private Conversations*   115
6 | *Exposures: Sex, Privacy, and Sensibility*   140
7 | *Trivial Pursuits*   167
8 | *Privacy as Enablement*   196

Afterword   223
Works Cited   229
Index   237

Acknowledgments

One of the pleasures of writing a book is talking with others as the manuscript takes shape. As always, I have profited greatly from conversation. Those whose reactions, insights, and comments proved especially valuable include Myra Jehlen, Deborah Kaplan, William Kates, Jerome McGann, Steven Marcus, Adrienne Munich, Bruce Redford, Margery Sabin, and Aubrey Williams, as well as many graduate students with whom I have worked at the University of Virginia. I feel particular gratitude to those who have read and commented on portions of the manuscript at various stages of its development: Deborah Kaplan, Steven Marcus, Adrienne Munich, and Margery Sabin. I am also indebted to the American Academy of Arts and Sciences, which provided me with a splendid working environment during my semester as a Visiting Fellow in the Humanities.

A section of chapter 4 appeared in "Privacy, Dissimulation, and Propriety: Frances Burney and Jane Austen," in *Eighteenth-Century Fiction* 12, no. 4 (2000): 515–31.

I | *Privacies*

The opposition between public and private, in most formulations, involves a distinction between large and limited arenas—between domestic and national politics, for example, or between the domestic and the civic. The competition thus implied, however, tells us little about privacy, which typically concerns the personal rather than the domestic. Indeed, privacy can ally itself with the "public" side of the public/private dichotomy by its frequent opposition to the domestic: the housewife wants privacy specifically to get away from her family for a time, and from her family responsibilities. Her very capacity to imagine "privacy" depends partly on social class. If significant public functioning, except as a problem for others, seldom belongs to the bottom classes, their lives, though "private," rarely enable physical privacy.

At the beginning of the twenty-first century, privacy figures almost obsessively in the media and inhabits an important place in national consciousness. My favorite symptom: I've noticed recently that in upscale hotels the tags that you put on your door to keep the maid from bothering you no longer read "Do Not Disturb." Instead, they say "Privacy Please." Condensing the force of a negative imperative into a single powerful noun that needs no verb, the new phrase suggests repudiation, rejection of other people, a Greta Garbo stance: I want to be alone. It eliminates the idea of disturbance, some local and limited interference with serenity or pleasure, only to indicate more categorical exclusion of everyone and everything outside the door. The nominally more polite formulation ("Please") in fact conveys greater insistence and a more determined will to be left alone. "Do Not Disturb" hints a desire for noninterference with some specific activity (sleeping, going through papers) for some limited space of time. "Privacy Please" imparts a wish for fundamental separation.

The word *privacy*, by way of its adjectival form, derives from a Latin word meaning *deprived:* specifically, deprived of public office; in other words, cut off from the full and appropriate functioning of a man. What originally designated a state of deprivation, however, has come, in the Western middle-class world, to refer to a condition alleged by some in the United States to be a constitutional right, a privileged condition of freedom and control. Indeed, one commentator differentiates privacy from "alienation, loneliness, ostracism, and isolation" precisely on the basis of its self-evident desirability: "alienation is suffered, loneliness is dreaded, ostracism and isolation are borne with resignation or panic, while privacy is sought after" (Weinstein 88).

The catalogue of the Harvard University libraries provides 1,384 entries under the heading "Privacy." An enormous preponderance of them— entries 75 through 1,384—cluster beneath the rubric "Privacy, Right of," a rubric mainly subdivided geographically: "Privacy, Right of—Lichtenstein," "Privacy, Right of—Manitoba." What our forebears considered a danger, we assume as our due; those signs on the door demand something that we feel entitled to. That fact in itself suggests our distance from an earlier ideal of communal responsibility and support.

Yet the situation is more complicated than this single piece of data might suggest. I hardly need mention the enormous contradictions that attend current attitudes toward privacy, or the wide range of issues now evoked by the concept. Journalistic media stimulate anxiety about the possibility that Internet circulation of data may damage our privacy. We reject past customs of housing extended families under a single roof in favor of nuclear families, detached dwellings, a separate bedroom for every child. The richer we are, the more likely we are to seek walled enclaves for our homes and secluded Caribbean beaches for our vacations. In other words, we want our privacy. On the other hand, a man who used to work for a newsmagazine told me that people yearn so deeply to appear on television—to have attention paid to them—that if you stick a microphone at them just after they've lost a child, they eagerly talk into it. A large audience appears to exist for twenty-four-hour-a-day filming of random individuals' intimate lives. We watch Oprah and Geraldo, we share our sexual problems with pop psychologists on the radio, we consider a television appearance on *Good Morning America* a mark of success.

That *we*, of course, is slippery. I myself don't watch Oprah, and neither do a lot of other people, although millions do. I have refused opportunities to appear on television. I've never set foot on a Caribbean beach, I find walled enclaves distasteful, and I am not unique. But if *we* can designate the culture at large, my sketch indeed suggests a set of contradictions that we all inhabit in one way or another. Social class presumably makes a difference in our specific attitudes as well as our possibilities for possessing privacy, and so do the values of our families and our communities—which is to say we all have our own assemblages of contradictions. Each of us establishes individual boundaries of privacy; each of us may willingly, even happily abandon privacy in different specific contexts. In practice, then, privacy carries in modern Western culture no fixed assignment of value. Sometimes we want the state it designates, sometimes we don't.

Or perhaps one should say, rather, that privacy, in our culture, carries with it the notion of choice. If privacy is not an incontrovertible right, it is an uncontestable privilege, and part of that privilege consists in the exercise of control over access to personal material. To talk to a reporter if one feels like it, to live behind a wall, to tell all to Oprah—such are the opportunities of a society that makes privacy possible. It is the absence of choice, perhaps, that exercises people so much about the prospect of governmental spying, of prying into our e-mail, of medical records exposed to unwanted view. A great many of the books cited in the Harvard catalogue concern just such matters.

As an abstract idea, privacy in our culture unquestionably possesses a powerful positive valence. Even those who find every microphone, every camera, appealing might claim to value their privacy—and might indeed value it in certain contexts. If England was indeed "the birthplace of privacy" (Ariès 5), the United States became its nursery, providing a social environment in which to cherish the idea more than the actuality of every individual's unalienable right to control over personal space. Legal and philosophic definitions of the word (some of which will appear later in my discussion) become ever more momentous, as the notion of privacy develops from a simple concept of being left alone into a way of condensing ideas about autonomy and integrity.

Privacy, I should emphasize once more, has relatively little to do with the much-debated split between "public" and "private." It has become received wisdom that the eighteenth century saw the creation of a new kind of public sphere, a newly defined division between private and public concerns, although much uncertainty remains about the definition of terms and the precise timing of events. Learned journals devote issues to the eighteenth-century "public," or to the nature of the private-public debate. Most scholars believe, at the very least, after several decades of controversy, that the concepts of public and private bear historical significance and that their nexus in the eighteenth century warrants special investigation.

The term *privacy* has received much less historicized attention, despite its ubiquity in current media discussion. The debate about private versus public of course bears on privacy, but the "private life" does not necessarily entail privacy (as Charlotte Perkins Gilman, for one, long ago pointed out), despite the fact that the noun derives etymologically from the adjective. Discussions of "private" versus "public" characteristically concern the operations of the state, the relation between members of the state in their communal and their individual functioning. The subject of privacy, in contrast, especially if considered historically, often demands focus on the ways people expose and guard themselves in relation to limited numbers of others. Within the private life—the life of people operating in the family, or in relatively small communities of friends—many forces impinge on the privacy of individuals, their capacity to protect themselves from other people's desire to know about them or to insist on their participation in social activity. As Gilman puts it, "Such privacy as we do have in our homes is family privacy, an aggregate privacy; and this does not insure—indeed, it prevents—individual privacy" (258). The dynamic of retreat and self-protection, as it was represented in the eighteenth century, provides the subject of this book.

Jürgen Habermas's seminal formulation of the modern relation between public and private exemplifies the way in which what might be called the third term of privacy gets elided in discussion. Initially, he ignores the subject, defining his key concept of the "bourgeois public sphere" without reference to privacy: "The bourgeois public sphere may be conceived above all as the sphere of private people come together as a public; they soon claimed the public sphere regulated from above against the public authorities themselves, to engage them in a debate over the general rules governing relations in the basically privatized but publicly relevant sphere of commodity exchange and social labor" (27). The precursor to this development, Habermas goes on to say, involved "a public sphere in apolitical form." By this, he apparently means that individual self-contemplation prepared the way for the assumption of power. This apolitical sphere "provided the training ground for a critical public reflection still preoccupied with itself—a process of self-clarification of private people focusing on the genuine experiences of their novel privateness" (29). Now Habermas involves privacy (I assume the equivalence of "privateness" and "privacy") in his public-private distinction, claiming the experience of privacy as a vital precursor to the development of a new public. He argues that the all-male coffeehouse society of eighteenth-century Britain contributed to the evolution of a self-aware public, but he claims also that the conjugal family, with its "self-image of its intimate sphere," served as an important "agency of society," especially in mediating the "strict conformity with societally necessary requirements" that the larger public required (47).

To value the state of privacy as a precursor to public functioning of course makes it only a means to a dramatically different end. Moreover, it elides the important differences between the person operating in privacy and one acting even within the limited sphere of the family. If the family, and those performing within it, serve as agents of society and encourage social conformity, no such claim could readily be made about the person secure within his or her privacy. Privacy can provide a venue for "self-clarification," but perhaps little encouragement for "strict conformity." Although Foucault and his successors have abundantly demonstrated how internalized principle polices private consciousness, it remains conceivable that the individual in privacy might at least explore some marginal realm of personally rather than publicly ordained standards. The relation between privacy and society, thus far largely unexamined, proves intricate: so literary discussions of that relation, devious and indirect though they often are, suggest. Although the state of privacy implies at least temporary self-sufficiency, it may involve diverse forms of dependence on the public sphere.

To look at the idea of privacy in an earlier stage of its development reveals, unsurprisingly, differences from our own situation as well as similarities to it. The debate over privacy in eighteenth-century Britain often took covert forms. Psychological privacy, rather than its physical counterpart, attracted the most insistent attention. Discussion did not begin from the premise that privacy was at least theoretically a good; its social disadvantages arguably outweighed its individual attraction. Privacy presented, many thought, clear and present dangers both to the social order and to vulnerable persons (women, the young) within that order. As a psychological possibility, it appeared to encourage hypocrisy, a major focus of anxiety in the period: people might employ masks of various kinds in order to retain control of secret thoughts, feelings, and imaginings. Possibly connected with secrecy and with performance, as well as with seclusion, the very idea of privacy could arouse fear.

All of which is not to say that individuals failed to seek privacy, or to value it. This was a period in which curiosity (as well as curiosities) played an important role (see Benedict). Inasmuch as curiosity operated on a personal level, it encouraged penetration into feelings and events that persons might prefer to conceal. Adding to the constraints of widely shared physical space, the efforts of individuals to violate psychic space must have felt like an enormous imposition. Textual evidence suggests that the matter loomed large for women, whose conventional lives deprived them in particular of opportunity for physical isolation. By late in the century, the poet William Cowper could declare at length the importance of privacy to his poetic and moral achievement. Diarists throughout the century left indications of their concern for the matter. Samuel Richardson's earliest novels could not exist without the idea and the imagined actuality of both physical and psychological privacy.

To look at textual records and registers of privacy holds particular interest because of the dual valence of writing for publication. Both the writer and the reader function simultaneously in privacy and as members of a community. The writer writes alone, in seclusion, but with awareness of an audience and within a historical and contemporaneous community of other writers. The solitary reader bears a similar metaphorical relation to a community of readers and exists in relationship—often affectionate, hostile, or both—with the writer. Readers and writers therefore inevitably know, at some level of consciousness, something about the complexities of privacy. Those complexities emerge vividly in the important literary genres of eighteenth-century Britain.

Eighteenth-century England did not originate the concept of privacy, but the evidence indicates a new level of attention to it during the period. Such evidence includes architectural history, which obviously bears on questions of physical privacy. Mark Girouard points out the "growing feeling for privacy which became noticeable in the seventeenth century. Households in the old style had the disadvantages of all tightly-knit communities. Everyone knew what everyone else was doing, and quarrels and intrigues were endemic right across the hierarchy. As soon as families began to value their privacy they inevitably started to escape from their servants" (11). Habermas likewise observes, speaking specifically of Great Britain, that "the privatization of life can be observed in change in architectural style" (44). The "revolutionary invention" (Girouard 138) of back stairs, a late-seventeenth-century development, definitively separated servants from masters. Previously, the great hall had provided a center for social activity and a gathering place for servants, guests, dependents, and petitioners, as well as the family. Now, gradually, various kinds of activity became divided from one another.

Girouard warns that "it would be a mistake to see country-house history in terms of greater and greater privacy." He comments on the "growing sociability" of country families and observes that "Privacy was perhaps at its greatest in the early eighteenth century, when servants had been moved out of the way, and individuals among both family and guests enjoyed the security of private apartments, each containing two or even three rooms" (11). Christopher Hussey, however, observes that such apartments, strung out along a single axis, often supplied the only means of passage to other parts of the house (21): they might be "private," in other words, but they did not necessarily provide privacy. Not until interior halls became commonplace, a development later in the eighteenth century, did the great houses offer dependable separation of individuals from one another.

Few people, of course, have ever inhabited great country houses. But what happened in the upper reaches of society suggests a shifting consciousness that would gradually permeate other social levels sufficiently prosperous to have the luxury of choice in matters of privacy. Toward the end of the seventeenth century, Pepys reported on his "very fine close stool"—which occupied his drawing room (Wright 76). In seventeenth-century France, the "Royal Stool" "played an official role. Kings, princes and even generals treated it as a throne at which audiences could be granted" (Wright 102). A hundred years later, human excretion occurred mainly in solitude. Something had changed radically.

Yet I do not mean to imply a steady, straightforward progress toward privacy. That would make a far less compelling story than the one I want to tell, which is above all a story of ambivalence and ambiguity. If textual evidence suggests that the possibility of psychological privacy presented a vexing social and moral issue for many eighteenth-century thinkers, the implications of that issue's discussions extend to physical privacy as well. Privacy, whatever its definition, always implies at least temporary separation from the social body. To seek or advocate it therefore entailed a degree of threat to the values of a society still hierarchical and still retaining ideas about the importance of the communal.

It remains something of a surprise to me that this book has turned out to concern itself primarily with what I've been calling "psychological privacy": the kind of privacy that entails self-protection of a sort not immediately visible to others. At the outset, I intended to write about physical privacy, assuming that literary discussion of the subject would accompany architectural evidence of its increasing importance. But it turns out that, after Richardson (whose treatment of privacy has attracted previous critics), few writers in letters, diaries, autobiographies, or fiction concern themselves significantly with the subject. Perhaps they assume the impossibility of physical privacy; perhaps they feel no need for it; perhaps they consider it a matter too trivial for discussion. In contrast, the matter of psychological privacy comes up everywhere—not necessarily (indeed, rather rarely) with reference to the word, but as a problem both social and personal. The topic generates anxiety about the degree to which social prescriptions should control individual lives and ingenuity about ways to avoid the restrictiveness of convention. It encourages reflection about the value of isolation and worry about the difficulty of controlling those who internally absent themselves.

In 1977, Richard Sennett published *The Fall of Public Man*, deploring the modern decline in civic responsibility. The book describes what Sennett considers a peculiarly modern—that is, twentieth-century—notion of privacy, in contrast to its Roman equivalent, which involved "a principle based on religious transcendence." "In private," Sennett writes, "we seek out not a principle but a reflection, that of what our psyches are, what is authentic in our feelings. We have tried to make the fact of being in privacy, alone with ourselves and with family and intimate friends, an end in itself" (4). No evidence indicates that eighteenth-century thinkers considered privacy an end in itself. But the idea of privacy as authenticity, as a space of self-discovery, proves intensely relevant to the meditations of poets, fictional characters, and diarists of this earlier period. Indeed, one might reformulate the eighteenth-century concern with what I have been calling "psychological privacy" as an effort to discern, comprehend, and properly place the individual reflection of the authentic.

Privacy is above all an imaginative category. If a remarkable act of imagination was required to conceive of back stairs, figuring out how to use the new possibilities of new architecture demanded comparable imaginative force. The kind of privacy at issue in this study, privacy of the mind and heart, depends yet more obviously on particular modes of self-imagining and of imagining the other. The connection between the increasing individualism of the eighteenth century and intensifying stress on privacy is obvious enough. But the development of individualism for individuals can be a tortuous matter in a society that assumes the primacy of family interests and the importance of community. Privacy marks a point of tension between individual and societal values. Investigation of that tension, the subject of this book, entails looking into records of imaginative energy focused on selves conceived as set apart, at least temporarily, from their kind. And set apart by choice: a crucial fact. The choosers, however, rarely imagined their condition of willed separation as permanent. Cowper, writing late in the century, is unusual in conceiving his privacy as an enduring state. For most who wrote about the matter, privacy comprised a breathing space, a kind of time-out from social pressure.

John Richetti, considering the relevance of Habermas's argument to the actual production of eighteenth-century English novelists, has argued that the evocations of life in fiction do not support Habermas's view. Richetti points out that in the course of defining the new kind of bourgeois "public" that developed in the eighteenth century, Habermas "always returns to what underlies and guarantees the public sphere: the so-called intimate sphere of private and domestic experience whereby those who meet in public acquire their subjective autonomy that makes them qualified to speak in public. The new, or at least newly conceived, privileges of privacy and domestic autonomy create the conditions that make the public sphere possible" (116). Considering this view in relation to the novels produced in the period, Richetti suggests that novelists typically imagine their characters as exceptions to social rules. The private realm, opposed to the corrupt public, is in fiction "the home of the good." And novelistic renditions "represent negotiations for identity and the material possessions that enforce it as political in a thickly local and specific historical sense that Habermas' scheme simplifies or even ignores" (116). Looking especially at *Roxana* and *Humphry Clinker*, Richetti concludes that "the novel in the course of the century becomes a voracious form in which other kinds of discourse, some of them resembling what Habermas associates with public political and economic debate, are appropriated or radically subordinated to that representation of self-expressive consciousness that we call the novel" (122). Novels operate both within and against the public sphere, generating their own kind of reality.

Well, yes. It is hardly a surprise that novelists imagine the world in terms different from, and partly opposed to, those of a philosopher. Or perhaps the point is that literary critics are likely to read in different ways from philosophers. But I think Richetti implies a crucial insight here, about precisely how novelists' imaginings of privacy differ from Habermas's. As Richetti rightly explains, Habermas considers that the "privileges of privacy . . . make the public sphere possible." Analysis of novels, however, calls attention to the fact that the "privileges of privacy" can work in quite different ways. Roxana's brooding about her life includes political perceptions about her situation as a woman, but it enables no entry into a wider sphere: on the contrary. The imagining of privacy in experiential terms produces consequences quite different from those of what one might call theoretical imaginings of privacy.

Eighteenth-century discussions of reading, both allusions within works of fiction and avowedly moralistic commentary, indicate uncertainty and concern about the consequences of reading even in relative privacy. They provide a case history of anxieties implicit in imagining the Other as existing in privacy. Before the great spread of literacy in the eighteenth century, communal reading aloud was a widespread activity. Reading aloud continued, of course, but increasing numbers of people found it possible to read to themselves, to read alone. Writers and narrators might express hope or faith that their readers nonetheless participated in an imaginative and moral community that, though unseen, could exercise normative force on an individual reader's consciousness. Or they might register excitement at the challenge of readers who felt and judged for themselves. Such feeling and judgment could best take place without witnesses. But the possibility of feeling and thinking without witnesses readily evoked danger. Especially when commentators imagined young people or women reading alone, reading in privacy, they often imagined dark contingencies: uncontrolled, uncontrollable fantasies leading inevitably to disaster. Only the network of voluntary spies that Austen evokes in *Northanger Abbey* protects the culture against the unruliness of unleashed imaginations, imaginations that might be stimulated by solitary reading. Reading was vicarious experience, which could only be undergone by individuals. But experience needed rationing, especially for female consumption: so, apparently, many thinkers believed.

The kind of vicarious experience generally considered most dangerous involved the imagining of other people's privacies—the subject matter of the evolving novel and, in a narrower sense, of the widely popular genre of romance. Romances concerned love, as moralist after moralist pointed out with professed or genuine alarm, and presumably encouraged their female readers in particular to think romantic love the most important, the most definitive, of emotions. Novels created a larger and more indeterminate sphere of danger as they contemplated the inner lives of their characters. Pamela and Clarissa, from the century's first half, both thought a great deal about love, but also about other things: about families, about social class, even about appropriate standards for judging men. An increase in what one might call interior independence, or at least an increase in the capacity to imagine its possibilities, might result for women reading fictions with such protagonists. The novel's implicit valuation of mental privacy could therefore entail real-world consequences.

Fiction thus supplied raw material for the concealed debate over privacy that continued in various forms through the century. The growing emphasis on "sensibility" in the novel calls attention to further perplexities of privacy as an issue. Preoccupation with sensibility both links the eighteenth century to the Romantic period and marks the earlier period's difference. By the early nineteenth century, concern with privacy had largely yielded to a desire for solitude less openly and directly tied to complex awareness of social actualities. The Romantics often aggressively rejected the society of their day, and they did not appear to care about that society's expectations in the way that even someone so reclusive as Cowper did. The cult of sensibility, as recent scholarship has revealed, responded directly to contemporaneous developments in economics and medicine. Although sensibility can seem at a distance in time only sentimental posturing, it has now become apparent that it had complicated social meanings. Often a target of mockery, as well as of celebration (Laurence Sterne, notoriously, combined the two), sensibility provided a way of organizing and of valuing feeling. Novels from midcentury on frequently insisted on it as a marker for the good woman; increasingly, for the good man as well. Clarissa was a woman of sensibility; her friend's suitor Hickman exemplified the man of sensibility, as, in some of his aspects, did Lovelace's friend Belford and on occasion even Lovelace himself, for all his heartlessness. If Jane Austen's character Wickham, in *Sense and Sensibility*, like his beloved Marianne, suggests the possible meretriciousness of sensibility, such figures as Fanny Price, in *Mansfield Park*, imply high valuation of the capacity for responsive feeling associated with the quality.

The connection between sensibility and privacy depends on the general eighteenth-century conviction that sensibility entails display on the body of the heart's deepest feelings. Sensibility thus would exist in opposition to privacy, making privacy in emotional matters impossible for the sensitive. Yet, as itself a mode of display, sensibility lends itself also to deception. Its manifestations are never unambiguous: if they express emotion, they do not explain its causes. Frances Burney focused with particular deftness on the incalculable consequences of feeling ambiguously revealed, its revelations carefully watched by observers whose interpretations depend more on their own natures than on what they behold. Although the word *privacy* does not recur in discussions of sensibility, those discussions frequently betray anxiety about what sensibility conceals as well as what it reveals. Concealment constitutes both the individual appeal and the social danger of psychological privacy.

At the opposite extreme from sensibility on a continuum of cultural practices, eighteenth-century emphasis on social decorum also entwines itself with problems of privacy. Eighteenth-century sensibility resembles nineteenth-century hysteria in its apparent ubiquity, uncontrollability, and symptomatic force. Like sensibility, hysteria registers feelings on the body. The definitive difference between the two depends on their different relation to social mandates. Sensibility, socially reinforced, expresses a philosophically sanctioned ideal of sensitive feelings that lead to benevolent action. Although its manifestations most readily associate themselves with women, men of sensibility might also be admired. Hysteria perhaps conforms equally well to its period's expectations for women, but society does not overtly sanction it; nor does it seem to have presented itself often as a male symptom. The emotions it conveys have been repressed, in accordance with the demands of decorum. The emotions of sensibility, in contrast, are generally assumed to be those of which the world at large approves: sympathy, pity, delicacy, modesty, tenderness. The woman of sensibility, like her male counterpart, both feels and expresses feeling in socially accepted ways. The hysterical woman demonstrates her lack of intellectual discipline, her inevitable inferiority to men. But both declare emotion uncontainable.

Eighteenth-century good manners, in contrast, proclaim their possessor's self-control. If concealment in itself amounts to a form of privacy, sometimes the only available form, the importance of propriety is manifest: ready-made concealment. Conduct books of the period recommend good manners as a way to cover up base impulses, but they also betray anxiety about the perception that manners may provide an impenetrable screen for unacceptable thoughts, feelings, and intentions. Burney shows her expertise with this subject too, making it clear that manners provide an important resource, especially for women, whose possibilities for self-concealment might seem as limited as their opportunities for free self-expression, given their existence under constant social surveillance. As Austen's Elinor Dashwood fully demonstrates, decorum creates a socially acceptable, and often convenient, form of privacy.

To employ etiquette as a device for self-concealment turns social convention to personal ends. Similarly, the practices of social conversation, as textually rendered, can open up possibilities for individual privacy. Still thought of as a form of performance for which successful practitioners must train themselves, conversation afforded many opportunities for self-concealment. Like personal letters, conversation might on occasion purport to reveal the heart, but—also like letters—it more often constructed a social mask. The principles of good manners of course governed polite conversation, so this subject overlaps with its predecessor. Yet the widespread presence of hypocrisy in social converse concerned commentators both before and after Swift.

The ubiquitous worry about hypocrisy—moral sin but perhaps social necessity—throughout the eighteenth century calls attention to the fundamental matter of privacy. Hypocrisy, a form of public performance, deliberately attempts to obfuscate a person's true intent. Its possibility exists everywhere. Moralists inveighed against it, despite the fact that their instructions to young women often recommended something very like it. Parents warned their children, both male and female, of its widespread presence in social life. Young people had to learn to penetrate the masks of others, but also to construct their own protective coverings. And the point holds also for privacy in a larger sense: everyone needed some measure of it; everyone might worry about what other people's privacies made inaccessible.

Suspicion of erotic fantasies and erotic actualities somewhere unknown hovered about the subject of hypocrisy, as about reading and sensibility as topics of discussion. The idea of privacy always carries about it some aura of the erotic. Those "Privacy Please" signs on the outside of a door suggest the possibility of couples at play inside the rooms they protect; the impeccable politeness of the well-bred young woman allows the viewer to construct wild hypotheses about what's going on within her head and heart. So the subject of pornography becomes closely implicated with that of privacy. The inconsistencies of our own historical period—the enormous interest in the sex lives of the rich and famous combined with protectiveness about our e-mail—had their prelude in the late eighteenth century, when scandalous reports of upper-class adulteries abounded in the press while many members of the higher social strata resolutely preserved their concealing decorums. The appeal of pornography depends partly on its illusion of revealing what conventionally remains hidden. Pornography flourished during the eighteenth century, but it was mostly imported into England. A more typical British genre was the first-person narrative, fictional or factual, that skirted sexual explicitness, characteristically promising more shocking material than it actually delivered. Works in this mode held obvious appeal for a wide audience. Their special interest in relation to privacy derives from the fact that they appear to violate the privacy of their writers (literal or fictional), telling exactly the kind of story most people wish to conceal about themselves. Yet one may wonder whether self-violation of privacy is possible or a contradiction in terms. Do the boundaries of privacy shift with genre, or does the fact of personal choice in the matter change the paradigm? Another way of putting the same question might focus on how writers guard their own privacy while appearing to reveal intimate detail. Perhaps the preservation of privacy as a mode of self-protection depends less on the nature than on the tactics of revelation.

To read diaries from the past may enlarge the concept of what private disclosure entails. Boswell's journals perhaps come to mind first when one thinks of eighteenth-century diaries; their material notoriously includes considerable sexual revelation, the conventional stuff of privacy. More surprising from a literary point of view, though perhaps not at all surprising when we think about our own lives: some diaries, even diaries written in cipher, hence ostensibly not available to any eye other than the writer's, dwell on relentlessly trivial data from experience. And they too may attract wide audiences when published. Perhaps readers want reassurance about the inherent interest of their own lives. Perhaps, alternatively, they want assurance that the happenings of others' days and years hold no more excitement than their own. At any rate, such records raise questions about what, exactly, privacy protects. The conventional notion that it guards against revelation of the scandalous or of intimate details about such matters as sex, finances, and illness fails to acknowledge the probability that people zealously protect also the privacy of their lives' monotony and the privacy of their obsessive concern with the events or nonevents defining that monotony. The transformation of the trivial into the significant marks one achievement of the realistic novel. Diaries often accomplish the same end by strikingly different means.

The assumption that privacy protects implies a specific view of what the concept means. Much eighteenth-century fiction (again, especially fiction about women) relies on just this view: women in particular, as rendered in fiction, feel the need to defend their feelings against the metaphoric gaze of the social world or that of a would-be or prospective lover. But if privacy implies freedom *from*—from watchers, judges, gossips, sensation-seekers—it also connotes freedom *to:* to explore possibilities without fear of external censure. Privacy can constitute a form of enablement. Eighteenth-century writers explored this eventuality too, especially in the final quarter-century. Cowper provides a particularly useful case in point, becoming a productive poet, by his own account, despite crippling psychosis, specifically because his circumstances made it possible for him to choose privacy, both physical and psychological, as a condition of life. That privacy turns into a central subject of his poetry. More crucial to his poetic effects: the tension it creates, between a sense of social responsibility and a desire for seclusion, accounts for much of the sometimes bewildering tonal and substantive movement of *The Task*—between vituperation and celebration, for instance; or between the evils of card playing and the pleasures of cucumber raising.

The issues I have sketched—the relation of privacy to reading, to sensibility, to propriety, to conversation, to scandalous narrative, to diaries filled with trivia, and to a personal sense of enablement—organize the present account. Each subject provides a different angle of vision for the misty large topic of privacy; each subject thus helps to clarify different aspects of a problem. They do not add up to a systematic history. Rather, they allow for a series of speculations. Individual chapters will explore each topic by analyzing textual instances. Together, the chapters engage with several literary genres. The tangle of ideas and feelings associated with the not-yet-fully-defined subject of privacy in the eighteenth century should unwind a bit as a result. Such a tangle, however, will not yield a single strand of meaning. The tangle itself is the subject: the intertwined, sometimes contradictory attitudes and emotions aroused by reflection on the subject of privacy in a time when, a place where, privacy had no legal status and in which its social meanings remained ambiguous and confused. Privacy might imply hiding, secrecy, hypocrisy, hence untrustworthiness, danger, potential subversion. Or it could enable dignity and proper concern for others. It might represent a way of preserving threatened selfhood or a state of self-humiliation. (I think, for instance, of a diarist who obsessively worries about the possibility that he has bad breath.) It could deny and refuse communication or hint messages that could not be openly conveyed. All these modes, and others, emerge openly or covertly in the period's writing.

To tease out the subject of privacy in a varied body of eighteenth-century literature also illuminates the texts itself. Such an investigation helps to clarify just what it might mean in specific terms to connect the rise of the novel to that of individualism and suggests ways that developing individualism may have affected other literary genres as well. Looking carefully at privacy as an issue uncovers case histories of how imaginative writers used their craft as a way of pondering psychological and social issues and reveals subtleties of observation and insight. It calls attention to thematic connections among works in various genres. It elucidates understudied aspects of individual writers' accomplishment, demonstrating, for example, how Cowper's discussions of social ills relate to his preoccupation with the natural world. And it provides fresh ways of investigating such familiar subjects as Fielding's addresses to the reader in *Tom Jones*.

The possibilities become clearer as one examines a specific text: *Clarissa*, for instance, to which I have already referred, a novel energized by its intricate dynamic of privacy and publicity and richly revelatory of privacy's ambiguities. The novel's first letter, from Anna Howe, calls attention to privacy as a desirable state, attainable only with difficulty. Clarissa, Anna emphasizes, has always been "desirous . . . of sliding through life to the end of it unnoted" (1:2). Now, though, because of the duel between her brother and her would-be lover, "Every eye . . . is upon" her (1:3). Anna wants a full account of Clarissa's past and present situation to offer for justification— in other words, to publicize. Through no fault of her own, Clarissa appears to have lost the right to privacy.

At first reading, Anna's request for information may seem a rather clumsy narrative device, a pretext for providing necessary knowledge to the reader. But it inaugurates a novel that dwells obsessively on the tensions the request implies. Clarissa's story by the very fact of its telling insists on the individual's power to determine the degree to which and the ways in which she is known. Lovelace's part of the narrative dramatizes an unfailing need for self-display; Clarissa's reveals the uses of privacy as both a defensive and an enabling resource.

The defensive value of privacy for Clarissa is readily apparent. The heroine's preternatural prudence—after her single fatal episode of imprudence, meeting Lovelace at the garden gate—causes her unfailingly to protect her physical privacy, in such instances as her refusal to share a bed with another woman, allegedly a visitor, but actually a whore planning to further Lovelace's nefarious ends. She guards her living quarters as she guards her interiority, refusing to allow anyone in. As her death approaches, she calls attention to the ultimate privacy of the coffin, that fine and private place where (a fact of special relevance to Clarissa) none embrace. The coffin inhabits her room, emphasizing to her few visitors the imminence of her escape and the power and uncontrollability of her will. Despite the fact that her protracted dying becomes a spectacle, both immediately, for the scanty number of her attendants and visitors, and, in the form of narrative, indirectly for many others, that process of dying reiterates the unknowability of the interior life. It contrasts in this respect as in others with the equally spectacular dying of Mrs. Sinclair, whose semicoherent utterances seem to reveal all she knows and feels.

The relation between Clarissa's impeccable behavior (always excepting that one disastrous mistake) and her unknowability has irritated and perplexed readers since Dr. Johnson, with his notorious remark that there was always something Clarissa preferred to the truth. Through the eyes of others within the text, Clarissa emerges as the perfect lady, paragon of conduct, invariably behaving as she ought. She wants to go to church; she does not wish to attend plays. She appears virtually always well groomed, even in prison. Anna tells us how generously she allots her time to the needs of others and to the demands of her spiritual life: in large matters as well as small, she embodies her culture's ideal of female comportment. Lovelace's need to rape her comes from his literalized desire to penetrate the smooth surface, to prove definitively that Clarissa is mere woman, physical, vulnerable, possessed of uncontrollable feelings. The now familiar dynamic of the psychologically oriented novel leads the reader to desire comparable, if less literal, penetration. And indeed Richardson appears to offer abundant data about what goes on beneath the decorous surface Clarissa presents to the world. Writing to her confidante, the protagonist analyzes her own thoughts and feelings, frequently protesting that she tells all. Yet Anna herself from time to time voices her suspicion that Clarissa either does not know or does not tell all—about, for instance, her feeling for

Lovelace. Told more and more, page after page (if you read it for the plot, you'd hang yourself, Johnson observed), the reader only feels more and more mistrustful that everything is being told. Everything in the novel suggests that depths matter more than surfaces—and everything reminds us that we never reach the final depth. An irreducible residue of privacy always remains.

Teaching *Clarissa* recently, I found myself beset by students' questions about Lovelace's ultimate fate. Does he repent and find salvation between his wounding and his death? Does he necessarily go to hell? Is it possible to imagine him reunited with Clarissa in heaven? The text in fact leaves little room to conceive the possibility of Lovelace's salvation, and these questions are from one point of view fairly bizarre. But they call attention to how forcibly the novel demands that the reader take it on its own terms. Twenty-first-century students do not customarily inquire about the destiny of characters' souls; Richardson makes them feel the urgency of the question. Similarly, he insists on the urgency and the difficulty of self-knowledge and self-revelation. We can never know enough about Clarissa to understand definitively the degree to which she is saintly, the extent to which she is manipulative, or the ultimate scope of her self-awareness. Like Lovelace, we can never answer our own questions about this remarkable heroine. Like Lovelace, we come up finally against a privacy that allows no recourse.

I may sound as though I have fallen into the trap that awaits so many students of *Clarissa* and Clarissa: confusing her existence with that of a real person. Clarissa, after all, has only textual reality. She exists as the product of words on a page—many words on many pages. Her "inner life" is the life Richardson has assigned her and linguistically evoked for her. The fact that it is possible to talk about, to *feel*, her privacy measures the magnitude of the novelist's accomplishment. He has provided so many layers of apparent knowledge and awareness that he creates the illusion of more layers still, the sense that there is always more to know.

The kind of privacy the figure of Clarissa evokes—what we might call the privacy of the soul—is not socially ordained or controlled. For Clarissa it serves defensive purposes, but she cannot control it either: she cannot choose not to possess it. Its existence is not peculiarly characteristic of eighteenth-century England. But the intense attention paid to it in eighteenth-century fiction underlines the anxiety associated with the period's often-noted preoccupation with hypocrisy, appearance, and theatricality. At best—given the most virtuous conceivable man or woman, the most intense self-examination—that irreducible residue of the unknowable remains. Whatever a given society mandates about the degree of privacy appropriate to the responsible individual, it cannot avoid the final fact of that individual's separateness.

This fact comes into play for readers as well as imagined and actual persons in other roles. Richardson's notorious efforts to exercise utter control over the reader's opinions of the characters in *Clarissa* reiterate in a different key the perception that people, finally unknowable, are as a consequence impossible to regulate with precision. Like Clarissa herself, Richardson's readers escape him. His obsessive revisions and interpolations dramatize an effort like Lovelace's, an effort doomed to failure, to comprehend the Other: alike the subject and the method of his fiction.

Privacy becomes not only a hypothesis but a powerful force in the plot of *Clarissa*. Inasmuch as privacy, both willed and unwilled, serves a defensive function for Clarissa, it works by fending off others, protecting the heroine's selfhood from the depredations of a hostile or irrelevant world. In its enabling capacity, it has the same effect, but the purpose of its self-protection is to create psychic space in which the individual can develop capacities that might otherwise be stunted. The drama of that development occupies much of the novel. For Clarissa, privacy remains urgent even after she is nominally "safe," in a refuge where Lovelace will not trouble her and where she has loving attention from authentic and willing caretakers. It enables her to lay her plans, to write her many "posthumous" letters, to perfect her soul. All these activities, too, become "spectacular," eagerly reported by Belford—who can, however, only see external facts and narrate appearances, supported by accounts of Clarissa's utterances. She fully realizes the potential paradox of Anna's initial letter. Desiring to slide through life unnoticed, she resolutely separates herself—physically, as much as she can; psychically, almost completely—from others, as the end approaches no longer wishing even response to her letters to her family. Yet all eyes are upon her: the eyes of all she encounters, but also, by her prearrangement, the eyes of all who survive her: not only family and friends, but potential readers of the book to be compiled by Belford, for which she also arranges. She wants to slide through life unnoticed; she also wants all eyes upon her. She wants privacy; she wants fame. This paradox by no means sums up Clarissa's rendered character. It ignores, for instance, the third term between her and "society": God, toward whom she resolutely directs her attention, and in relation to whom she neither needs nor desires privacy. But not all her spiritual effort, ardent though it is, can enable her to escape the fundamental problem of the individual's relation to the rest of the world, a problem summed up by the dilemma of privacy.

This sketchy account of some of privacy's perplexities in a single novel may at least hint the multiple issues and proliferating ramifications that attend literary examination of the subject. An entire book devotes itself to privacy in *Clarissa* (Christina Marsden Gillis, *The Paradox of Privacy: Epistolary Form in "Clarissa"*)—without touching on any of the concerns I have discussed. Gillis focuses on matters of physical space and on the meanings of Richardson's choice of epistolary form. Her illuminating treatment may remind one of the sheer breadth of privacy as a subject: she considers baffling issues, while leaving equally complicated concerns about privacy untouched.

Part of the difficulty of privacy as subject, certainly, derives from the diverse meanings attached to the term. I am quite aware that I have not yet defined it, in any of its meanings. Debate over the import of *privacy* belongs particularly to the twentieth century, when the word assumed legal weight and when threats to what people in general understood as privacy rapidly multiplied. When Samuel Warren and Louis Brandeis in 1890 effectively defined privacy as the "general right of the individual to be let alone" (82), they made the question of definition, to say nothing of the matter of privacy, seem simple, although they offered more assertion than argument in claiming the existence of such a right. (In some ways their definition remains more satisfactory than most of its more intricate successors.) Moreover, they inaugurated a century and more of commentary, influencing legal discourse in Great Britain as well as the United States. Subsequent commentators, legal, sociological, and philosophic, complicated the issue by perceiving ever broader implications in the concept. Many followed Warren and Brandeis in understanding privacy as a right; but they differed in their understanding of what the right entailed and why and how it mattered.

Some came to the conclusion that privacy could not be satisfactorily defined. In the wake of a series of scandals in public life, the British appointed the Younger committee to investigate the issue of privacy. That committee, although it produced some recommendations, concluded that privacy was not susceptible to definition. Its successor, the so-called Justice committee (*Justice* denoted the British Section of the International Commission of Jurists), similarly reached the view that "little purpose would be served in constructing a further definition on the grounds that the notion of privacy is largely emotional, often irrational and anyway subject to constant change" (Young 2). A recent commentator, after pointing out the range of definitions from narrow ("the right to control the possession and disclosure of specific facts about one's self") to broad ("the right 'to be let alone'"), takes "the position that any attempt at definitional encapsulation in any but the most metaphorical sense is misguided because in a definitional or descriptive sense, our right to privacy is structurally complex" (Neill 4). Nonetheless, even while granting emotionality, irrationality, and structural complexity, legal scholars and philosophers in particular have ventured elaborate definitions and engaged in elaborate disputes.

The principal issue has been whether privacy should be defined as a condition of limited access or as one of personal control. Julie C. Inness summarizes: "Privacy may work by separating a realm of the agent's life from the access of others, or it may work by providing the agent with control over a realm of her life. With regard to the content of privacy, the literature suggests that privacy covers either an agent's intimate decisions about her own actions, informational access to her, or general access to her" (23). The distinction between the concept of privacy focused on access and that stressing control corresponds to the difference between privacy *from* others and privacy *to* achieve desired ends.

Although the two broad categories of access and control (sometimes in combination) account for most definitions of privacy, the concept in its modern developments allows for a surprising range of variation. A philosopher can define it as "the state of a person who in the pursuit of the good justifiably can choose the nature and duration of contact with others" (Velecky 21). (He does not explain why privacy pertains only to the good—if, indeed, that is what he means.) Another commentator sees it as concerned only with "a realm of intimacy," explaining that "to claim that an act or activity is intimate is to claim that it draws its meaning and value from the agent's love, liking, or care" (Inness 56, 90). Yet another defines it by the different "states" it may include: "Privacy actually embodies several different states of psychological and physical relationship between an individual and the persons around him, which can be categorized as solitude, intimacy, anonymity, and reserve" (Flaherty 1). Many descriptive and definitional accounts call attention to the prevailing association between privacy and positive value. Michael Weinstein's careful (if ponderous) definition makes clear and explicit the connection between privacy and "good" purposes, explaining privacy as "a condition of voluntary limitation of communication to or from certain others, in a situation, with respect to specified information, for the purpose of conducting an activity in pursuit of a perceived good. The variables of choice, limited communication, relevant others, a situational context, activity, and a good to be attained must all be present in the full construction of privacy" (94). Occasionally a theorist will raise the possibility that privacy can serve dubious ends. More typically, the perception of privacy as a *right* entails the assumption that it automatically associates itself with the good.

A definition widely adopted by others comes from Alan F. Westin, a historian whose interest in privacy is both theoretical and pragmatic (he has contributed to the construction and implementation of several large surveys). I shall quote his explanation in its immediate context:

> Privacy is the claim of individuals, groups, or institutions to determine for
> themselves when, how, and to what extent information about them is com-
> municated to others. Viewed in terms of the relation of the individual to
> social participation, privacy is the voluntary and temporary withdrawal of a
> person from the general society through physical or psychological means,
> either in a state of solitude or small-group intimacy or, when among larger
> groups, in a condition of anonymity or reserve. The individual's desire for
> privacy is never absolute, since participation in society is an equally power-
> ful desire. Thus each individual is continually engaged in a personal adjust-
> ment process in which he balances the desire for privacy with the desire for
> disclosure and communication of himself to others. . . . The individual does
> so in the face of pressures from the curiosity of others and from the pro-
> cesses of surveillance that every society sets in order to enforce its social
> norms. (7)

Although Westin's definition in terms of information sounds limited in comparison with others, his elaboration of it specifies clearly and economically the range of situations—from physical solitude to psychological reserve—in which individuals can find privacy. He designates privacy as a "claim" rather than a right or privilege, thus emphasizing the fact that it belongs to the realm of individual choice rather than social or legal mandate. And he stresses the dynamic involved in every choice: a crucial dynamic of self and community. The lucidity and energy of his account have given it special authority in the broad field of utterances on the subject.

Philosophers who have considered the matter of privacy often appear to believe the state—or the "claim"—valuable as a means to important ends. The end most often specified is intimacy (Fried, Gerstein, Reiman, Gavison, Inness): without the possibility of privacy, the argument goes, intimate relationships would prove impossible. But some make yet larger claims. Gavison's summary covers the most important ground. She specifies "the functions privacy has in our lives" as "the promotion of liberty, autonomy, selfhood, and human relations, and furthering the existence of a free society" (347). Later, she adds growth and creativity as further consequences of privacy (361). But the issue of intimacy remains fundamental. Charles Fried puts the case eloquently:

> It is my thesis that privacy is not just one possible means among others to insure some other value, but that it is necessarily related to ends and relations of the most fundamental sort: respect, love, friendship and trust. Privacy is not merely a good technique for furthering these fundamental relations; rather without privacy they are simply inconceivable. . . . To respect, love, trust, feel affection for others and to regard ourselves as the objects of love, trust and affection is at the heart of our notion of ourselves as persons among persons, and privacy is the necessary atmosphere for these attitudes and actions, as oxygen is for combustion. (205)

In modern society, many value privacy highly who have never thought about the matter sufficiently to make or, perhaps, even to understand such large claims. In 1978, three out of four Americans believed that "the 'right to privacy' should be akin to the inalienable American right to life, liberty, and the pursuit of happiness" (*Dimensions* 5). Between January and December, 1978, the proportion of survey subjects characterizing themselves as "somewhat" or "very" concerned about threats to personal privacy rose from 47 percent to 64 percent (12). Eighteen years later, a Harris-Equifax poll of more than one thousand Americans "found that nearly 80 percent of them were 'somewhat' or 'very' concerned about threats to personal privacy, the highest percentage ever recorded by the polling agency on this subject." In 1997, a Harris-Westin poll revealed that 92 percent of respondents were "concerned"; 64 percent were "very concerned" (Etzioni 6). The status of privacy as a threatened individual value appears to have solidified in the United States.

Perhaps, by now, in England too; lacking comparable survey data, it is difficult to tell. Historically, British legal authorities have proved reluctant to intervene in questions of privacy. A judicial opinion from 1865, by J. Blackburn, is emphatic in its disclaimer of legal responsibility for matters of privacy:

> The law does not protect the right to privacy as it does that to light and air. It may be that the reason for this distinction given in the old cases, viz., that light and air are things of necessity, while prospect and privacy are but things of delight, is more quaint than satisfactory; but it is not, I believe, proposed by any one to disturb that distinction now. If it were proposed, I think more substantial reasons for supporting it might be assigned. (Quoted in Pratt 59)

The status of privacy as a "thing of delight" may have been precisely what made it seem so dubious a value in the previous century. Delight that separated individuals from their communities was arguably reprehensible. Indeed, it remains arguably reprehensible. More provocative than the varying definitions of privacy in recent times are the varying emphases of discussions about privacy's implications for the social fabric. Arnold Simmel observes, "As a value privacy does not exist in isolation, but is part and parcel of the system of values that regulates action in society" (71). At one extreme, certain thinkers argue that privacy and social life, mutually implicated, depend on one another: "If the various needs and motivations that lead us into forming social relationships constitute the bricks of social life, then privacy and its related aspects constitute the mortar. The one depends upon the other" (Ingham 55). Or, as Ferdinand David Schoeman puts it, given a proper understanding of privacy "we appreciate that it is central to social life and not a principle that stands in opposition to it" (137). Yet another formulation: "Not only does belonging to oneself call for privacy, but so too does belonging to others in the sense of participating in the world and using one's talents for positive contributions" (Allen 47).

Not everyone, however, feels so sanguine about the comfortable relation between concern for privacy and responsibility to society. Morris Ernst and Alan Schwartz argue that "The very word [*privacy*] connotes a necessary alienation between the individual and his society, an alienation or distance that is at the core of all our civil liberties" (1). They do not explore the implications of this perception. More detailed, and more alarming, is the self-styled "communitarian" Amitai Etzioni, who maintains, "In principle and in practice, there is no escaping the basic tension between our profound desire for privacy and our deep concern for public safety and public health" (3). He sees privacy as a "highly privileged value" in American society (3) and believes that "the common good is being systematically neglected out of excessive deference to privacy" (4). Although he grants the status of privacy as "an individual right," he argues that it must "be balanced with concerns for the common good" (4). He understands the current passionate concern for privacy as a product of "growing individualism and neglect of the common good" (195), and he recommends a return to more emphasis on the needs of the entire human community.

Etzioni writes out of his perception of the social situation at the very end of the twentieth century. His worries and his prescriptions are more concrete, pragmatic, and specific than those of his eighteenth-century counterparts, but the connection he makes between privacy and individualism suggests a continuum between eighteenth-century England and the

United States at the dawn of the twenty-first century. The development of individualism in the eighteenth century, Schoeman suggests, depends on choice in relationships. "One way of describing the emergence of 'the individual,'" he writes, "is to think that what is emerging in the eighteenth century is the significance of the relationships one makes for oneself, and a diminution of those over which one has no control" (131). Choice is a defining element of privacy (solitude is not identical to privacy precisely because it does not necessarily entail choice); the difference between relationships chosen and those inflicted involves the playing out of a dynamic of privacy. (The relationship unchosen necessarily interferes with privacy; the freely elected one enlarges privacy's possibilities.) Just such playing out provides the crucial subject for much eighteenth-century writing.

My argument in this book does not depend upon or derive from the definitions, explanations, and descriptions I have sketched here. Indeed, it was largely formulated before I read most of these discussions, which of course illuminate the late twentieth and early twenty-first centuries more cogently than they bear on the past. Not even the word *privacy* functions importantly in most of the texts considered in the subsequent chapters; eighteenth-century thinkers had not consolidated their understanding of the dynamic of individual and society under a single rubric. My own conceptualization belongs to a later time; I bring together early modern treatments of something that we dwellers in the twenty-first century can see as a distinct topic but that our forebears would not necessarily have understood as connected at all.

I have been surprised and enlightened, though, to discover how sharply twentieth-century theoretical discussions of privacy formulate the precise issues that attract the attention of eighteenth-century imaginative writers. Problems of personhood, intimacy, and autonomy lie at the center of novels and poetry from the earlier period. Problems of control over information help to explain the structure and content of diaries. The issue of hypocrisy, deeply implicated with the possibilities of what Westin calls "reserve," at least in eighteenth-century accounts, involves how one appears in society. Recent commentators provide a vocabulary that helps to clarify the writings of men and women operating in a different context, but a context that bears recognizable resemblances to our own.

For my purposes, the straightforward if vague definition of privacy as the right to be let alone works remarkably well in most instances. That's exactly what I shall be talking about: the strategies writers devise or describe for being let alone, and the anxieties that develop about what it might mean to let one another alone. But I have inevitably been influenced by more elaborate interpretations of privacy as an idea, given their often unexpected relevance to textually rendered eighteenth-century social and personal situations. For instance: "privacy is the measure of the extent an individual is afforded the social and legal space to develop the emotional, cognitive, spiritual, and moral powers of an autonomous agent" (Schoeman 13). I think of Tom Jones, always cheerfully surrounded by others, then isolated (spiritually, if not literally) in prison, only thus enabled to acknowledge responsibility for his own actions. I think of Clarissa and her dramatic self-development, but also of Burney's Cecilia, systematically deprived of "social and legal space" and consequently kept from any semblance of autonomy. The accounts of privacy offered by twentieth-century thinkers often illuminate the fictional structures and social perceptions of much earlier writers; I shall draw on them frequently in this study.

It will come as no surprise that the "novel of manners" from the late eighteenth century has proved particularly apposite to my concerns. Such novels operate with an exact and subtle understanding of how "society" works in specific ways and how it informs the experience of its participants. Frances Burney, with her especially detailed understanding of such matters, therefore figures importantly here. Burney's special meaning in this study derives also from her gender. Perhaps it is also unsurprising that privacy is a peculiarly emphatic issue for eighteenth-century women, both within fiction (e.g., Clarissa) and as writers of fiction, poetry, and diaries. Given the complex web of social restrictions within which middle- and upper-class women functioned, finding ways to protect their intimate lives would have been particularly urgent. To say so is not to reinforce the old association of women with the "private," men with the "public." Lawrence Klein has written compellingly about his perception that, in the eighteenth century, "the public and private realms are less well segregated from one another and less exclusively gendered than they are sometimes represented to be" (102). I find his argument entirely persuasive, but the issue of privacy does not depend on "segregation" or its absence. A man might feel the need to seek privacy in a public setting; a woman might find the private realm quite devoid of privacy. Because of women's comparative lack of freedom, their strategies for privacy display special ingenuity, and sometimes a certain desperation. They therefore hold a large place in this study.

The book also attends, however, to such canonical novelists as Defoe, Richardson, Fielding, Sterne, and Goldsmith. I have dealt in detail with only two poets, Cowper and Charlotte Smith, by no means "representative," but crucial to my enterprise because of Cowper's near-obsession with the matter of privacy and Smith's sharp articulation of its psychological overtones. The diaries and works of pornography and near-pornography here considered are fairly random choices. They *are*, I think, representative, in the sense that the aspects of their writing that I focus on might be found as readily in many other texts of the same kind.

In its various psychological and social meanings, as I have tried to suggest, privacy figures importantly as an issue in eighteenth-century writing: an issue that both illuminates the specific operations of a broad community more closely knit than those we are accustomed to and elucidates patterns common to fiction, diaries, and even some poetry. But we might begin by contemplating the situation of readers of such works—readers both literal and figurative.

2

Privacies of Reading

Diffuse anxiety—the multiplied anxiety of individuals—accompanied what can be seen from a distance in time as an increasing focus on the individual in eighteenth-century England. The widespread concern over the possible effects of novel reading registers an aspect of that anxiety: worry over what it might mean for people to read in solitude. For women and the young, in particular, the solitary experience of others' fantasies would perhaps encourage their own, and perhaps those fantasies would result in dangerous action (meaning, in most cases, sexual action).

In the twenty-first century it is—as, for that matter, in the twentieth and nineteenth centuries it was—hard to imagine how people could read except as individuals, locked in the cocooned privacy of the text. Cecile M. Jagodzinski, however, argues that such reading developed at a particular historical moment, partly as a result of "the social, religious, and political upheavals of the late sixteenth and seventeenth centuries." She continues, "the chance to get 'lost in a book' unsettled long-held notions about the relation of the individual to God, to religious, political, and social structures, and to his or her own interior life and consciousness. The ability to read granted independence from all those communal structures. . . . In short, readers in seventeenth-century England, because they read, began to develop a sense of the private self" (2). Precise historical location of such a development must necessarily remain somewhat dubious, but many historians and critics agree that something new happened to the nature of reading at some point between the late sixteenth and the late eighteenth centuries.

Novel reading in particular marks a zone of privacy. J. Paul Hunter has argued that the eighteenth-century development of the novel helped to construct an "anti-social" reader (*Before Novels* 42). We think of novel reading as occurring in privacy not merely because of the physical solitude of the isolated reader, but because such reading provides special stimulation for unshared individual fantasy. The fantasies encouraged by fiction may speak to the self's deepest longings and can separate their possessors from the actualities of their outer experience. Women surveyed about their enthusiasm for popular romances, for instance, consistently mention that such reading provides them with valued time of separation from the encroachments of their families (see Radway). It puts them, they say, into their own space. When I was a little girl, grade school teachers were fond of reciting for our edification the opening lines of a poem by Emily Dickinson that begins, "There is no Frigate like a Book / To take us Lands away." The point, in the teachers' version of things, was that we could escape through books. They didn't specify what we might want to escape *from*, but one obvious possibility is that we might want to get away from other people.

The act of engrossing oneself in a book self-evidently creates its own privacy. Roger Chartier explicates the connection: "The hours spent in the library are hours of withdrawal in two senses, which define the essence of privacy in the modern era: withdrawal from the public sphere, from civic responsibility, from the affairs of city and state; and withdrawal from the family, from the household, from the social responsibilities of domestic intimacy. In retreat, the individual is free, master of his time" (Chartier 136). To make a deliberate choice of fictionality intensifies privacy by guaranteeing a heightened degree of separation through the substitution of imagined for literal substantiality.

When Dickinson declares an analogy between a book and a boat, she hints the imaginative power of reading—the power of books to arouse, involve, and enlarge the imaginations of those who partake of them. Books carry us away not only by establishing an alternate reality but by stimulating us in such ways that preexistent forms of reality—the cluttered room, the irritating colleague—assume new meanings, reveal new possibilities. Or perhaps it would be more accurate to say that we understand new aspects of ourselves as a result of reading novels, and the new forms of self-imagining immediately affect our perceptions of the world outside ourselves. We pay attention to new things, in new ways. I associate such imaginative transformations with privacy because they are unique to each individual who experiences them, unknowable to others unless the possessor decides to communicate them, and quite possibly at odds with communal assumptions. They belong to the realm of self-enclosure and of potential resistance that we connect with privacy.

In a simpler sense, the experience of absorbing oneself in a book is one of privacy because it necessarily shuts out the world. I can still vividly remember the resentful note in my mother's voice as she said over and over during my childhood, "That girl always has her nose in a book." I knew her resentment justified: I was, for the time of reading, rejecting her and home and housework and even school. I had taken possession of my privacy. The Warren and Brandeis formulation is quite to the point here: privacy expresses "the general right of the individual to be let alone."

I claimed my privacy through reading, as do many other readers, in a more positive sense as well. The opportunity to explore and solidify the self belongs to privacy. Reading novels provides opportunity for such exploration, such solidification, and for the processes of discovery that necessarily precede these activities. The discovery takes place, of course, at the level of fantasy. Through the imaginative activity of identification and differentiation in relation to fictional characters, fictional actions, one learns to be more grandly oneself.

The value of imaginative privacy, however, has not always been so readily apparent. When Jane Eyre huddles in her window seat, her feet drawn up, behind red curtains, for the delicious indulgence of reading, she creates a memorable image for reading's self-enclosure. But it is a peculiarly nineteenth-century image. Brontë's novel, published in 1847, draws on and helps to solidify the metaphors of romanticism. If it had been published a century before, Jane would not have inhabited the same setting or thought of reading in the same way. If she read for the sake of imaginative stimulation in 1747 or thereabouts, her creator would probably have introduced even into a fictional text some warning about the danger of such stimulation. The kind of anxiety that now attends, for many, consideration of images of violence on television or pornography on the Internet—how might they affect children?—once belonged to the idea of novel reading, specifically because of its privacy and that space for fantasy which privacy creates. An eighteenth-century clergyman, James Fordyce, writing in 1766 for an audience of young women, offers an exemplary statement:

> There seem to be very few [books], in the style of Novel, that you can read with safety, and yet fewer that you can read with advantage.—What shall we say of certain books, which we are assured (for we have not read them) are in their nature so shameful, in their tendency so pestiferous, and contain such rank treason against the royalty of Virtue, such horrible violation of all decorum, that she who can bear to peruse them must in her soul be a prostitute, let her reputation in life be what it will. (1:148)

Fordyce worries not only about the "nature," or content, of novels but about their "tendency"—that is, roughly, how their readers might interpret and use them. The possibility that a woman might be a prostitute "in her soul" while leading an outwardly exemplary existence horrifies, and perhaps terrifies, him. His anxiety stems from the impossibility of policing the inner life. The privacy of novel reading is inviolable: one cannot penetrate the reader's consciousness. *Anything* might be going on in there.

This sense of the privacy of reading, however, originates in a specific historical period, however dubious its precise moment. In my view, it develops gradually and unevenly, concurrently with emphasis on reading communities, in the course of the eighteenth century. Many questions have been raised, as H. J. Jackson observes in her book on marginalia, about "the supposedly solitary experience of reading in the period. Not only did public reading out loud persist as an important part of the culture (notably in churches), but there was a great expansion in domestic reading, that is, reading aloud in small circles of family or friends" (66). Jackson goes on to note that "Even so-called private reading—silent reading to oneself—was seldom really solitary, being carried on in shared household space or outside the house in coffee shops, bookshops, and circulating libraries" (66–67). Moreover, book clubs and reading groups were common among woman, a legitimating social form of entertainment (Pearson 160–61). Of course lack of physical solitude, as we shall see, by no means precludes the possibility of experienced privacy, and the existence of "social" reading does not obviate that of its solitary equivalent.

Deidre Lynch claims that Jane Austen's novels mark the moment when the privacy of reading fiction became fully established and valued, but in fact Austen's novels provide indications of continuing conflict between the notion of reading as purely personal and the conviction that readers belong, necessarily and importantly, to moral communities, at least, if not others. Unlike earlier novelists, Austen rarely addresses imaginary versions of her readers, but she explores in her fictions the actual processes of reading. *Pride and Prejudice* provides an exemplary instance. Its famous opening sentence inaugurates a narrative that will grapple with the problem of reading, literal and metaphorical, specifically in relation to issues of privacy and community. The truth that a rich man must want a wife is "universally acknowledged." What comprises the relevant universe, and does it really have the authority to determine "truth"? If not, how can one discover where truth lies?

Although the Bennet sisters belong to the gentry, that fact guarantees them little physical privacy. To be sure, they have their bedrooms (it's not clear how many of them share rooms). But they also have their social obligations. The only time we see Elizabeth Bennet reading a book, she does so in a drawing room full of other people, one of whom soon interrupts to demand her engagement in another kind of activity. Elizabeth's propensity for long solitary walks partly reflects her need to find space for private reflection. She understands, though, that privacy does not altogether depend on physical situation (a truth more fully elaborated in *Sense and Sensibility* and *Mansfield Park*), and her private internal commentary on what she sees and feels continues unabated in company.

In a novel so self-evidently concerned with problems of interpretation, reading might be expected to play an important part. Books appear from time to time, mainly as props. Mr. Collins reads aloud to the Bennet sisters, Mary Bennet proclaims her preference for books over people, Miss Bingley praises Darcy's family library, Mr. Bennet reads while the rest of the family attends a ball. But it is the reading of personal letters that best locates, complicates, and eventually clarifies the dilemma of interpretation. Lynch considers such reading part of Austen's training of her readers: "Austen identifies to her readers the proper means of and motives for literary experience when she demonstrates that the truth of a letter is situated beneath or beyond the face of the page" (131). Darcy's letter of self-explanation after his botched proposal provides the richest instance, but others have preceded it: notably Miss Bingley's letter from London, explaining their sudden departure, which Jane reads as having one meaning and Elizabeth as having a completely different one. In the case of Darcy's letter, Elizabeth must play the part of both readers, the one willing to believe the best about the writer and the suspicious one. And she must confront the undependability of public opinion, as well as of her own.

"Everybody" has decided Darcy's nature from the time of his first appearance. By the end of the ball at which he declines dancing with Elizabeth, "His character was decided. He was the proudest, most disagreeable man in the world, and every body hoped that he would never come there again" (12). Indeed, long before the time of the crucial letter it has become a truth universally acknowledged that Wickham epitomizes male attractiveness and that Darcy has no regard for other people.

The process by which Elizabeth comes to reverse these judgments, through successive readings of Darcy's letter, demonstrates the arduousness of interpretation. In her first reading, shaped by her rage over his insulting proposal and over the harm he has done to her beloved sister, she finds his explanations unpersuasive. But she acknowledges her own "prejudice." She tries hard to allow reason to form her judgment. In her second reading, she "commanded herself to examine the meaning of every sentence" (169). Putting down the letters, she weighs "every circumstance with what she meant to be impartiality—deliberated on the probability of each statement—but with little success. On both sides it was only assertion" (169). Unable to rely on textual exegesis alone, she brings to bear the evidence of her memory, with detailed analysis of her past experience and of other people's responses. She wanders the lane for two hours, "giving way to every variety of thought; re-considering events, determining probabilities, and reconciling herself as well as she could, to a change so sudden and so important" (173)—a change, that is, in her understanding of Darcy and of Wickham, and in her own judgment. Darcy has convinced her, but only by virtue of her own ardent participation in the process of interpretation.

Elizabeth is an exemplary reader. But there are no guarantees of her rightness, even after her exhaustive and exhausting effort. Emotion has interfered with her capacity to interpret accurately, and emotion remains as a potential distorting force. *IRONY,* undergraduates like to write in the margin next to Elizabeth's self-critical comment, "Had I been in love, I could not have been more wretchedly blind" (171). Even on a first reading of *Pride and Prejudice,* one suspects that she *is* in love and doesn't know it; subsequent readings make the fact altogether obvious. Unaware of her feelings for Darcy, Elizabeth may not assess his self-exculpation correctly. Or she may: the reader can't know for certain, and neither, ever, can she.

Elizabeth has much at stake in interpreting Darcy's letter, more by far than anyone coming to terms with a work of fiction. Yet she stands as a model for novel readers. She tells us of the urgency of "private" reading, and of its dangers. The urgency depends on the fact that the community Austen imagines—a community of judgment rather than of readership— is often wrong. Echoes of Elizabeth's procedure, as well as of its results, reverberate back and forth through *Pride and Prejudice.* Elizabeth's new comprehension, for instance, sharply suggests that truths universally acknowledged are more likely than not untrue. Austen has more fun with cliché and platitude in *Pride and Prejudice* than in any other of her novels. Mary Bennet's conduct book maxims, Mr. Collins's obtuse commonplaces, and Sir William Lucas's predictable sentiments remind us that what the community accepts as self-evident need not prove accurate, relevant, or even meaningful. What the community accepts can create obstacles to thought. "Private" reading and speaking, therefore, provide the only inlet to clarity. Elizabeth's total immersion in the text and its problems, her effort both to use feeling and to prevent it from overpowering thought, her capacity for imaginative participation and imaginative expansion (she entertains herself by fancying—prophetically—how Lady Catherine might respond to the news of her marriage to Darcy)—the way Elizabeth reads the crucial letter exemplifies the best possibility for interpretation.

But even the best possibility yields relatively little moral clarity. Elizabeth's endeavors of interpretation include and rely on the testimony of her feelings, perception, and intelligence, draw on her memory and her sympathetic imagination, demand the effort to divest herself of "prejudice." Yet her most careful efforts can produce at most provisional and personal clarity, along with a certain exhilaration, the exhilaration of the private reader. Despite the fact that it offers such moderate rewards, Elizabeth and her sister Jane both understand the exigency of interpretation. Their understanding differentiates them from the rest of their family and from others in their neighborhood, who relax in the comfort of the taken-for-granted. Elizabeth and Jane know that one must "read" constantly—read people and events and conversations as well as letters and books. Although they have each other, they know also that one must read alone. And if they can enjoy at some level the pressures of the need to interpret, they can never enjoy the sense of any external authority sustaining their readings.

It is a commonplace reiterated by generations of critics—one more truth universally acknowledged—that Jane Austen interests herself in "society," in microcosmic societies that illustrate the tensions and the comforts of living within group conventions. Equally commonplace is the perception that she anatomizes the inner life of individuals. In many ways, the group—an essentially secular group, although all its members go to church—supports the individuals within it. But in the crucial process of interpretation as Austen renders it, the individual must stand alone, understanding her own ultimate undependability. When Darcy proposes for the second time and is accepted, he recurs to the subject of the letter. Now he, its author, has reinterpreted what he has written: "When I wrote that letter, . . . I believed myself perfectly calm and cool, but I am since convinced that it was written in a dreadful bitterness of spirit" (296–97). Elizabeth insists that they talk no more of the letter, since the feelings of both have radically changed since its writing. Now it would be written differently, now it would be differently read. The fluctuations of private interpretation destabilize meaning until the only recourse is to ignore the text—a possible tactic only because literal human contact has in this instance succeeded its textual equivalent.

Most readers now would readily agree about the necessary ambiguity of interpretation and the degree to which personal elements may dictate perceptions about a text, and they would agree that reading is a private matter. Austen's rich appeal to audiences almost three centuries after she wrote may derive partly from the familiarity of such ideas. But a larger moral program embeds the kind of reading that Elizabeth Bennet practices: a program of self-scrutiny, self-discipline, and constant effort. To contemplate this program, perhaps less readily assimilable to current assumptions than is the kind of reading I have described, may make one suspicious about the foregoing description itself, which is in fact based on my own highly selective reading.

All reading is selective, of course, conditioned by individual and collective experience. We filter out aspects of a novel that seem irrelevant and notice what makes most sense to us, reading in our own historical moment and our own personal circumstances. My account of *Pride and Prejudice* ignores elements of Elizabeth's reading that seem less immediately appealing to twenty-first-century readers than her attention to her own feelings. Her way of reading, like her larger moral effort, participates in the Romantic debate over the place of the individual, fully conscious self in the human community. David Bromwich speaks of "the imaginative identification of a self with the community of humankind" as an aspect of "Romantic idealism" (72). Austen is rather less grandiose in her imagining of community—not an undiscriminated mass of other people, but a body of individuals connected to one another in specific ways. She uses the strenuous interpretive endeavors of Darcy and Elizabeth primarily as a basis for adumbrating a new kind of community, that of the like-minded.

Jacqueline Pearson emphasizes the importance and the problematic aspects of the reading communities in which women participated. "The most legitimate pleasures offered women by reading," she writes, "were those of domesticity, family and community, and reading was 'idealised as the basis for the formation of community.' . . . However, if reading could figure and facilitate community, it could construct not only traditional domestic communities but other extended or nontraditional communities, whose significance could be subversive or even consciously revolutionary" (96; internal quotation from Kilgour). Elizabeth is neither revolutionary nor subversive, although the idea of what I have called "a community of the like-minded" has subversive potential. She does not emphasize her own religious commitment, but she tries to judge according to moral principles that belong to an existing community. She is not a twenty-first-century reader but an early-nineteenth-century one. Elizabeth reads, to the degree that she can, with the whole of herself: her experience, her feelings, her knowledge, and her principles. Although she recognizes and values her uniqueness, she also values the ideas she has inherited. Her very determination to be just to everyone reflects her consciousness of ethical obligation. To call her a "private" reader fails to acknowledge the degree to which she understands the necessary participation of the private in the social. Austen infuses her fiction, after all, with inherited values.

The alternatives I suggest here (by no means mutually exclusive), privacy and community, differ importantly from the antithesis Lynch con-

structs between the private person and the crowd. A crowd, with little re-
semblance to a community, represents the social as unpredictable and incoherent. The proliferation of "new editions" in the early nineteenth century, Lynch suggests, "made novel reading the activity of a crowd" (221).
More fully:

> even in reading by and for oneself, one reads in a crowd. In the inside sto-
> ries of the novel of manners, the romantic reader finds the means to sound
> the depths of her own special self and manifest her distinctive sensibility. In
> an age of steam-powered printing presses and circulating libraries, how-
> ever, the silent reader's intimate transactions with the inner meanings
> of literature are public-spirited in a couple of senses: from such pursuits
> of individual distinction a public sphere is composed, and such pursuits of
> individual distinction are haunted by the murmuring spirit of mass con-
> sumption. (209–10)

The historical argument that Lynch constructs accords with the general current assumption of antagonism between the effort to maintain
a realm of uncoerced interiority and ever-intensifying pressures toward
"mass consumption" from a proliferating commercial establishment. As
careful reading of any newspaper will confirm, the third term I have suggested, *community*, now occupies a place of diminishing importance and
scope, often invoked in sentimental terms but rarely perceived as powerful. Perhaps less ideologically useful than the notion of masses or crowds,
the idea of community often allows itself to be forgotten. In the eighteenth
century it remained a vital concept, although diminishment had already
begun. Well before Austen wrote, the canonical early novelists also conveyed and at least indirectly pondered the relation between reading as an
autonomous process of the individual consciousness, indeed a way of developing such consciousness, and reading as a communal act. Despite the
recent proliferation of studies of reading, we still lack adequate evidence of
actual reading procedures and assumptions in the eighteenth century, but
textual clues abound for the hopes, fears, and expectations of writers about
their readers. Fielding and Sterne, with their insistent addresses to imaginary readers, have already attracted much critical attention. Less explicit
novelists also reward investigation.

But Fielding still provides a plausible place to start, partly because he
insists so vociferously on positing the multiplicity and variety of his readers, ostensibly rejecting the possibility that anything beyond the act of
reading his novel binds those readers together. A random collection of
metaphorical travelers, his readers remain free to accept or reject the bill

of fare he offers, free to go elsewhere if they like (*Tom Jones* 31–32). They may or may not understand what the author wishes to convey; they may have assumptions opposed to his; they are certainly less profound and less clever than he (e.g., *TJ* 46–47). They are unpredictable: "we cannot possibly divine what Complexion our Reader may be of" (*TJ* 59; and cf. 523). They are likely to make mistakes (e.g., *TJ* 135). In short, many of the narrator's explicit evocations of his readers stress the diverse possibilities they embody.

Nicholas Hudson, writing in 1989, summarizing previous commentary on the "implied reader" in Fielding, emphasizes the "divided and paradoxical," "torn and ambivalent" aspects of that reader (177). Without disagreeing with Wolfgang Iser's contention that Fielding sets out to lead his reader to moral enlightenment, Hudson investigates the manipulations by which the author hopes to achieve such an end. He calls emphatic attention to the difference between "the addressed 'reader'" and the "true reader" (179)—a difference with extensive implications.

Despite his genial tone, Fielding's narrator often appears to expect little of the reader he addresses, who, he anticipates, will frequently misjudge situations and will not share his values. He uses that imaginary figure as a stalking horse in his effort to lead actual readers to the proper conclusions. Iser emphasizes the degree to which Fielding's reader "has to [like *must* a recurrent verb in his analysis] produce the meaning for himself" (46); Hudson stresses, rather, the ways in which Fielding pushes those who encounter his text toward a desired meaning.

Agreeing with Hudson both about the nature and the degree of manipulation, I yet find myself perplexed by questions that his account avoids. When—to use the example that Hudson starts with—Fielding's narrator apparently assumes that "the discerning Reader" will sympathize with the "sober, discreet and pious" Blifil (*TJ* 118) rather than with "thoughtless, giddy" Tom (134), how can he feel confident, or even hopeful, that the literal reader will not accept that "discerning" reader's judgment, or at least feel swayed by it? If, as most critics agree, Fielding operates by means of layers of irony, what allows him to conclude that readers will recognize or respond to his ironies? The insistent references to readers' existence preclude the possibility that the writer simply doesn't care what others think; the increasingly complicated characterizations of conceivable readers provide clues about the basis for the narrator's trust.

To assert the narrator's trust flies in the face of his frequent protestations of mistrust. With increasing frequency he raises the possibility of a "bad" reader, usually meaning a reader of insufficient moral discrimination, unable to judge character adequately or to feel appropriate responses to delineated action. Such a reader will expect Tom to be hanged and may even look forward to this denouement. Readers of this kind will consider Tom's mercy to a would-be highwayman "as a Want of Regard to that Justice which every Man owes his Country" (681). They may, indeed, condemn "all Compassion as a Folly, and pernicious to Society" (392); they presumably operate themselves on other bases than feeling. They will blame Tom for his rather consistent failure to look after his own interests (171). The reader's primary responsibility, the narrator makes abundantly clear, is to interpret character accurately. The narration itself repeatedly reveals this task's difficulty, as even the most admirable figures in the novel fall into their own interpretive mistakes. No wonder, then, that readers make errors, errors likely to multiply if the interpreter is dominated by self-interest and cynicism.

Yet I would still argue for the fundamental fact of trust, its ground a sense of what "humanity" means. The fullest account of humanity as a virtue in *Tom Jones* occurs not in a direct address to the reader but in an account of the writer's necessary attributes, which include "Genius," "Learning," and "Experience," in addition to "Humanity," figured as "almost the constant Attendant on true Genius" (686). Humanity brings with it "tender Sensations," for "Not without these the tender Scene is painted. From these alone proceed the noble, disinterested Friendship, the melting Love, the generous Sentiment, the ardent Gratitude, the soft Compassion, the candid Opinion; and all those strong Energies of a good Mind, which fill the moistened Eyes with Tears, the glowing Cheeks with Blood, and swell the Heart with Tides of Grief, Joy, and Benevolence" (687).

The paragraphs elaborating the concepts of genius, learning, and experience all dwell specifically on the value of the qualities to the writer. Humanity is another matter. It enables the writer to paint "the tender Scene," but its other attributes appear to have nothing to do with writing. They concern, rather, the nature not only of "a good Mind" but of a good man or woman. Most of these qualities belong conspicuously to Tom, within the narrative. They might well belong also to the good reader.

The imagined "good reader" appears more consistently in *Amelia*—a somewhat surprising fact, considering the novel's severe skepticism about the motives and conduct of most human beings in its fictional world. The narrator gestures occasionally toward the possibility that readers might disagree, as when he announces his intention of placing Booth's account of "Scenes of Tenderness" in a separate chapter, "which we desire all our Readers who do not love, or who perhaps do not know the Pleasure of Tenderness, to pass over" (*Amelia* 101). More characteristic, though, is the assumption that readers will share the narrator's version of "humanity":

"The Scene that followed, during some Minutes, is beyond my Power of Description: I must beg the Readers' Hearts to suggest it to themselves" (316). The imaginary community of good readers compensates morally for the diminished community of good within the text.

Nicholas Hudson, in his concern for Fielding's techniques of rhetorical manipulation, concludes that the good reader can be no more than a fiction. He cites Mark Kinkead-Weekes as a critic who takes seriously the possibility of a reader with sensitivity and judgment, then comments that "this very recognition is delusive, and disguises from the reader a process which is, in important ways, at odds with Fielding's professed moral doctrine: the sensitivity and judgment we perceive in ourselves is both the creation of subtle rhetorical coercion, and a screen for that coercion" (191). But manipulation, readily identifiable in Fielding, is not identical with coercion, which cannot be demonstrated. In fact the reader—*pace* Iser— does not *have to* do anything at all. Readers can stop reading; they can skip; they can read the end before the beginning; they can prefer bad characters to good ones, minor characters to major ones; they can declare plots implausible and metaphors inept. If Fielding subtly urges the reader toward self-perception as sensitive and judicious, such persuasion is of course readily acceptable, but it does not necessarily create or alter the reader's sense of self.

Good men and women exist within Fielding's texts. The narrator also posits their existence beyond the text; the reader may well belong to their number. When the narrator evokes "Humanity" as characteristic of a good writer, he also mentions two conspicuous real-world possessors of the quality, Lord Lyttelton and Ralph Allen (*TJ* 687), both much praised for their benevolence also by Fielding's contemporaries. The reminder of such actual presences denies the necessary fictionality of any construction of the "good." (One may assume a certain amount of mythologizing in the versions of Lyttelton and Allen promulgated by Pope and Fielding, but the fact remains: these people exist in the world, and they do good.) This particular construction of goodness, based entirely on emotion (friendship, love, sentiment, gratitude, compassion, emanating in tears, blushes, and swelling hearts) calls attention to the foundation of Fielding's sense of existent and potential communities.

References to a community of feeling abound in novels of sensibility from later in the eighteenth century. Fielding only adumbrates this kind of linkage among men and women of good will by his repeated suggestions that readers lacking certain kinds of emotional capacity will not understand Tom's actions or, on occasion, the narrator's comments. Within the narrative, the same point emerges through Blifil's inability to grasp Tom's feelings or motives. Blifil, altogether self-interested, understands others by analogy to himself and therefore necessarily fails to comprehend "Humanity" in all its manifestations. The reader who lacks "Humanity" will prove unable to grasp the operations of a novelist who has invoked this virtue right along with "Genius." The company of those possessing what Adam Smith, less than a decade later, would celebrate as "sympathy" accepts the bonds of a common condition and a common capacity for emotion, bonds that necessarily unite them.

Privacy is neither a value nor a possibility in the world of *Tom Jones.* The novelistic action systematically uncovers secrets. Every time Tom goes to bed with someone—an action epitomizing the conventionally private—that fact is certain to be revealed. The vision of naked Square, ludicrously bent into Molly Seagrim's closet, provides an appropriate emblem for the situation of the sexually active, sure to be exposed. If the narrator intermittently flaunts his own knowledge of secrets that for a time he may withhold, he eventually tells all—or, at any rate, all he thinks we need to know. The novel's structure, with the omniscient narrator in conspicuous control, insists on the moral value and the fictional urgency of exposure. The story preserves its own decorums, but it never acknowledges the importance of privacy.

It conveys clearly, however, the importance of community. J. Paul Hunter, in an essay primarily focused on Fielding, mentions Swift's earlier practice in *A Tale of a Tub.* Swift, Hunter reminds us, addresses many different kinds of readers individually. In the process, Hunter suggests, he acknowledges "that personal attention must be gotten hold of for specific purposes but lament[s] lost community" ("Fielding" 10). In the same essay, Hunter, exploring the eighteenth-century appeal of didacticism, maintains that "there can be little doubt about the commonality of *understanding* of literary purpose or about the expectations of eighteenth-century readers that writers will address them directly and anticipate Results. Those expectations have an astonishing similarity regardless of generic particulars, the kind of utility the work aims at, or the social or educational background of author or reader" (7). Certainly both statements are true: Swift laments lost community; eighteenth-century writers and readers appear to share common expectations. But in fact those common expectations, crossing lines of class and education, establish their own fundamental community.

The specific common expectations that interest Hunter derive from shared assumptions about the proper nature of reading and writing. Those assumptions almost certainly extend beyond the notion that the author will "have designs on" the reader and will try to instruct him or her. They probably include confident expectation that a novelist or a poet, or even a philosopher (as Hunter says, generic divisions don't make much difference here) will appeal to the anticipated audience on the basis of shared feelings as well as shared convictions. It is shared feelings above all that provide human connections—reminding individuals of their common "Humanity."

Swift might appropriately lament the disappearance of community: many of the old forms had disappeared, and English men and women no longer shared as much as they once had. But *community* is a relative term. Communities may be more or less large, more or less tight, more or less closely connected. Even three centuries after Swift, communities remain: smaller, less inclusive, perhaps precarious, but often sources of reassurance for those who inhabit them. In Fielding's time, close to Swift's, some basis for wide community yet survived. At the very least, such a basis could be imagined and repeatedly invoked by the novelist—perhaps the more emphatically if the sense of actual community was becoming more precarious.

The narrator's abundant comments on "bad" and "good" readers, then, particularly conspicuous in *Tom Jones*, comprise more than manipulation. "Every Reader, I believe, will be able to answer for the worthy Woman [Mrs. Miller, whom Allworthy has invited to join him in visiting Tom in prison]; but they must have a great deal of Good-Nature, and be well acquainted with Friendship, who can feel what she felt on this Occasion. Few, I hope, are capable of feeling what now past in the Mind of *Blifil*" (933–34). This typical intervention, toward the very end of the story, attaches value to one kind of feeling and opprobrium to another. It asserts the existence within the narrative of both emotional stances and posits the possibility of comparable feelings in those beyond the text. Since it does not specify the precise nature of Mrs. Miller's feelings, it both demands the reader's effort and declares all effort futile without the good nature and friendship—in short, "Humanity"—that would enable Mrs. Miller's sentiments to be duplicated. It suggests the existence of that community of good feeling I have been claiming, as well as the conceivability of a community of bad feeling, a community symbolically centered on Blifil, which the narrator "hopes" will remain small.

The explicit links between characters within and readers outside the text call attention to an idea latent in *Pride and Prejudice:* the claimed moral continuity between real world and printed rendition, a continuity on which "realism" of plot or its alternatives have no bearing. In Austen's novel, that conceivable moral continuity derives from the reader's exercise of the same kind of interpretive discipline that Elizabeth enacts. Not only does a community of value link Elizabeth and Darcy; it also connects both of them with their forebears and their peers and, in rather different terms, with their interpreters: the interpreters of Austen's novel. The "value" involved, *Pride and Prejudice* implies, demands the proper use of emotion in conjunction with judgment. For Fielding, the realm of communal value appears to entail only feeling. The existence of the "right" emotions in itself declares moral excellence. Their specific functioning and consequences hardly matter.

The argument I have constructed suggests that the concept of private reading would be irrelevant for Fielding. His novel does not celebrate privacy in its action; his direct addresses to imaginary readers, whether he figures those readers as "good" or "bad," indicate that he conceives them within categories that connect them to characters within the fiction. Yet those addresses—even granting the point that the "readers" they imply bear no necessary relation to actual readers—may betray consciousness of private reading as a possibility, and of its dangers. The perception or fantasy of a community of readers with shared, predictable emotional responses is after all not altogether solid. One can read the emphasis on the diverse characters and reactions of conceivable readers as registering anxiety lest emotion prove uncontrollable. Such "bad" characters as Blifil acknowledge the possibility that emotion can direct itself entirely toward the interests of the self, obviating moral schemes like Adam Smith's that depend upon the posited universality of sympathetic regard for others. Once the universal no longer exists, even the communal may fail. The impulse toward privacy in reading, like Blifil's impulses toward secrecy, threatens the vision of a feeling community of readers or of friends. In celebrating the man of good feeling (good feeling finally guided by prudence), Fielding simultaneously evokes the reader of his choice; he may also defend against the insulated and self-indulgent kind of reading that Brontë would lovingly evoke. His use of first-person plural pronouns suggests both the hope of making common cause with his readers and the fear that no such cause may exist. "When we find such Vices attended with their evil Consequence to our favourite Characters, we are not only taught to shun them for our own Sake, but to hate them for the Mischiefs they have already brought on those we love" (527). That "love" belongs, ideally, to novelist and readers alike. Yet a sentence later, the narrator refers to this confident statement of what "we are . . . taught" as one of his "Admonitions" to the reader: the outline of a desired outcome rather than an actuality.

In one of the narrator's most emphatic comments about the uncontrollable reader, he moves from another sequence governed by the first-person plural (e.g., "This is one Instance of that Adulation which we bestow on our own Minds, and this almost universally") to an injunction to the reader: "Examine your Heart, my good Reader, and resolve whether you do believe these matters with me" (271). A gap has opened in the *we*. The writer posits a universal, or near-universal, only to fall into doubt that registers both commitment to the idea and uncertainty about the continuing fact of community. The private reader, whose convictions cannot be taken for granted, menaces the fundamental structure of much eighteenth-century fiction.

However appealing, however a matter of assumption the idea of private reading may be for current readers, it can hardly seem appealing to any novelist who thinks seriously about it. The concept itself calls attention to readers' unruliness, to the fact that writers cannot dictate responses in those willing to commit themselves to textual perusal. That fact could, of course, assume more than one valence. *The Female Quixote*, a work centrally concerned with the consequences of private reading, leaves room for a twenty-first-century reader, and for many twentieth-century critics (e.g., Langbauer, Ross, Spacks), to suspect a subversive undertone in Charlotte Lennox's treatment of this subject as of other aspects of the female condition. What eighteenth-century female readers thought about the matter we can only surmise: I have been unable to unearth convincing testimony. The most prominent male readers—Samuel Johnson, Henry Fielding—found Lennox's book a triumph of orthodoxy, warning young women against excessive indulgence in the reading of romances. That message, though, is hedged with ambiguities, at least for recent readers. *The Female Quixote* suggests that for women private reading, feared by men as a female indulgence, becomes inevitable as a consequence of male restriction.

At the novel's opening, a man disillusioned with public life chooses privacy as his condition, retiring from court and company, and inflicts that condition on his uncomplaining wife, who solaces herself by reading romances. She does not live long. Her daughter, likewise deprived of all society, seeing other people only at church, follows her mother in her choice of reading and, having no experience of the actual world to counter the messages of that reading, comes to believe the fictions she encounters all true. The novel's action concerns the process by which Arabella realizes her mistakes and accepts her fate of marriage. As she begins to live in the social world from which she has previously been excluded, she offers harsh indictments of prevailing fashion and custom, seeing the moral inadequacy of what "society" has to offer. Her creator, however, need not take full responsibility for these indictments, since Arabella's condition has been posited as delusional.

Very little reading takes place in this novel about reading. Arabella has already completed the reading that defines her; although she may look back at her chosen texts, she reads nothing new. She commands her would-be lover, Glanville, to read certain romances himself, but to him these texts remain illegible. Glanville's sister, an ignoramus who embodies the assumptions of society, appears to have read nothing at all and certainly reads nothing new. Sir George, a past reader of romances, uses his reading to entrap Arabella but does no reading in the present. Lennox interests herself, rather, in reading's consequences. The difference between the results of romance reading in Arabella and Sir George depends not only on the man's moral corruption and eagerness to manipulate others but also on the contrast between private reading and comparable transactions occurring in the context of community. Sir George's "community" in its nature largely duplicates Miss Glanville's. It partakes of and is principally defined by social depravity. It nonetheless provides a check against the propensity of private reading to mislead. Arabella, with apparently innate goodness, yet lacks an appropriate sense of how a woman must (and must not) behave. She can learn the rules only by inhabiting and taking seriously a social world.

But many recent readers, reflecting on Arabella's manifest moral superiority to the likes of Miss Glanville as well as on her capacity to imagine and, however ludicrously, even to undertake significant female action, have perceived ambiguity in Lennox's account of a young woman's inadvertent alienation. Arabella's reading enables her imaginative energy and her indirect commentary on the female situation in the world. That reading's privacy, which implies its, and her, separation from an immediate social context, gives it potency.

One must wonder what kind of community of readers Lennox imagined for herself. "Subversive" readings of *The Female Quixote* implicitly raise the possibility of a double community. On the one hand, the novel offers its message for Dr. Johnson and his peers, men particularly, but women too, committed to and more or less content with established values and supported by social givens. More covertly, the narrative speaks to quite a different community: of the discontented, the alienated, the depressed. And it conveys the message that they are not alone. Arabella embodies at least the temporary possibility of making a world for oneself. Although she emphatically rejects that world in the end, aligning herself with orthodoxy, her private life, the life nourished by reading, has allowed her briefly to exercise force.

Charlotte Lennox does not typically address readers real or imagined. Her coy chapter title for book 9, chapter 11 ("Being in the Author's Opinion, the best Chapter in this History") implicitly offers a pointer, straightforward or ironic, for the reader, but its stress on opinion raises the possibility that the author is talking to herself or to someone offstage (Johnson? The critics?) rather than to those who will read her book primarily for pleasure or enlightenment. Only in the novel's final sentence does a reader make a transient appearance: "We chuse, Reader, to express this Circumstance, though the same, in different Words" (383). Like the chapter title cited above, this explanation (which turns on the moral difference between Arabella's marriage and Miss Glanville's) hints a didactic purpose. The undifferentiated reader, invoked in the singular, is assigned no character and no community. In privacy she learns what Lennox has to teach. She may, like Arabella, dramatize what she has learned, using it as a principle for her life. On the other hand, she—if she *is* a *she*—may choose to keep it to herself, a woman's secret.

Keeping it to herself, of course, exerts no effect in the world. Lennox sketches fairly bleak alternatives: conventional marriage or eccentric individualism; making insight public, in an effort to control one's own life, and winning only ridicule; or keeping it private and controlling nothing. A woman's attempt to move from the privacy of her reading into a wider domain is doomed to failure. To be sure, Arabella's attempt is ridiculous, but it provides a revealing allegory of impossibility. The limited efficacy of private reading for Arabella reminds Lennox's readers of the danger of delusional fantasy implicit in separation from the community. But it may remind some readers as well of the special situation of women, for whom speaking in Parliament—which Glanville's father declares possible for Arabella by virtue of her talents, but impossible by virtue of her sex—must always remain forbidden, and private fantasy provides the only outlet of aspiration.

For Austen, Henry Fielding, and Lennox, altogether private reading, in its separation from direct experience and from the values of the community, proves dangerous because of its inherent lack of discipline and its consequent unpredictability. Sarah Fielding complicates the issue by arguing that private reading—most often in its metaphoric sense: "reading" of other people—provides the best basis for community. In *David Simple* she uses a literal instance of private reading to undergird the more expansive point. Cynthia, eventually a participant in the little community that forms around David, has suffered a miserable early existence, largely because of her passion for reading. Unlike Arabella, she favors books that will improve her knowledge of the actual world. As she says of herself—prefacing the account by the assertion that she has never experienced happiness—

I loved reading, and had a great Desire of attaining Knowledge; but whenever I asked Questions of any kind whatsoever, I was always told, *such Things were not proper for Girls of my Age to know:* If I was pleased with any Book above the most silly Story or Romance, it was taken from me. For *Miss must not enquire too far into things, it would turn her Brain; she had better mind her Needle-work, and such Things as were useful for Women; reading and poring on Books, would never get me a Husband.* Thus was I condemned to spend my Youth, the Time when our Imagination is at the highest, and we are capable of most Pleasure, without being indulged in any one thing I liked. (101)

This narrative neatly encapsulates a view of female reading often represented in eighteenth-century works by women. Indeed, such a view may stand behind the story of Arabella, whose unchecked indulgence in romances could reflect the attitude of even a loving father: romances can be thought the most appropriate reading for a girl, who is not expected or desired to know much about the world. Needlework is useful for a woman; knowledge is not.

Cynthia's reading is "private" in a new sense: exclusionary. Her sisters, constantly taunting her about her pretensions to "wit," understand her reading as a way of separating herself from them and from the community of mindless women. Her own narrative of her experience hints that she would have been willing to share, to engage in constructive conversation, but the sisters' perception insists that she considers herself different from them. The misery of her girlhood derives partly from her being forced into difference.

A more conventional female reader, whom David also encounters, finds no impediment to her extravagant reading of romances, an acceptable, if sometimes moralistically criticized, form of female indulgence. The unnamed wife who tells her story reports how readily she succumbed to her first letter from a would-be lover: it "was writ so much in the strain of some of my favourite Books, that I was over-joyed at the Thoughts of such an Adventure" (54). The adventure leads her into an unfortunate marriage, from which David finds her suffering. Like Arabella, she has read for herself; unlike Arabella, she finds no moral guide to rescue her from the consequences.

The "good" characters *David Simple* evokes occupy themselves extensively in reading those they meet. They vary in their capacity to penetrate plausible but misleading appearances, characteristically hoping to find in others charity of spirit like their own. David is particularly obtuse, always expecting the best, but often encountering evidence of corruption and debilitating self-interest. Like Cynthia, David, whose conscious and consistent desire focuses on community (he sets out into the world in search of "a friend"), finds himself inadvertently doomed to separation and difference because of his "reading" of other people, which tells him over and over of hypocrisy and corruption and emphasizes for him the ways in which he diverges from common expectations and standards. Roughly the first third of Sarah Fielding's novel dwells on his unsuccessful effort to find a good man or woman. Like many protagonists of sentimental fiction a feminized male, he initiates little action beyond that of interpretation. But interpretation matters enormously. It supplies the necessary preliminary to friendship and ultimately to community. The "bad" people David encounters don't bother to interpret. They explain character, with great insouciance, according to what they have heard, or what they wish, or what appears to serve their immediate interests in relation to David. If he must learn the deceptive possibilities of appearances, he must also discover that he cannot trust everything he is told.

The other men and women whom David rather readily comes to love offer him, in lavish detail, their stories, which he must also "read" for evidence of character as well as experience. Those stories center in every instance on persecution and suffering, delineating their tellers as victims of injustice both familial and social. Suffering validates character for David, securely placing its victim beyond the realm of appearances. The community he develops on the basis of his benevolence, as he shares his money with the virtuous who need it, rests on the assumption of mutual obligation to help and sustain. As Sarah Fielding elaborates her narrative, she specifies diverse modes of support and of mutuality, responsive both to open and to covert need.

But the community David forms is inevitably small. It exists under constant threat because of the posited corruption of the "polite world" where power and wealth reside. The precarious alliance of good people survives and procreates for a considerable time, but its members, although they die in conditions of faith and hope, die also in earthly misery. If the novel celebrates the notion of community, it denigrates that of society, predicated as it is on the assumption that the world flourishes on the basis of depravity.

The implicit understanding of readership in the novel is implicated with this vision of the world. Good readers, too, constitute a small and threatened community. The chapter titles often sound confident in their pointing of moral emphasis: "In which are seen the terrible Consequences which attend Envy and Selfishness" (1:2); "In which is plainly proved, that it is possible for a Woman to be so strongly fix'd in her Affection for one Man, as to take no pleasure in hearing Love from any other" (3:4); "Which proves the great Difference of those wrong Actions which arise from violent Passions, and those which have their Source in the Malignity of a rancorous Heart" (4:8). The verb *prove* and its cognates, frequently reiterated, insist on the incontrovertibility of the moral insights provided. Yet the events that "prove" the strength of a woman's fidelity do not prevent men from testing it; the distinction between passion and malignity never becomes self-evident.

Many of the narrator's references to readers suggest the affinity between good readers and the good people depicted in the text. Camilla looks at David "with an Air of Softness and Gratitude, in which our Hero's Sensibility read as much as in any thing [s]he could have said" (129). Two pages later: "What this poor Creature, whose Heart was naturally tender and grateful, felt at seeing himself loaded with Benefits from a Stranger, I leave to the Imagination of every Reader, who can have any Sense of Obligations" (131). Sympathetic imagination allows David to understand a woman's "Air" as easily as he could understand her words; precisely the same quality is required of the reader. Often the narrator declares herself incapable of rendering some emotionally complex situation. The difficulties of expressing and those of understanding are identical: "What he felt during that Interval, is not to be expressed or understood, but by the few who are capable of real Tenderness" (18). The book is written for, as well as about, those few.

Within the story, good people often refrain from saying what might cause pain to others, and other good people understand what is said without words. Accordingly, the narrator need not describe delicate feeling. "But as Tenderness, when it is come to the height, is not to be described, I shall pass over the rest of this Scene in Silence" (185). The reader, too, will understand without words. The text, then, only provides a kind of signpost, to be first deciphered, then elaborated on the basis both of experience and of what one might call emotional character. Reminders of what the narrator fails to say, what the reader should comprehend nonverbally, proliferate until the narrative seems to deny its own utterance. What it states assumes less importance than what it only hints, because the hints test not only the acumen but, more importantly, the character of the individual reader.

That reader will prove adequate or inadequate not so much by virtue of values shared or rejected as by feelings responsive to other, imagined feelings. The reader necessarily functions as an individual, indulging, like figures within the text, in seductive but morally sanctioned pleasures of sympathy and compassion. The experience of reading unites the private and the communal. Inasmuch as the reader sympathizes with those whose imagined experiences lead them to forming a community, he or she becomes imaginatively part of the same community. In any case, the emotion of sympathy declares the whole world kin, depending on an idea of community for its very existence. Yet the reader feels that emotion in literal isolation and enjoys it as a private pleasure.

The assertions of inexpressible feeling and the claim that only readers with finely adjusted emotional equipment will be able to respond adequately to the text became familiar in later sentimental fiction, but Sarah Fielding helped to originate this way of imagining text and reader and the relation between the two. In the final paragraph of *Volume the Last*, the 1753 sequel to *David Simple* (now printed continuously with the earlier work, first published in 1744), however, Sarah Fielding complicates the vision of a possible reader and exposes the ambiguities of such a reader's role. The preceding paragraph concludes with David on his deathbed, a scene less prolonged than that of Clarissa's dying, but equally edifying. Then comes this extraordinary utterance:

> But now will I draw the Veil, and if any of my Readers chuse to drag *David Simple* from the Grave, to struggle again in this World, and to reflect, every Day, on the Vanity of its utmost Enjoyments, they may use their own Imaginations, and fancy *David Simple* still bustling about on this Earth. But I chuse to think he is escaped from the Possibility of falling into any future Afflictions, and that neither the Malice of his pretended Friends, nor the Sufferings of his real ones, can ever again rend and torment his honest Heart. (432)

Positioning the writer and the reader as equal imaginative participants—either could choose to drag David from the grave—the first-person speaker conveys a shadow of resentment at the reader's imaginative freedom. The reader who wants to fancy David still bustling about the earth lacks compassion: only death can free from suffering the good man whom the narrative has delineated. The account of his deathbed has stressed his piety, his Christian hope. This concluding vision suggests that death means only surcease from pain, not ascension to a better state. It also conveys the arbitrariness of fictional invention. Matters can always be otherwise than as they are described; the reader can make them otherwise. So the narrator's choices lack final authority—authority that the text seems deliberately to give away.

It is of course true once more that this is an imagined, not an actual, reader. But to imagine the reader thus entails reflection on the consequences of privacy. The situation of the private reader indeed implies the possibility of doing—that is, thinking—anything at all. Henry Fielding, in his elaborate manipulations of the reader, hinted at least a faint fantasy of control, a fantasy supported by the idea of shared values. His sister reveals no such hope or dream. As she evokes a reader largely governed by and profoundly responsive to emotion, she necessarily relinquishes belief in the possibility that such a reader would belong to a large community. David's community remains small and threatened because surrounded by a corrupt world. The community of feeling readers must inhabit a comparable position. And to fancy readers as primarily governed by feeling is to adumbrate their intransigence.

Sarah Fielding suggests in every respect a vision of the world darker than her brother's. The smallness of her imagined community of feeling, both within and beyond the text, like the difficulty of interpretation, indicates how precarious and arduous the situation of the good person necessarily remains. The self-interested, corrupt, and wicked take advantage of David and his friends, who have no meaningful protection against exploitation. Virtue makes one vulnerable in society. The reader's conceivable virtue enables the pleasure of reading, but also entails social vulnerability. As for privacy: the good don't want it. David and Cynthia and Camilla and their friends expose everything to one another. The telling of intimate stories appears to constitute a primary activity of virtuous people. The little community shares everything: wealth, knowledge, action. The small community of readers seeks the pleasure of intimate knowledge about imagined figures, a trope for such sharing in actual experience. The bad have secrets; like Henry Fielding's Blifil, they alone require privacy. Sarah Fielding conveys no image of the private reader, but the logic of her text suggests that she would disapprove. Yet she claims no power to enforce her disapproval.

It remained for Laurence Sterne to explore the full implications of imagining a reader profoundly autonomous and separate. Like Sarah Fielding, he conceives a reader who, resembling him in this respect, is governed by both feeling and imagination. His implicit address to that reader—sir or madam, hostile critic or amused dilettante, skeptic or devotee—says, over and over, "Anything you can do, I can do better." Always, Sterne, in the persona of Tristram or Yorick, is there first, wherever "there" may be. One can hardly speak of a "typical" passage in *Tristram Shandy*, but this early set of injunctions to the reader at least typifies the debonair insistence with which the storyteller asserts his power:

> Therefore, my dear friend and companion, if you should think me somewhat sparing of my narrative on my first setting out,—bear with me,—and let me go on, and tell my story my own way:—or if I should seem now and then to trifle upon the road,—or should sometimes put on a fool's cap with

a bell to it, for a moment or two as we pass along,—don't fly off,—but rather courteously give me credit for a little more wisdom than appears upon my outside;—and as we jogg on, either laugh with me, or at me, or in short, do any thing,—only keep your temper. (11)

The deployment of *seem* masterfully establishes the narrator's claim of control. The reader can only deal in *seemings*; the narrator knows facts. All superficial appearance of folly, he claims, only conceals wisdom. Alleging the reader's position as his "dear friend and companion," he ends by offering the kind of moral lesson one might give a child: be courteous, keep your temper. All conceivable negative judgment can be subsumed under the categories of discourtesy or bad temper.

Tristram shifts ground rapidly and disconcertingly. He warns the reader against "the indiscreet reception of such guests" as his father's hypotheses (53), posits the reader's "thorough knowledge of human nature" as justification for not elaborating a point (28), taunts the reader for inattentiveness (56). When he wants to call attention to bawdy double entendres, he usually invokes a female reader. He guides the reader in elaborate imaginative sequences (e.g., 109) and tells the reader what he or she remembers and expects (e.g., 292). His dominant tone in reference to the reader is teasing. He mocks anyone who has difficulty grasping the precise geographical contours of Uncle Toby's garden: "If the reader has not a clear conception of the rood and the half of ground which lay at the bottom of my uncle *Toby*'s kitchen garden, and which was the scene of so many of his delicious hours,—the fault is not in me,—but in his imagination;— for I am sure I gave him so minute a description, I was almost ashamed of it" (443). He deliberately encourages false, tormenting expectations, promising, for instance, a fifty-page digression about an irrelevant historical figure (486). Not only does he shift ground; one can never be quite sure where, exactly, he is.

Barbara Benedict, commenting on these manipulations, points out that they involve prompting the reader's reactions. "These reactions, however," she adds, "paradoxically dramatize the separation of the reader from the fiction, the characters, and even the narrator" (*Framing* 80). Benedict claims that "conversation or communication paradoxically marks alienation, and Tristram continually attempts to co-opt all the imaginative possibilities in the text" (81). In making this claim, she calls attention to one way in which Sterne forces the reader to experience aspects of the psychic action within the text—the duplicity and frustration involved in attempts at communication among the characters.

Yet Yorick persistently conveys at least a fantasy of another sort of communication with the reader. He suggests rather clearly the nature of his desired relation to his readers. Long before he specifies a failure in the imagination as the cause of the reader's inability to "see" Uncle Toby's battlefield, he bursts out, in the context of a bitter complaint about "the cant of criticism," "I would go fifty miles on foot, for I have not a horse worth riding on, to kiss the hand of that man whose generous heart will give up the reins of his imagination into his author's hands,—be pleased he knows not why, and cares not wherefore" (182). The ideal bond between narrator and reader depends on willing submission, acceptance of guidance for the unruly imagination. Again, a moral term (*generous*) carries much weight. The submissive reader obviates the necessity for the narrator to mock and tease and cajole. It is an act of true generosity freely to allow the storyteller that dominance that he will insistently claim with or without the reader's consent. Such a reader, to be sure, does not necessarily exist. Tristram wishes for him; he does not necessarily have faith in this imagined being's actuality.

In this supremely self-centered narrative, it is not surprising that the reader is implicitly conceived in the image of the narrator. Tristram feels governed by his emotions and his imagination; the reader, he assumes, will operate the same way. The character's sequences of language come to him by way of association of ideas; he has Locke's authority for believing that the reader's mind will work in comparable fashion. The notion of a community of assumption would be inconceivable in the solipsistic universe Tristram evokes. Despite all the tender feeling manifest in Uncle Toby and Corporal Trim, neither demonstrates much capacity to grasp the operations of another consciousness. Each man rides his own hobby horse; the few women in the narrative figure as adjuncts to male dramas. It is possible to sympathize—Uncle Toby can sympathize even with a fly—without comprehending. The novel as a whole emphasizes the unavoidable separateness, the final privacy, of every human being.

But it also claims the commonalty of feeling: the ground of Tristram's/Sterne's manipulation of readers. The narrative's dramatic shifts of tone demand the reader's participation as well as attention. When Corporal Trim weeps over the sermon he is reading aloud, because the hypothetical narrative in the text reminds him of possible happenings in his brother's life, he calls attention to the situation of ideal readers moved by events occurring in the lives of imaginary characters to reflect on happenings in their own experience or that of those they care for. Tristram both alternates and combines the ludicrous and the pathetic. The story of his infantile accidents, for instance, evokes laughter as well as sympathy. The imagined future death of Uncle Toby will ideally make the reader as well as the narrator shed a tear. The pressure to do so may come at least partly from the reader's desire to make common cause with a narrator who, in the absence of shared responses, will mock and scorn the recalcitrant peruser of his text.

This putative readerly desire for alliance provides a counterpart for the narrator's desire, focused on that sense of community that implies the possibility of control. Given assurance that common assumptions govern narrator and reader, the teller of the story can feel confident of possessing the power to manipulate a reader about whom he knows (or believes) something crucial. Conversely, the reader can feel assured that the narrator will not disturb any of the fundamental assumptions governing worldly as well as literary experience. Yet both sides perhaps sense also the tenuousness of such assurance, given the unknowability of interior lives. The community of feeling, on which Henry Fielding built so much, for Sterne appears to provide at best a precarious foundation.

So Tristram turns to other bases for fictional construction, exposing and exploiting the fact of his own unknowability. His incalculable leaps of the imagination dramatize his eccentricity, comparable to that of every other man and woman. The marbled page that he provides as emblem of his work would, in eighteenth-century printings, have possessed a unique form in its every instance (a point I owe to Bruce Redford)—appropriate mark of the unpredictable effects of every reader's consciousness on the representations offered by the knowing narrator, who knows, among other things, that he can never know enough. The reader's privacy constitutes the narrator's problem, as the narrator's flaunted inaccessibility constitutes the reader's.

On the whole, *Tristram Shandy* adumbrates the situation of privacy as one of necessary doom rather than possible privilege. The deprivation entailed in privacy consists not only in separation from public life, the state suggested by the word's etymology, but also, more importantly, in removal from certainty and from dependable interpersonal communion. The novel's characters endure their own forms of privacy, with attendant false certainties (Walter Shandy's convictions about naming, for example, or Tristram's assertion that digressions are the sunshine of reading), and the narrator often sounds at least faintly desperate in his implicit acknowledgments of the reader's corresponding privacy. Privacy by definition implies relative or absolute isolation, psychological or physical or both. The lack of successful communication in the world of *Tristram Shandy* provides one index of its consequences.

Yet Tristram as narrator employs an ostensibly, even ostentatiously, conversational tone, apparently implying his confidence in the ease of establishing intimate contact with his individual readers. In its structure and its substance, though, the story he tells undermines any claim of confidence, as it demonstrates the characteristic meaninglessness of what passes for conversation: people talking at cross-purposes. The conversational tone can be only bravado. Privacy defeats communication by making it always incomplete, often nonexistent.

If Jane Eyre's secluded reading supplies an image for the delight of the reader's privacy, Tristram's linguistic flourishes call attention to the potential horror of the same condition. In the sequence of novels I have investigated, Sterne's novel provides an appropriate end point. Henry Fielding appears to worry about what private reading might mean, but he can believe that a moral community of feeling would check its conceivable excesses. Charlotte Lennox emphasizes the danger of private reading, the degree to which it might separate its practitioner from the security of social and linguistic convention, but also hints that such reading provides a resource for establishing an individual sense of power and possibility. Sarah Fielding, despite her suggestions that private reading might provide the basis for solid moral community, deplores the possible irresponsibility of the autonomous reader. Sterne, without the ominous moralizing that occasionally characterizes the others, goes farther than the rest in insisting on the ultimate separation of one human being from another even within a social context. He understands the private reader as a special case of the private person, functioning like other persons in final isolation, demonstrating repeatedly the imaginary nature of conversation and other forms of putative communication.

This sequence, roughly chronological though it is, does not point to any simple or clear social change. Throughout the eighteenth century, writers provide indications of concern about the implications of private reading, yet by the early nineteenth century the writers who succeeded them often appear to take for granted such reading as a source of pleasure. The sequence of increasing concern, in other words, did not issue in rejection of private reading as an idea.

But the meditations on the private reader that make their way into eighteenth-century fiction call attention to the period's sense of ambiguity about the right of the individual to be let alone, and about the propriety of the privilege. The right or privilege of privacy, from some perspectives, might when realized appear more like a loss than a gain: a decline in social comfort rather than, or as well as, an acquisition of personal freedom. Unlike Swift, or even Henry Fielding, Sterne betrays no nostalgia for an imagined or remembered period of fuller community. Unlike Sarah Fielding, he expresses no vivid longing for personal association. He makes comedy of isolation—but the comic viewpoint does not obviate the potential pain and danger of that isolation. Getting away from other people, which I suggested as an innocent childhood delight, may carry high costs. It entails the absence of support as well as of interference; it can mean frustration as well as liberation.

If Sterne and the others convey the negative aspects of private reading—and, by extension, the ambiguities of privacy as a large concept—they also on occasion hint the exhilaration that may accompany a flight from the social realm so vital to eighteenth-century self-imagining. Lennox suggests privacy as a recourse for women, a way of turning to their own advantage restrictions externally imposed upon them. Sterne's representations have broader implications. Tristram's rollicking narrative reveals impossibilities of human exchange, but it also conveys the storyteller's glee in the comedy of cross-purposes, his affection for the participants, his amusement at the futile struggles individuals pursue. One cannot escape the human condition: he entirely understands that fact. But he understands, too, the appeal of solipsism as well as its more sinister aspects. He vigorously indulges in it himself, and the gusto of his self-indulgence declares the pleasure as well as the pain of living to oneself.

3

The Performance of Sensibility

People do not know, she said, what satisfaction there is in weeping over one's own sufferings and those of others. Sensibility always brings to the soul a certain self-contentment independent of fortune and events. Rousseau

The community of feeling that eighteenth-century novelists invoke on occasion depends especially on the capacity for sympathy. That capacity, an eighteenth-century thinker could believe, potentially united all or most of humankind; that, one might depend on. Yet, as my last chapter indicated, not even faith in feeling could alleviate uncertainty about the kind of response that a given textual maneuver might elicit in any particular reader.

The recorded anxiety about the inaccessibility of the reader's consciousness calls attention to a deeper worry: the period's pervasive fear of human opacity. Recognition that human beings remain finally unknowable could create anxiety in itself, but the possibility that people might consciously *make themselves* unknowable threatened the social value of every ritual of manners and morals. The rites of masking in the fiction of Eliza Haywood and her contemporaries, the prevalence of the masquerade as trope throughout the century, the explicit preoccupation with hypocrisy in Henry Fielding and others, the detailed investigation of such antiheroes as Lovelace, Proteus-like from start to finish of his career: such signs testify to widespread awareness and concern. *English Literature in the Age of Disguise* (Novak), the title of a 1977 collection of critical essays on the eighteenth century, appropriately suggests the issue's pervasiveness. Praise for "openness," warnings against hypocrisy and affectation, close supervision of the young and of women: no such tactics could alleviate the possibility that persons might conceal—even from those who most needed to know—precisely what should define them. Such concealment willfully separated its practitioner from the community. It constituted, in other words, an expedient for privacy, a set of tactics that could protect the individual from unwanted observation by disguising personality or at least obscuring immediate reactions. "No act of transgression, other than ultimate mind control, can ever fully penetrate and expose inviolate personality," writes Elizabeth Neill (111). The need to protect "inviolate personality" looms large in much eighteenth-century writing, especially by women. Yet the same writing often expresses also the period's intense concern about the ubiquity and impenetrability of disguise. When hypocrisy serves as an almost universal social strategy, substituting for unavailable forms of privacy, such concern would seem justified.

In the context of worries about self-concealment, the cult of sensibility that developed around the middle of the century takes on new meaning. Sensibility, the kind of personal consciousness that allows—indeed, guarantees—fine responsiveness, was thought to originate in the nervous system. Women tended to demonstrate it to a higher degree than men because of their "finer nerves." Since its signs registered on the body, it opened emotion to public view. Weeping, blushing, fainting, "brain fever"—such evidence of psychic states might be read by any onlooker. Although ambiguity remained (did a father's illness occasion a young woman's tears, or did they attest to the existence of a lover?), the mythology of sensibility encouraged fantasies of accessibility. Not even a determined will to privacy, according to this mythology, could protect women in particular from offering inadvertent testimony to their inner states.

In practice, though, the relation between sensibility and privacy proved complex and contradictory. On the one hand, sensibility can function as self-display, a deliberate and often flamboyant abjuration of privacy; on the other, sensibility itself may serve as a form of concealment or emphasize the ultimate fact of concealment. I began this chapter with a quotation from Rousseau's *Julie, or, The New Heloise*, that virtual textbook of eighteenth-century sensibility (understood as such by many contemporaries), which exemplifies both sensibility as performance and sensibility as participating in concealment. The passage comes from an account of Julie's death by her "cold" husband, Wolmar, written for the benefit of her former lover, St. Preux. As Wolmar reports it, Julie's deathbed summation of her life includes this panegyric to sensibility, valued for its emotional benefits to its possessor. Her remarks take on special interest in conjunction with an earlier narrative, this one by St. Preux, providing evidence of Wolmar's sensibility. According to St. Preux's account, Wolmar enters a room where Julie and her beloved cousin Claire both lie unconscious, having fainted from joy at their reunion. Also present are Claire's daughter, Henriette, crying and screaming; Julie's servant Fanchon, at her mistress's side; and St. Preux himself, striding "erratically about the room" without knowing what he is doing, uttering "broken exclamations, and in a convulsive spasm" he is unable to control. Instead of intervening in the chaotic scene, "this happy husband threw himself into an armchair to watch avidly this ravishing spectacle. Have no fear, he said, perceiving our solicitude. These Scenes of pleasure and joy exhaust nature for a moment only to revive her with a new vigor; they are never dangerous. Let me savor the happiness which I am enjoying and which you share" (Rousseau 490).

Like Julie herself, Wolmar, however cold, values sensibility's private satisfactions. He perceives the scene of sensibility, quite appropriately, as "spectacle," partly designed for the observer. He recognizes the women's fainting as signs of their sensibility and indulges his own by "avidly" watching rather than by helping. To be sure, no help is needed. Wolmar is quite right in saying that nothing dangerous has happened and in predicting that the cousins will revive soon. Nonetheless, the scene provides dramatic evidence of the self-gratification provided by indulged sensibility and of its manifestations' ambiguity. Wolmar's sensibility expresses itself in a passivity that might readily be taken to indicate lack of feeling; correspondingly, the scene opens the possibility that tears and fainting and blushing and the rest, the most extravagant signs, the opposite of Wolmar's apparent inertness, might "mean" not responsiveness to others but indulgence of the self.

Introducing his study of theatricality (which deals mainly with the eighteenth century), David Marshall writes, "I will trace the interplay between the threat of the theatrical position of appearing as a spectacle before spectators; the protection of dramatic impersonations that would conceal the self from those who would see, name, or know it; and the dream of an act of sympathy that would allow those who face each other as actor and spectator to transcend theatrical distance through a transfer of parts and persons" (2). The terms he here establishes are precisely relevant to Rousseau's scene, in which Julie and her friends occupy the "theatrical position," with Wolmar as spectator, and in which, as I shall argue, "dramatic impersonations" help to conceal the self, establishing privacy, while the claim of "sympathy" justifies much that happens.

If, as Julie claims, sensibility provides independent "self-contentment," its display can signify self-satisfying performance rather than outward-directed concern. The quality celebrated for its evidence of the power of sympathy lends itself also to solipsistic gratification. The exercise of sensibility sometimes constitutes emotional masturbation. Sensibility as spectacle feeds on itself and generates ever more self-dramatization.

I put the case in extreme terms to emphasize the intensity of a paradox that others have noted less emphatically. Recent scholarship, placing the movement or "cult" of sensibility in social context, has stressed the social significance of eighteenth-century concern with the capacity for emotional responsiveness (e.g., Brissenden, Van Sant). The connections of ideas about sensibility with everything from medical theory to consumerism have been provocatively explored by scholars who recognize also the degree to which the interest in sensibility encouraged individual concentration on inner states (see especially Barker-Benfield, Mullan, Ellis). Indeed, toward the end of the period that saw the fullest development of this interest, Frances Burney clearly articulated sensibility's double valence. In a fiction relying heavily on a rhetoric of sensibility, she observed that sensibility, leading its possessor to disinterested concern for others, also encouraged one to "forget all mankind, to watch the pulsations of its [i.e., sensibility's] own fancies" (Burney, *Camilla* 680). The disturbing discrepancy between disinterested concern and complete forgetting, between turning outward and inward, creates a gap not readily bridgeable. Burney herself does not attempt to bridge it: her characters generally manifest either the self-regarding or the outward-turning kind of sensibility, not both.

The implicit division of sensibility into "good" and "bad" varieties becomes familiar in the 1790s. The distinction between the two, for most novelists, depends on the intervention of reason. Sensibility controlled and directed by reason, as Wollstonecraft and Radcliffe insist, generates humanitarian action; sensibility without reason encourages navel-gazing and, worse still, sexual indulgence. But such an attempt to resolve the paradox of sensibility neither clarifies the problem of how a literature of sensibility affects the reader nor resolves the ambiguity of individual manifestations.

Julie makes its problems of sensibility vivid. In one exemplary sequence, Julie tends her dying mother. According to her cousin's account,

> Her heart seems suffocated with affliction, and the excess of the sentiments that oppress her lends her an air of stupefaction more frightening than sharp cries. She stays day and night on her knees at her mother's bedside, absently, her eyes riveted to the ground, keeping an absolute silence; serving her with more attention and intensity than ever; then suddenly falling back into a state of prostration that makes her appear a different person. Very clearly it is the mother's illness that maintains the daughter's strength, and if eagerness to serve her did not quicken her zeal, her vacant eyes, her

pallor, her extreme dejection would make me fear lest she herself have great need of the care she is providing her mother. (Rousseau 252)

The vacant eye and pallor that declare Julie's sensibility derive immediately from her guilt over her affair with St. Preux, which her mother has discovered and which the culprit sometimes declares responsible for her mother's illness. But her sensibility also expresses itself in her selfless service to her mother, and the "excess of the sentiments that oppress her" originates in the double burden of guilt and grief. Both reflect high consciousness of, and responsibility toward, others. Julie dramatizes her magnanimity by her service, but also by her self-castigation. She demonstrates how completely sensibility depends on the existence of others—as recipients of benevolence, but also as audience for the highly orchestrated physical signs that declare what "seems" her emotional state.

By the end of the letter describing Julie's activity and condition, though, Claire sounds a new note, commenting on "the abasement to which remorse and shame have reduced her" (254). No longer, the writer suggests, does the heroine possess the profound sensibility that previously impelled her actions. "She is still, I admit, gentle, generous, compassionate; the endearing habit of doing good she cannot possibly lose; but it has become merely a blind habit, an unreflected [unconsidered] taste. She does all the same things, but she no longer does them with the same zeal; those sublime sentiments have waned" (254). This summary grounds Claire's appeal to St. Preux to renounce Julie utterly: presumably he will restore her sensibility by thus exercising his own. He does so, pledging to Julie's mother that he will neither see nor write to his beloved. Then he in turn appeals to Claire to absolve him of responsibility for Mme. d'Étange's death. She responds by renarrating the daughter's grief in a way that may prepare the reader for Julie's self-satisfied deathbed account of the pleasures inherent in weeping for oneself and for others. You should not believe what Julie's sufferings say, Claire explains: "the imaginary motive with which it pleases her to exacerbate them is but a pretext to justify their excess. That tender soul always fears she grieves too little, and it is a sort of pleasure for her to add to the sentiment of her pains whatever can render them more acute. She is misleading herself, be sure of that; she is not sincere with herself" (264).

The notorious ambiguities of epistolary narrative of course operate here. One must understand Claire's letters (like those of others) as designed to affect their recipients in specific ways. When the writer wants St. Preux to renounce, she stresses Julie's pathos; to supply comfort, she emphasizes performance. Presumably both terms simultaneously apply: Julie embodies but also performs pathos. Her theatricality serves as a mode of relationship. Consciousness of audience can hardly be far from her mind, in a social environment predicated on the endless exchange of letters analyzing every emotional nuance of self and others. Julie, St. Preux, and Claire, the chief correspondents, brood over one another's thoughts, feelings, actions, and language. They offer interpretations only to revise them. Even as they suffer, they relish the intense drama of their interactions, a drama they construct as they respond to every experience with profound feeling. Suffused with sensibility, they appear sometimes to vie for supremacy of pain (although Claire, whose self-definition carefully differentiates her from Julie, does not often compete). Their revelations to one another help to shape their self-conceptions; their individual performances contribute to an ensemble but also proclaim the uniqueness of each actor.

In a situation that so encourages—indeed, demands—self-exposure, the idea of privacy, in the sense of individual withdrawal, may seem irrelevant. The fact that, despite all the revelations, mysteries of personality yet remain concealed suggests, however, that some degree of privacy is implicit in the very insistence of the self-display. Marshall characterizes Defoe as wanting "a world in which social relations are theatrical" (Marshall 157). Julie and the rest possess just such a world. Their ardent performances finally protect them from view—despite the fact that they are constantly watched. The letters that comprise the novel apparently constitute a concerted effort to make the inner recesses of the self accessible to at least a few others; the novel composed of those letters extends the effort more widely. The success of the little "family" in shutting out the world emphasizes the loss of separateness for each of its individual members. No notion of boundaries interferes with the insistent collective endeavor to open the heart to view. Nonetheless, recesses survive.

The interest of *Julie* for twenty-first-century readers inheres largely in its ramifying ambiguities, which focus intensely on the problematic aspects of privacy. Julie and St. Preux expose their hearts to one another, but the very process of self-exposure reveals its own ambiguities. Inasmuch as it comes to constitute a ritual, an observance conventional according to the rules of the small society, artifice inheres in the demonstration of sincerity. The concerted display of sensibility comes to emphasize the infinite regress of privacy: behind the feeling elaborately confessed, always further feeling unacknowledged; the self watching a self that can never be fully exposed and taking implicit pleasure in the watching; every confession of sensibility generating yet more sensibility. *Sensibility always brings to the soul a certain self-contentment.* That self-contentment suggests the presence of an irreducible realm of privacy, where, finally, no confession occurs.

The reader must in some sense participate in Rousseau's drama of sensibility and privacy. Even if readers serve only as witnesses, they find themselves implicated. They witness as Wolmar witnesses, watching a "ravishing spectacle" of imagined suffering, with no obligation to do anything. Like Julie, they experience some version of the "self-contentment" of sensibility. Like all the novel's main characters, they sink into a sea of feeling. If they thus partake of an imagined communal experience, they also separate themselves from the world of responsibility and action for the sake of emotional indulgence. All alone, each reader enjoys cost-free suffering. In a sense, readers, like Rousseau's characters, must receive pleasure from the contemplation as well as the activity of their own sensibilities. As the reader undergoes it, the experience of sensibility has no real outward-turning component: it provides purely private gratification. Maria Edgeworth, writing at the end of the eighteenth century, articulates the point clearly:

> You ask, why exercise does not increase sensibility, and why sympathy with imaginary distress will not always increase the disposition to sympathize with what is real?—Because pity should, I think, always be associated with the active desire to relieve. If it be suffered to become a *passive sensation*, it is a *useless weakness*, not a virtue. The species of reading you speak of must be hurtful, even in this respect, to the mind, as it indulges all the luxury of woe in sympathy with fictitious distress, without requiring the exertion which reality demands. (45–46)

The moral ambiguity of sensibility, apparent even at the time when philosophers like Hume and Adam Smith were claiming feeling as the source of morality, becomes especially vivid, as Edgeworth suggests, in the situation of those who consume the literature of sensibility. Like Richardson before him, Rousseau, in his role as "editor" of the letters, betrays anxiety about the reader's responses to the emotional drama he has constructed. Characteristically, his anxiety expresses itself in the guise of confidence: he doesn't care about the reader's reaction anyhow; good people will like his story, and the others don't matter; if readers find his narrative morally dangerous (because of Julie's unpunished premarital sexual activity with a man other than her destined husband), that fact only shows the corruption of those living in cities or frequenting courts. These rationalizations all appear in the second preface, called "Conversation about Novels between the Editor and a Man of Letters." The man of letters takes a pragmatic view; the editor presents himself as an idealist with a project of introducing "reason" into novels. Nonetheless, the chief appeal of the letters he offers comes, he says, from their "sentiment," which will appeal not to the worldly but to those who dwell far from urban corruption. "Sentiment there is, it is communicated to the heart by degrees, and it alone ultimately makes up for all the rest" (12). When one lives in isolation, the editor continues, reading makes a greater impression. "Writings intended for Solitary Folk must speak the language of Solitary Folk" (15). His narrative speaks just such a language.

If one posits a continuum from "private" to "public" life, "Solitary Folk," existing in isolation, inhabit the private end of the scale. But they do not necessarily live in privacy. Like Julie and her companions, they may create and enjoy small communities, or they may thrive in existing communities, their "isolation" only relative, their solitude measured by its distance from the crowds of city and court. Rousseau seems to think, though, that a heightened degree of isolation will intensify susceptibility to the "sentiment" he offers: the more privacy envelops readers, the more readily they serve as undistracted audience, feeling the emotions that the novelist tries to induce. Yet the editorial footnotes Rousseau scatters through his text suggest his uneasiness lest serving as feeling audience be not enough. In one telling moment, Julie, writing to St. Preux during the period of their affair, offers a bit of literary criticism: "I for one have no other manner of judging my Readings than to sound the dispositions in which they leave my soul, and I scarcely imagine what sort of goodness a book can possess when it does not lead its readers to do good." Rousseau's note as editor reads, "If the reader approves this rule, and uses it to judge this collection, the editor will not appeal his judgment" (214).

The disposition of Julie's soul appears to impel her action. Rousseau in his guise as editor hopes that those reading of good people will be inspired to virtuous activity by the encouraged disposition of their souls. But his representation of those people raises another possibility. The image of Wolmar in his chair, avidly watching, doing nothing, epitomizes the situation of the literary consumer. If, as Wolmar claims, nothing is really at stake in the scene of two unconscious women, how much less is at issue when one reads a book! Reading the fiction of sensibility may gratify desires for subtle sensation. It does not necessarily generate any corresponding desire for noble action. The act of reading takes place without the operation of overt community sanctions. Despite the fact that, as my previous chapter argued, the reader may inhabit an imagined community, reading yet encourages privacy's indulgences.

In other words, the ideal balance between the outward and inward impulses associated with sensibility is unlikely to occur in the reading of sensibility-dominated fiction. Julie herself, paragon though she is, acknowledges the self-satisfaction of sensibility. Performer and audience alike—both Julie and Wolmar—may feel it. If Julie does not explicitly acknowledge the temptation implicit in the prospect or possibility of such self-satisfaction, her creator's apparent uneasiness over the moral effects of his work tacitly recognizes exactly that.

By its very nature, the novel of sensibility lends itself particularly well to the evocation of uneasiness and anxiety—not just the author's, obviously, but the characters'. With its minute attention to shades of feeling, it aggrandizes emotion of every kind. Frances Burney directs her attention to the uncertainties of a woman's life in the social world, reminding her readers that emotion derives not only from personal situations—as Rousseau suggests, by isolating his characters from any larger social context— but especially from the consequences of inhabiting a sphere beyond the personal. *Camilla, or, A Picture of Youth*, as long a work as *Julie*, offers equally heartrending episodes and equally intense displays of sensibility. Its psychic drama depends heavily on ambiguity, uncertainty, and concern about the extent to which sensibility should expose itself to view. It argues, through its action, that privacy can be constituted by society to comprise an imposition rather than a mode of freedom.

Like many of her female literary contemporaries, Burney pays lip service to the idea that reason should control sensibility. In practice, that dictum often means that sensibility should be concealed. One cannot readily avoid feeling what one feels, but one can, according to common assumption, avoid making feeling apparent: such is the discipline that reason characteristically provides. If blushes do not fall within a woman's conscious control, she yet can leave a scene of observation, or use her fan judiciously for concealment, or provide (usually indirectly) a plausible, misleading, but unembarrassing explanation for her color. *Camilla* narrates the experience of a young woman who endures extraordinarily intense surveillance, principally by her doubtful lover and by her father. Edgar, the rich, handsome, virtuous man she loves, loves her too, but his upright tutor, Dr. Marchmont, misled by his own unhappy experience with women, persuades Edgar to watch Camilla steadily before entangling himself with her. He must watch to see if she really loves him (this despite the universal mandate of conduct books warning woman not to reveal their love until they know it reciprocated, and perhaps not even then), and to discern whether she is, as Dr. Marchmont expects, coquettish, unstable, indiscreet. Predictably, Camilla cannot sustain such undeviating and distrustful scrutiny. Despite—indeed, partly because of—her good heart and warm impulse to do good, she embroils herself in ambiguous relationships and circumstances. Under the eyes of suspicion, she appears flirtatious, extravagant, and imprudent, using bad judgment in choosing her friends, remaining loyal to a woman whose reputation is gone. Like Cecilia, the protagonist of Burney's previous novel, she finds herself in a climactic situation of solitude, illness, and near-madness. To generate a happy ending out of such a condition requires some maneuvering by the author, but only to make Edgar change his mind once more. Within the novel's social environment, he can change his mind as often as he wishes, with no imputation of instability. Different rules govern women.

Different, and inherently ambiguous. Take the matter of sensibility: plausible though it may sound to recommend that women use reason to control and obscure the manifestations of feeling, such a recommendation does not fully respond to the actual female situation. The apparent ambivalence of such writers as Burney, Wollstonecraft, and Radcliffe about sensibility stems from recognition that the quality provides one of women's most valuable resources for constructing and sustaining relationships. Hence the drama of concealment and revelation, the tension between acknowledging feeling only in privacy and displaying it to others. Only by such display can a woman reveal her nature. Yet she also makes herself severely vulnerable by indulging in it.

Burney characteristically populates her large novels with a cast of characters designed to represent a spectrum of possibility. In *Camilla*, the cousins Indiana and Eugenia exemplify polar opposites in handling sensibility. Indiana apparently feels nothing but self-love. A striking beauty, she expects amorous worship from every side. One instrument for achieving it, she believes, is the display of sensibility. Taught to "nourish every fear as becoming" (132), she exploits a repertoire of hesitations, starts, exclamations, and tears, attracting the attention and the help of the men around her. Romantic Melmond, captivated by her beauty, accepts as genuine the evidence she offers of fear, weakness, and dependency—all of which captivate him yet more. When Indiana elopes with an army officer, although engaged to Melmond, she unequivocally demonstrates her self-absorption and frivolity, but her displays of false sensibility have made the same point long before. They have also illustrated her obsessive need for an audience. Without one, she would hardly exist. To her, privacy means nothing.

At the opposite extreme is Camilla's sister Eugenia, all virtue. Maimed and scarred by childhood accident and illness, she has lived a sheltered life with her family, unaware that her appearance could be seen as grotesque. She has cultivated her mind and her compassion, making herself a tower of strength for her sisters. When a series of accidents reveals to her that others will judge her harshly, her first impulse is to sequester herself. Entwining herself in the window curtain for emblematic and real concealment, she cries, "O hide me! hide me! From every human eye, from every thing that lives and breathes!" (295). Again, when her love for Melmond is accidentally betrayed, she sees extreme privacy as the remedy for embarrassment, announcing that "she would inhabit only her own apartment for the rest of her life" (677). Sensibility leads directly to the will to solitude: Eugenia's feelings are too tender for ordinary social intercourse. But Eugenia, despite her admirable character, is wrong in this respect: the text makes that point perfectly clear. Her invariably right father devises a bizarre scene involving a beautiful madwoman to demonstrate to Eugenia that she should not mourn her own fate. The proper course involves continuing to be and do good among others. One must pursue moderation in privacy as in everything else.

The precise nature of moderation, however, may be hard to discern. Camilla proceeds by a series of lurches, alternately hiding and helplessly revealing herself. Her wise father may recommend a uniform course of self-protection, but such a course not only seems difficult to manage but in some instances dubiously effective. "Ah! who is like you!" Edgar exclaims, at the beginning of their romance, going on to explain what he admires: "so lively—yet so feeling!" (152). In her childhood and early teens, Camilla openly reveals what she feels, as guileless as her uncle, Sir Hugh, who, lacking worldly experience, expresses and acts upon his every impulse. But Sir Hugh is a man, and rich at that. Although he may provide a subject for gentle mockery, no serious criticism appears to attach to him even when he makes dreadful mistakes, mistakes damaging the lives of others. Camilla seldom makes mistakes of this order, but that fact does not protect her from harsh criticism. Her revelations of sensibility draw Edgar to her. Seeing her red eyes, trembling voice, bent head, hasty exits, he determines to propose—"from the rising influence of warmer sympathy, which bids me sooth her in distress, shield her from danger, strengthen all her virtues, and participate in their emanations!" (173). At other junctures too, Camilla's display of sensibility proves attractive. When she sees the young man threatened by a bulldog, Edgar perceives "in her countenance terror the most undisguised, and tenderness that went straight to his soul" (539); he reveals immediate romantic interest in her as a result. But Indiana's governess, Miss Margland, watches every sign of sensibility to make of it a cause for criticism; Eugenia tells her sister that she has no valid reason for anguish when she suffers over the accusation that she has tried to lure Edgar away from her cousin; Dr. Marchmont hints that displays of sensibility may be signs of vanity. Alternately blushing and turning pale at the news that Edgar has disclaimed romantic interest in her, Camilla becomes the focus of Miss Margland's malicious attention. Sensibility betrays its possessor. But concealing sensibility may betray her too, as Camilla's mother points out. Talking with Edgar about the evil entailed when a man abandons "an innocent female," Mrs. Tyrold observes that "the more exquisite her feelings, the stronger will be the impulse of her delicacy to suffer uncomplaining; and the deluder of her esteem commonly confides, for averting her reproach, to the very sensibility through which he has ensnared her good opinion" (233). Delicacy and sensibility, those greatly admired female traits, leave a woman susceptible to suffering and incapable of self-defense.

Camilla's father specifies at length and in revealing detail the case for concealment: for preserving feelings in the privacy of the heart. Warning Camilla that others have noticed and commented on her state of depression, he summarizes, "Risk not, my dear girl, to others, those outward marks of sensibility which, to common or unfeeling observers, seem but the effect of an unbecoming remissness in the self-command which should dignify every female who would do herself honour" (348).

Self-command consists in eliminating "outward marks," not in stamping out feeling. Mr. Tyrold disapproved of Eugenia's desire for physical separation from the community, but he strongly advocates its psychological equivalent—what Alan Westin would call "reserve"—for the young woman of sensibility. The sensibility that worries him is the kind that, communicated, might betray a woman's potentially erotic interest in a man. Warnings to females almost always turn out to have sexual implications, and this is no exception. The father's advice both advocates and carefully rationalizes dissimulation. One must watch steadily, Mr. Tyrold tells his daughter, to avoid self-revelation: "There are so many ways of communication independent of speech, that silence is but one point in the ordinances of discretion" (360). Nothing can be more disastrous than a woman's revealing to a man her interest in him. He will be flattered, but he will lose respect for her because her social value diminishes as she expresses too much feeling. "Carefully, then, beyond all other care, shut up every avenue by which a secret which should die untold can further escape you" (360). The emphasis and detail of these recommendations suggest that the woman's full energy and intelligence must enlist themselves in the service of repression. The reason for such effort is momentous. True, Mr. Tyrold acknowledges, a woman's emotion toward a man "may be considered as a mark of discerning sensibility" (361). But it must somehow be discovered without being revealed: "that it should be betrayed uncalled for, is commonly, however ungenerously, imagined rather to indicate ungoverned passions, than refined selection" (361). Such a judgment may be unjust, yet a woman who allows herself to be open about such feeling, who makes it possible for an observer to notice, obviously does not respect herself. (Mr. Tyrold does not explain how he reaches this conclusion.) Even if her weakness originates in "artlessness" and "innocence," much-praised female qualities, it remains nonetheless reprehensible.

Given the enormous social danger of female self-revelation, the woman must learn to play an actress's part, realizing the omnipresence of critical audience. Camilla hasn't learned yet, Mr. Tyrold realizes, but she needs to do so. Finally the father justifies what sounds very much like an earnest recommendation of hypocrisy, only to continue: "Discriminate, nevertheless, between hypocrisy and discretion. The first is a vice; the second a conciliation to virtue. It is the bond that keeps society from disunion; the veil that shades our weakness from exposure, giving time for that interior correction, which the publication of our infirmities would else, with respect to mankind, make of no avail" (361). The dissimulation of discretion justifies itself as a means to virtue, a device for gaining time in which failings of feeling—interior emotional excess—might be corrected. And its primary value is to "society," which it keeps from "disunion."

Yet Mr. Tyrold appears to feel some qualms about his own prescriptions. It would be better, he concludes, if we could all reveal ourselves utterly to our fellow human beings. A world without privacy would be a better world. Since humankind is fallen, though, one must remain cognizant of the fact that people judge one another harshly. "Discretion" thus becomes an urgent virtue, privacy a social imperative.

Nowhere else in eighteenth-century writing have I found so full and clear a statement of the importance, for women, of the psychological privacy that consists in withholding of affect. The philosopher Elizabeth Neill, writing in and about the twenty-first century, suggests that "while privacy is represented as the dignity of self-concealment, autonomy is represented as the dignity of agency" (65). Her formulation is almost eerily appropriate to the situation Burney represents. Mr. Tyrold recommends self-concealment as the only possible means to retain dignity in a world that allows the unmarried woman virtually no autonomy. The dignity of agency is hardly available to Camilla; the dignity of self-concealment is more readily achieved. Yet its proximity to hypocrisy may remain troubling. Although the father urges his daughter to discriminate between hypocrisy and discretion, he offers no principles for making such a discrimination, except by labeling one a vice, the other a virtue. The difference between them is presumably their motivation. An unkind judge, unable to know motives, however, might readily interpret "discretion" as hypocrisy, since it too involves deliberate masking and conscious effort to mislead observers. Edgar's mistakes in interpreting Camilla emphasize the point that to obey prescriptions for female conduct may entail damaging consequences because such obedience systematically makes women opaque.

Mr. Tyrold provides social justification for the practice of "discretion" when he attributes to it the bond preventing social disintegration. The preservation of individual emotional privacy, in other words, serves the interests of others. As Claudia L. Johnson puts the point, in her full and revealing treatment of this passage, to conceal female frailty "carries a national agenda" (156). But the series of recommendations offered to Camilla consistently expresses a sense that the "others," the faceless members of society, constitute a potentially hostile audience, ready to leap to damaging conclusions. According to the virtuous clergyman's understanding of the world, sincerity, forthrightness, and honesty hold little value as attributes of the woman in love, who demonstrates her uprightness by her misleading performance of imperturbability. Prudence dictates performance; performance protects privacy; privacy protects not only the individual woman but the very structure of society in a fallen world. A woman demonstrates her virtuous femininity partly by her possession of delicate sensibility, yet the same system of conventions that dictates tender feelings demands also their judicious concealment.

In other words, the element of choice crucial to most understandings of privacy does not operate—*should* not operate, according to her father's views—for Camilla. Mr. Tyrold's speech epitomizes Burney's astute, melancholy perception of social impingements on female freedom. The conforming woman does not choose privacy in emotional matters; she has privacy thrust upon her. In circumstances where the open expression of sensibility conveys weakness and "delicacy"—circumstances of alarm or embarrassment, say—a good woman performs her emotion. (So does a reprehensible woman like Indiana, who understands the social attractiveness of such performance.) In situations where feeling might conceivably connote individualistic self-assertion, she keeps it to herself. The prescription of privacy becomes one more social imposition.

Camilla's efforts to follow that prescription do not suffice. As usual in a Burney novel, disaster succeeds disaster toward the end. Camilla, doing the best she can in a difficult situation, finds herself alone and penniless in a roadside inn, where, plagued by horrifying dream-visions, eschewing food, she sinks ever deeper into illness. Her repeated efforts to communicate with her parents fail because of various accidents. Her mother finally appears at her bedside, but not because of Camilla's letters. The more morally rigid of her parents, that mother is quick to condemn her: "'Camilla,' said Mrs. Tyrold, steadily, 'it is time to conquer this impetuous sensibility, which already, in its effects, has nearly broken all our hearts.'" She goes on to describe Camilla to herself as possessing "a soul of feeling . . . but too much alive," and as having "been wrought upon by your own sorrows to forget the sorrows you inflict" (864).

Mrs. Tyrold does not at this juncture have full possession of the facts, and she sounds less severe when she knows more of what Camilla has suffered. But her initial assumption that indulged sensibility is the source of difficulty and that it entails a failure of responsibility toward others underlines the implications of her husband's maxims. It is not clear exactly what Mrs. Tyrold knows, but a twenty-first-century reader may find it difficult to understand how "impetuous sensibility" can be said to account for Camilla's exigencies, even given only partial awareness of what they are. Sensibility does not explain her financial difficulties or her recourse to a moneylender, the immediate cause of her family's dire straits. She has never forgotten the sorrows she inflicted on her family—indeed, her consciousness of the burden she has placed on them is a principal cause of her own distress. Mrs. Tyrold's criticism of her daughter seems almost generic: if an eighteenth-century young woman gets in trouble, excessive sensibility must be the cause. Excessive sensibility, or excessive imagination, or—the hidden fear linked with both—excessive sexuality.

The narrator's account of Camilla early specifies that "an imagination that submitted to no control" constitutes "the reigning and radical defect of her character" (84). In this respect too she resembles her uncle, Sir Hugh, possessor of an imagination "neither regulated by wisdom, nor disciplined by experience" (34). What in a man contributes to comic weakness, in a woman comprises mortal danger. Yet only dubiously is it Camilla's particular danger. Although Camilla undeniably contributes, by several forms of indiscretion, to the desperate situation in which she ultimately finds herself, her indiscretions derive from inexperience. She does not know enough about the world to know when she should be suspicious of others or how much things are likely to cost or how to avoid casual pressure to spend money. She does not know the system of disguise her father recommends to her. She has neither learned how not to feel nor how to conceal the feelings she has. She has not learned to perform—rather than simply to be—herself. She lacks awareness of the range of human complexity. None of these failures of knowledge or awareness derives from excessive imagination, nor does sensibility explain them.

Almost the first introduction of Camilla into the text includes a sentimental panegyric to innocence, occasioned by the heroine's manifestation of that quality: "Every look was a smile, every step was a spring, every thought was a hope, every feeling was joy! and the early felicity of her mind was without allay. O blissful state of innocence, purity, and delight, why must it fleet so fast? Why scarcely but by retrospection is its happiness known?" (13). Several subplots of the novel, like the central story of Camilla herself, explore the nature of the progress from innocence to experience. Eugenia, her innocence prolonged by seclusion, learns painfully about human falseness—particularly about the false display of sensibility. Lionel, brother of the two girls, experiences vice in his own person, victimizing others rather than becoming a victim himself. Even Sir Hugh, largely untouched by experience, learns that he cannot achieve wisdom by studying the classic languages. Camilla learns almost entirely through her own mistakes—and learns how many different kinds of mistake are available.

In every case, although to varying degree, the movement from innocence to experience involves also a shift from openness to self-concealment. Lionel, ever more flamboyant in manner and action, confesses to thus hiding feelings that he does not know how to deal with. Eugenia acts cheerful by day and weeps alone in her bed at night. Camilla, whose father explicitly recommended a program of dissimulation under the label of discretion, tries consciously and assiduously to hide from all observers what she feels. An unfallen world, a world of innocence, would make privacy unnecessary. In it, all would be open to everyone's charitable view. The actual world, the world of forbidden knowledge, of difficult experience, and of social imposition, makes the attempt at privacy urgent, since few viewers are charitable. It also makes the kind of privacy I have been speaking about, that of emotions systematically withdrawn from observation, exceedingly difficult to attain, because individuals within the social system work assiduously to penetrate one another's privacy.

The scribes and Pharisees, according to Jesus, were hypocrites who thus resembled whited sepulchers, "which indeed appear beautiful outward, but are within full of dead men's bones, and of all uncleanness" (Matt. 23:27). John Silber ends a provocative essay on privacy and masking by offering a "Brechtian paean to scribes and Pharisees and even to whited sepulchers: All may be necessary in the community of men from which God is absent and in which privacy must be guaranteed" (235). In Camilla's community of men and women, God is frequently invoked and privacy is hardly guaranteed. All the more need for Pharisees and whited sepulchers: only pretense protects from penetration, although what is hidden may prove less sinister than dead men's bones.

Particularly menacing to privacy is interpretation, which declares its object not only knowable but known. From the beginning to the end of Burney's disturbing novel, Camilla figures as object of interpretation—for Indiana, Miss Margland, Mrs. Albery and her friends, Dr. Marchmont, Edgar, her parents, and occasional others. That individual interpretations of her differ according to the temperament and situation of the interpreter has no bearing on my point. In every instance, someone attempts psychologically to control Camilla by enforcing a specific sense of what her behavior means. The dreadful episode in which a crowd of onlookers divide between interpreting Camilla and her companion as shoplifters or as madwomen, behaving to the two women according to the kind of pathology they attribute to them, condenses the implications of the novel as a whole. Excessive sensibility and excessive imagination in the eighteenth century provided familiar and favored interpretations of female behavior. The authority of a narrator and of a parent support the readings of Camilla as dominated by one or the other. By the novel's end, the young woman accepts others' versions of her and promises subservience: she will be what she is told she is and do what she is told to do. Yet the novelistic action undermines the verbal authority of the explanation by sensibility or imagination. That action renders a process of endurance and growth that depends not on asserted characterological weakness but on attempted resistance to intolerable external pressure.

Mr. Tyrold recommends that his daughter preserve her privacy but assumes his own right of total access to her interior life, as does Mrs. Tyrold. However Camilla obscures her feelings to others, she should remain transparent to her parents and her husband. The demand of privacy and the demand of openness alike amount to bondage in Burney's figuration: choice has disappeared from both.

In suggesting that a powerful cultural interpretation finally controls Camilla, I do not mean to imply that she manifests no behavior that would justify it. Like most of the young people depicted in Burney's novel, Camilla provides many displays of sensibility, although she never controls them for theatrical purposes. She demonstrates violent shifts of feeling about Edgar; she suffers on behalf of the poor (and offers benevolence); she responds powerfully to babies. Her eyes glisten and her tears flow at the slightest provocation. The same description—except for the babies—applies to Edgar, who admires Camilla for her sensibility as she admires him for his. The reader is likewise invited to approve the evidence of emotional responsiveness both lovers reveal. But Camilla would not, like Julie, claim the "self-contentment" of sensibility, despite the fact that she obviously on occasion enjoys emotional indulgence. Her feelings characteristically extend outward. She shows relatively little of sensibility's potential narcissism.

Other characters in the novel display more. Melmond, for instance, makes a career of sensibility, with his recitations of poetry and his dramatic mooning over Indiana; Mrs. Berlinton provides his female equivalent. Bellamy yet more dramatically protests his desperate emotion over Eugenia, all of it false, but all belonging to a conventional repertoire of sensibility. Indiana likewise performs rather than feels sensibility. Both use sensibility's trappings as a mode of seduction, thus implying a critique of revealed feeling that the novel does not fully develop. They employ sensibility, in other words, not for the sake of others but in order to make use of others for their own purposes. Although they make every attempt to keep their motives private, their projects depend on public performance of sensibility.

Camilla, after all her valiant efforts to keep her sensibility to herself, finds herself called upon to make it available to selected others. She will gain neither the advantages of widely displayed sensibility nor those of sensibility concealed. Instead, she must expose herself to those who claim the authority to interpret her and her feelings and to control both. Although, like Burney's other three novels, *Camilla* ends in a desired marriage, the tone of the ending is the darkest of the four. More specifically than any of the other novels, *Camilla* demonstrates the susceptibility of women to external interpretation, the degree to which such interpretation subverts the bounds of privacy, and the power of sensibility as a cultural concept marking female subordination to social imperatives.

Despite its unusually intense focus on the difficulty of life for young women, which differentiates it from other novels of sensibility, *Camilla* characterizes its protagonist in a fashion familiar from other eighteenth-century fiction. Camilla suffers in more complicated and more socially significant ways than most other contemporaneous heroines of sensibility, but her modes of response resemble those of other fictional figures from the same period. Miss Milner, a central character in Elizabeth Inchbald's *A Simple Story*, produced in the same decade as *Camilla*, appears by comparison far less conventional, daring to fall in love with a Catholic priest, openly struggling with him for power after circumstances allow him to propose, and expressing anger at her husband by having an adulterous affair (for which, however, she is duly punished by death). Her spirit and assertiveness create the ground of her interest for most recent readers. Less conspicuous, but equally important, is her powerful sensibility (a quality she shares with her lover), by means of which Inchbald conveys some of the same ideas as Burney. She also takes the opportunity to examine contrasting manifestations of sensibility that appear strongly marked by gender. Less given than Burney to open didacticism, she too demonstrates complicated awareness of how the social impinges on the personal in the realm of privacy as well as that of public performance. Specifically, she explores relations between power and privacy.

Before Miss Milner appears on the scene, her newly appointed guardian, the priest Dorriforth, attempts to ascertain her nature by talking with acquaintances of hers. The intrusiveness of interpretation becomes apparent as two women discuss Dorriforth's ward specifically in terms of her feelings. One of the women emphasizes Miss Milner's frivolity and heartlessness—which, Miss Woodley points out, might be reformed by "good company, good books, experience, and the misfortunes of others" (10–11). (The misfortunes of others, inasmuch as they arouse response, allegedly have a moral effect.) The other commentator suggests that Miss Milner already reacts to such misfortunes, emphasizing the young woman's benevolence, her extended acts of charity. Relieved by this account, Dorriforth yet reserves the right to make his own interpretation. Both views of the young woman conform to social stereotypes of the female nature—superficial and frivolous or selflessly compassionate. To go beyond stereotypes in perception, as Dorriforth will temporarily do, requires a depth of understanding difficult to sustain.

As Miss Milner becomes the novel's central focus, she at least sporadically demonstrates her capacity to feel compassion—for Sandford's headache or Dorriforth's wounded arm, for a neglected child. (Her "heart was a receptacle for the unfortunate," the text informs us [34].) On the whole, though, her sensibility displays itself as an adjunct to her love. It manifests itself lavishly in the blushes, pallor, and weeping conspicuous in other heroines, as well as in less stereotypical physical signs: a knife and fork jumping in Miss Milner's hand, or her sudden inability to eat. Of course it finds verbal expression as well. Long-suffering Miss Woodley must listen to extensive and emphatic revelations of feeling that demonstrate how fundamentally Miss Milner's responses are founded on her emotions. Although she has considerable capacity for logical thought, engaging in intellectual sparring matches with the Jesuit Sandford, reason plays little part in determining her actions and decisions. Sensibility controls her, making her immediately appealing—and culturally recognizable despite her "unfeminine" brashness. Sensibility brings about her downfall: piqued at her husband's apparent neglect, she renews an old attachment and indulges sexuality quite without love. Sensibility apparently causes her death, although she lingers for almost twenty years after her expulsion from her husband's house, and determines her decision to leave no will: she chooses, she says, to have no will but her husband's.

In *Camilla*, as in *Julie*, sensibility manifests itself in similar ways (blushes, tears, voice quavers) and for similar reasons in men and women. The second-generation plot of *A Simple Story*, involving Rushbrook and Matilda, continues the stress on emotional self-display, with the young couple manifesting their worthiness of one another by comparable displays of feeling. But Dorriforth (who later becomes Lord Elmwood) and Miss Milner pursue a more complicated course. For them, the drama of sensibility depends largely on concealment. Both try hard—not for social but for personal reasons—to protect the privacy of feeling. The emotions they lavishly display for specific audiences often fail to correspond to those they actually feel. Both employ gender stereotypes as self-protection, Lord Elmwood performing male imperturbability as Miss Milner enacts female frivolity. The consequences of concealment, however, differ dramatically for the man and the woman: less because of the simple fact of gender than because of power inequalities.

Miss Milner at first needs to hide a range of feelings because of their social unacceptability. She has fallen in love with a Catholic priest. Her love cannot achieve fulfillment, so its revelation would humiliate her. She flirts and mocks, therefore; she allows others to think her in love with a young peer; she thrusts her head out the window to conceal her blushes. Later, after she has consented to marry Lord Elmwood, she involves herself in a struggle for control that threatens the very possibility of the marriage she ardently desires. Displaying every evidence of frivolity, extravagance, and inconsistency, she appears "in the highest spirits; sung, laugh'd, and never heaved a sigh, but when she was alone" (168). Finally she provokes her lover to nullify the engagement. At this point, she only intensifies her false performance of good cheer, although with less complete success than before. The misleading appearance, however, seems urgent to her, signifying her "fortitude"—"fortitude to bid him farewell without discovering one affected, or one real pang, though her death should be the immediate consequence" (176).

At the height of her premarital power over her declared lover, as well as in the brief period after he breaks the engagement, Miss Milner more or less successfully obscures her true feelings. The main resources available to her consist in the superficial indulgences of her sex. To show herself powerful, she conforms to every derogatory cultural stereotype. She flirts, deliberately buys extravagant and useless items, attends a masquerade in a revealing costume. She acts like a being of pure impulse, exaggerating the dominance of unworthy emotions in order to hide her true tenderness.

Her acting is performative in a double sense: both theatrical and directly functional. But it is not altogether successful with its desired audience: in order to prove Elmwood worthy of her love, she proves herself unworthy of his.

The inequality of the power struggle manifests itself in the force of negative interpretation of Miss Milner, long held by Sandford, recurrently by Lord Elmwood, and finally by the narrator as well. I referred to "the height of her premarital power," but that "height" is largely illusory. Miss Milner risks her own happiness in her compulsive challenges to her fiancé partly because she is altogether dependent on his decisions. If the energy of her desire has drawn the man to her despite opposition and obstacles, kindling his answering desire, he yet retains the culturally assigned right of absolute choice. Miss Milner's challenges to him seem grotesque, petty, and inevitably futile. She can only play at power, constructing ineffectual fantasies. The reader may admire her spirit but can hardly respect her judgment, either in her premarital risk-taking or in her postmarital infidelity. Her disguises of sensibility prove self-destructive. The woman like Matilda, daughter of Lord Elmwood and the former Miss Milner, capable of concealing little and of concealing only briefly, a being virtually defined by her utter compliance, will find greater happiness.

The Jesuit Sandford, penetrating to the feeling lying beneath the apparent equanimity of both lovers, brings about their marriage, but the novelist has little perceptible interest in the immediate workings of the marital relationship. She dwells, rather, on its dissolution, caused by yet another pattern of concealment. Elmwood, tending to his estate in the West Indies, hides from his wife the fact of his illness and leads her to think that he wantonly neglects her. Lady Elmwood, angry at this treatment, pretends to be in love with the man who has previously courted her and engages in an adulterous liaison. After Lord Elmwood's return, both man and wife express real feeling openly: Lord Elmwood mutilates his rival in a duel; Lady Elmwood flees in penitence and lives in self-humiliation and disgrace. Early in the second part of the novel, she dies.

Her death does not inaugurate but it intensifies the pattern of emotional dissimulation that Lord Elmwood has entered upon. Far more compelling than the course of young love in the novel's second section is the representation of what happens to male sensibility under stress. With much more power than Miss Milner's false frivolities, Lord Elmwood's claim to emotional privacy affects the economic as well as psychological situation of his numerous dependents—his servants; his nephew and heir, Rushbrook; his daughter Matilda; and Matilda's immediate protectors, Sandford and Miss Woodley. A rich and well-born male, he has the full right his wife could never have: to impose his feelings and desires on others without negative consequences. He enforces his claim to privacy by forbidding all about him ever to mention his wife and daughter. Violators—including Matilda herself, who accidentally encounters him and faints in his arms—suffer immediate banishment. The narrator explains that even Lord Elmwood's calmness after his wife's betrayal was of a "sensible and feeling kind," and continues:

> it was this sensibility, which urged him to fly from its more keen recollection as much as possible—this he alledged as the reason he would never suffer Lady Elmwood, or even her child, to be named in his hearing. But this injunction . . . was, by many people, suspected rather to proceed from his resentment, than his tenderness; nor did he himself deny, that resentment mingled with his prudence; for prudence he called it not to remind himself of happiness he could never taste again, and of ingratitude that might impel him to hatred; and prudence he called it, not to form another attachment near to his heart; more especially so near as a parent's, which might a second time expose him to all the torments of ingratitude, from one whom he affectionately loved. (203–4)

The multiplication of moral/psychological terminology in this sequence generates its own confusion. Sensibility, resentment, tenderness, prudence: the labels shift and merge. The designations in fact provide a series of synonyms for sensibility, although to term Lord Elmwood's unwillingness to face his pain "prudence" gives moral dignity to what might in another character, or in other circumstances, be called cowardice. Memory exacerbates sensibility. Lord Elmwood chooses to try to expunge memory by eliminating reference to it. He hides his sensibility by denying its correlatives.

Sensibility gone sour, one might say: a bizarre case, utterly atypical. And indeed I cannot think of another eighteenth-century fictional figure who greatly resembles the embittered Lord Elmwood. Yet in a sense it is his typicality that makes him significant. He typifies the disguise of sensibility that manifests itself as frequently as sensibility's self-displays, and he represents the male social impunity that dramatically contrasts with female vulnerability. Although one may lean out a window to hide a blush, the higher discipline involves not blushing at all. When Lord Elmwood reads of his wife's death, he lays down his newspaper, rests his head on his hand for a few minutes, walks across the room two or three times, and resumes reading the paper. The narrator comments:

Nor let the vociferous mourner, or the perpetual weeper, here complain of his want of sensibility—but let them remember Lord Elmwood was a man—a man of understanding—of courage—of fortitude—with all, a man of the nicest feelings—and who shall say, but that at the time he leaned his head upon his hand, and rose to walk away the sense of what he felt, he might not feel as much as Lady Elmwood did in her last moments. (204–5)

(It is notable that Lord Elmwood's "fortitude," like Miss Milner's when she confronts the end of her engagement, reveals itself in his preservation of emotional privacy.) A man of courage and fortitude, a man of the nicest feelings: Lord Elmwood embodies and allegedly reconciles conflicting ideals of masculine and feminine virtue. The same two ideals are invoked for Camilla, commanded to show courage, doomed to show sensibility. "Sensibility controlled by fortitude" often seems a more cogent formulation than "sensibility governed by reason" for the balance of qualities considered desirable in the late eighteenth century.

Yet Lord Elmwood in his self-control is not consistently represented as an object of admiration. His concealment and conversion of his feelings turn readily to brutality, as when he expels his daughter from the house because of her accidental encounter with him or discharges an old servant for inadvertently mentioning his wife's name. His possession of immense social power, a result of his rank and wealth, frees him for self-indulgence, which takes the form, in his case, of arbitrary impositions. In a sense he cripples himself—restricts his capacity for self-knowledge and self-expression—by disguising his sensibilities. Moreover, he uses other people, making them counters in his serious game of self-concealment. But there may also be a subtler reason, from an eighteenth-century point of view, for disapproving of Lord Elmwood's behavior. Despite the rhetorical praise of controlled sensibility that marks particularly the late century, literary treatments of sensibility's amorphous manifestations tend to dwell lovingly on the flamboyant. Camilla must learn to keep herself under wraps, but she becomes appealing because she feels so much and shows her feelings so clearly. In *A Simple Story*, Matilda, the second-generation heroine, proves her possession of "a proper education" (an education, it turns out, in adversity) by fits of weeping and by a dramatic physical decline after her father's expulsion of her. Although she is to a twenty-first-century reader less attractive than her misguided and self-willed mother, she is by the narrator's explicit judgment much more worthy than that mother. Theoretically, sensibility must be kept under control. In practice, its more dramatic manifestations declare a character's merit. Moreover, Matilda's physical deterioration, which makes her feelings manifest, demonstrates loudly that she has nothing to hide. Unlike Camilla's, her exacerbated sensibility declares grief rather than love: society dictates no concealment in such a case. On the contrary, it mandates performance. A young woman demonstrating her weakness conforms utterly to the established order of things.

The matter of privacy is at least covertly at issue here. Lord Elmwood's distorted enactments of his feelings conceal the true nature of those feelings to all observers. Matilda's physical deterioration, in contrast, makes her feelings manifest. Someone who has something to hide, and who succeeds in the act of hiding, represents, at least in the abstract, a kind of social danger. The reestablishment of order at the end of *A Simple Story* necessarily involves Lord Elmwood's dropping of his mask, since that mask—however "prudent," however definable as "dissimulation" rather than "hypocrisy"—by making its possessor unknowable separates him from the community. The powerful man can choose to wear such a mask, but its operations remain socially disturbing. Despite such recommendations as those of Camilla's father, in favor of prudent dissimulation; despite the injunctions of conduct books about the dangers of excessive sensibility; despite the warnings of even such radical writers as Mary Wollstonecraft—despite all official rhetoric of control, the evidence suggests widespread residual anxiety about the social implications of a consistent practice of concealment, even if the object of concealment consists in potentially dangerous feeling.

Inchbald's apparent interest in the male vicissitudes of sensibility under pressure plays itself out in the second important male character represented in the final third of *A Simple Story*, Lord Elmwood's nephew and heir, Rushbrook, who falls in love with Matilda, essentially at first sight, and works hard to conceal his feelings from his uncle, who is planning another marriage for him. The difference between Rushbrook's hiding of sensibility and Lord Elmwood's derives partly from their differences in character. Lord Elmwood, older than Rushbrook and far more practiced in suffering, does a better job of obscuring what he feels. But the inequality of roles between the two men hints also that the power to enforce one's will facilitates concealment. Rushbrook, in an altogether dependent position, suffers a kind of danger out of the question for his uncle. His vulnerability and consequent insecurity heighten his emotional instability and its manifestations. Try as he will to maintain emotional privacy, he cannot succeed—a fact that may guarantee his eventual happiness, but that also demonstrates his social weakness. In the structural position of a woman, moneyless and powerless except by virtue of his uncle's benevolence, Rushbrook is, like Camilla, subject to the close observation and interrogation of an authority figure. Like a woman, he must use illness (an illness closely associated with his sensibility, since it appears to be exacerbated by his love for Matilda) as virtually his only available defense. Like a woman, he has as little right to autonomy as to privacy.

Inchbald's novel systematically surveys the scene of sensibility, to demonstrate the inequalities of possibility, the temptations and the dangers of concealment, and the social advantages—for the weak—of sensitive feelings openly displayed. Like many works of its period, it reveals the tension between celebration of virtuous dissimulation and concern about the implications of successful self-disguise. Like Burney's explorations of the self in society, it explores individual consequences of social systems, revealing costs and benefits of power and of weakness and linking privacy firmly to power.

Discussion of sensibility, like discussion of imagined and real readers, leads me, inevitably, again to Laurence Sterne, whose fiction probably exemplifies more fully and insistently than any other eighteenth-century text the tension and balance between desire to reveal and desire to conceal. Its anomalies of tone simultaneously express feeling and make it opaque, declare the writer transparent and preserve his privacy. The unstable ironies of *A Sentimental Journey*, for instance, while delineating Yorick as a man of quivering sensitivity, also suggest his awareness that mockery might greet a full commitment to sensibility. Sensibility causes him to reject the need for privacy; sensibility makes him protect himself, irony his instrument.

To speak of "unstable ironies" immediately implicates the reader, compelled to reach at least tentative conclusions but provided with no firm ground from which to attain them. The reader's position (and I speak now of real, not imagined, readers) is always at issue in Sterne. Some readers, firmly rejecting ambiguity, read with insistence on ascertainable meanings and find them. Thus Thomas Jefferson could write to his nephew Peter Carr (10 August 1787), "Read good books because they will encourage as well as direct your feelings. The writings of Sterne particularly form the best course of morality that ever was written" (quoted in Imbarrato 112). One can readily comprehend how Sterne might "encourage" a young man's feelings; it is more ambiguous how he would "direct" them. Yet if we take Yorick at face value, he celebrates consistently and emphatically the importance and value of the kind of sensibility that involves tender feeling for the misfortunes of others. The young man "directed" by him would presumably respond powerfully to the emotional situations of those he encounters. (He would not, however, necessarily do anything to help the unfortunate, aside from weeping over them.) The ambiguity I alleged about the nature of Sterne's direction involves not what he says—that appears straightforward and unvarying, disclosed in anecdotes about others as well as in self-referential utterances by the narrator: a programmatic advocacy of tender feeling—but how he says it. Barbara Benedict finds in "how he says it" the meaning of Sterne's novels, arguing that "he preserves a slippery flexibility and multiplicity of rhetorical attitudes that attempt simultaneously to applaud and to attack the new influences on literary culture and the traditional values opposing them" (*Framing* 92). His techniques, she maintains, "construct a stylistics of sentimentalism that undermines its own liberal claims for instinct and sociability by exclusionary and fragmented rhetoric" (92). She may be right—but such assertions don't help much when it comes to parsing individual episodes.

The difficulties of Sterne's tone have long been notorious. The possibilities of concealment extend beyond the narrator, Yorick, to the author, whose regard for his own privacy becomes increasingly apparent even as his character apparently tells all. A single example may suffice to recall the contradictory possibilities that envelop virtually every statement, every story. Arbitrarily, we might consider the end of the chapter called "The Rose," in which an old French officer explains to Yorick a mysterious episode at the theater, ending his account by praising travel because "by seeing a great deal both of men and manners; it taught us mutual toleration; and mutual toleration, concluded he, making me a bow, taught us mutual love" (Sterne, *Sentimental Journey* 84–85). Yorick finds the officer appealing, but soon realizes the self-referentiality of his judgment: "I thought I loved the man; but I fear I mistook the object—'twas my own way of thinking—the difference was, I could not have expressed it half so well" (85). This reflection leads, by a non sequitur, to a comment about horses. It is a nuisance to rider and horse alike, Yorick says, "if the latter goes pricking up his ears, and starting all the way at every object which he never saw before." This, it seems, is a metaphorical horse, standing for Yorick himself: "I honestly confess, that many a thing gave me pain, and that I blushed at many a word the first month—which I found inconsequent and perfectly innocent the second." We are then offered the story of Madame de Rambouliet, who, after six weeks' acquaintance with Yorick, takes him on an expedition in her coach. She is correct, virtuous, and pure, the narrator tells us. She stops the carriage unexpectedly because she wants "*Rien que pisser*": "Grieve not, gentle traveller, to let Madame de Rambouliet p——ss on—And ye fair mystic nymphs! Go each one *pluck your rose*, and scatter them in your path—for Madame de Rambouliet did no more—I handed Madame de Rambouliet out of the coach; and had I been the priest of the chaste CASTALIA, I could not have served at her fountain with a more respectful decorum" (85). Thus the chapter ends.

The rose alluded to in the chapter title is presumably that scattered by each nymph, jarringly equivalent to urine, since the plucking and scattering of roses here metaphorically correspond to the act of urinating. (The French verb *roser*, meaning "to water," adds an extra level to the joke.) The lady's pissing is glorified as possessed of virtually mystical significance. Despite this glorification, Yorick also carefully reminds his readers of the event's physicality, with his reference to Castalia's fountain. The deliberate outrageousness of the equation between urination and flower scattering, underlined by the chapter title, exemplifies Yorick's constant challenge to the reader, who feels always in danger of being declared lacking in the subtle feelings that characterize the narrator.

With the recognition that he admires himself in admiring the old officer, Yorick undercuts possible condemnation of his narcissism. He sees around himself faster than the reader can see. The horse metaphor detoxifies the notion of conventional "indecency" by declaring an equivalence between something that offends modesty and something that simply has not been seen before. The French lady in her lack of embarrassment about body functions might violate conventional standards of modesty, but, understood as just a new phenomenon, her behavior becomes interesting rather than offensive.

These rhetorical manipulations of the reader, however, hardly prepare for the actual glorification of violation. Here the matter of tone becomes crucial. Are we to take Yorick at face value in his celebration? Is he mocking the reader for a probable response of shock? Is his explosion of feeling evidence of his unusual capacity for responsiveness, of his gift for satire, or of his innocent playfulness (with language and with episodes)? Or all of the above, and, if so, how does one reconcile the apparently incompatible attitudes?

These questions are unanswerable. Their indeterminacy may irritate, amuse, or perplex the reader. The novel creates these effects and others by insisting on the opacity of another mind. Like Rousseau's characters, Yorick makes every effort to function outside conventional assumptions about what must be withheld from view. Still, privacy is inevitable, Yorick suggests. No matter how one pours oneself out, the residue of mystery remains. Interpretation, which I earlier declared the enemy of privacy, only intensifies the mystery. Interpretation illuminates not its object, but the interpreter, who may achieve an illusion of penetration yet merely imagines the possibility of comprehending another mind. Because of the inherent ambiguity of language and the intricacy of consciousness, people are simply not available to one another's knowledge. The necessary residue of privacy may be curse or blessing—but in either case it remains necessary.

So, at any rate, *A Sentimental Journey* suggests, in individual anecdotes and in its total structure. But Yorick's preservation of privacy does not always by any means derive from necessity. That people are ultimately unknowable is a commonplace. That they can deliberately make themselves unknowable, as I have already suggested, carries more disturbing social implications. Yorick's performance of sensibility calls so much attention to itself that it demands reflection about the difference between the performative and the "authentic." When, for instance, the character deliberately summons up the figure of a prisoner in the Bastille, summons it up for the explicit purpose of exercising his feelings, his reflections hover uneasily between self-consciousness and spontaneity. He begins with the idea of the "millions of my fellow-creatures born to no inheritance but slavery," but finds that he cannot bring the "picture" of so many to life. Consequently, he focuses his attention on imagining a single captive: "having first shut him up in his dungeon, I then looked through the twilight of his grated door to take his picture" (97). This act of "looking" produces such distress in the imagining spectator that he finds himself "forced to go on with another part of the portrait" (98). He "sees" his victim keeping track of the days. "I heard his chains upon his legs, as he turned his body to lay his little stick upon the bundle—He gave a deep sigh—I saw the iron enter into his soul—I burst into tears—I could not sustain the picture of confinement which my fancy had drawn" (98).

Yorick experiences himself simultaneously as creator and manipulator of the scene and as sensitive, suffering, helpless observer. The power of his imagination generates the details that harrow his imagination, and he is altogether conscious of this fact. Implicitly he claims the delicacy and responsiveness of his feeling; explicitly he observes the factitiousness of its cause. He publicizes his emotion while keeping private any self-judgment. Nor does he offer the reader clear grounds for judgment, beyond the general celebration of feeling that creates its own uneasiness, both by the fantasy consistently associated with its conception and by the extravagance of its manifestations.

Yorick's insistence on making his feelings public—emphatically drawing the reader's attention to them and making them apparent to all observers within the fiction—challenges the conventional category of privacy. What he most wishes to expose to view, it seems, is what many (in fiction and in fact) hide. His constant performance of sensibility assumes and depends upon an audience. The anxiety that pervades Sterne's novel, beginning with Yorick's decision, narrated on the first page, to go to France in order to combat his servant's tacit mockery—this anxiety derives from the narrator's incessant awareness of audience. Locked within himself by narcissism, he proclaims his responsiveness to others, but that responsiveness, as the notorious episode with the madwoman Maria reveals with particular vividness, only feeds the self's needs.

The quotation I used as epigraph takes on fuller meaning in relation to the situation exposed in Yorick's experience: "People do not know . . . what satisfaction there is in weeping over one's own sufferings and those of others. Sensibility always brings to the soul a certain self-contentment independent of fortune and events." Yorick claims precisely the satisfaction sketched in the first sentence. Although he declares little suffering of his own, his weeping over Maria's suffering, or an ass's, brings him gratification that he feels unembarrassed to announce. The independence of fortune and events that he manifests stems from his heavy reliance on his own imagination, progenitor of sensibility. But sensibility's performative aspect implies that the weeper remains dependent on other people, if not on external happenings. Its "self-contentment" is not entirely self-contained. Sensibility requires watchers. Rousseau demonstrates the point at great length; Sterne makes it yet more emphatic.

The reader, implicitly urged to participate in the drama of sensibility as reactor to suffering, must also fill the position of watcher to not only the sufferers but the responders within the text. The efflorescence of writing about sensibility emphasizes the urgency of audience, the appeal to a public in even the most apparently private experience. And *A Sentimental Journey*, with its extraordinary self-consciousness, may heighten a reader's uneasy awareness of the paradoxes involved in such a commitment as Yorick's. Dedicated to the cultivation and pursuit of sensibility, he focuses all his attention on his internal life, using other people (the monk, the grisette, his fellow travelers, Maria—everyone) as means to heighten his own feelings, even inventing other people (the Bastille prisoner, the shepherd discovering a dead sheep) to serve the same purpose. He creates artifices of self-excitement to foster the sensitivity and responsiveness he values in himself. Yet his concentration on feeling does not imply a life of privacy. On the contrary, Yorick's is an existence of self-display. If he does not have an immediate audience, he must imagine one—the audience for whom he writes, revealing himself on the stage of his own fantasies. The internal life is not a private life. Sensibility entails its own performance, ever demanding publicity.

In the context of the other novels considered in this chapter, the implications of Sterne's work become especially pointed. In the light of Yorick's need to be watched and admired, for instance, one may perceive comparable patterns in fictions that appear less aggressive toward the reader than Sterne's. The small group at the center of *Julie* is manifestly composed of men and women who perpetually watch—even study—one another. The sense of constant surveillance in *Camilla* perhaps only emphasizes the natural environment of sensibility, the atmosphere in which performances of feeling flourish. The revelations and concealments, interpretations and reinterpretations of *A Simple Story* proclaim the novel's implication in the same ambience, a milieu in which people's displays and disguises alike dramatize the intricacies of lives of feeling led within a social setting.

It is true, then, that sensibility is a form of publicity, an aspect of the private life presented for public consumption. But it is equally true that to hide sensibility makes part of its crucial drama. And the ambiguous figure of Yorick suggests a third possibility, implicit also in the characters of *Julie* and perhaps in the other novels as well: that sensibility itself can constitute a form of hiding. The more Yorick tells us every detail of his feeling, the more we may suspect that there's a lot he's not telling us. The fundamental paradox of human openness operates: given our knowledge of the mystery of what we call personality, we can rarely believe in even the possibility of transparency. Proclamations of its presence only announce its absence. If sensibility involves performance, as it obviously does, it can also involve pose: the pose that operates to preserve the ultimate realm of privacy.

The dynamic of sensibility and privacy in the four novels considered here suggests both the cultural force that dictates individual expressive possibilities and the cultural ambivalence that causes them to inhabit paradoxical systems. Yorick and the little community that Rousseau imagines consider themselves unconventional, different from those who operate unthinkingly according to the dictates of society. Yet they conform as completely as do their more orthodox counterparts to the imperatives of a world in which the presence of an audience is always assumed. Of course the reader serves as audience for the constructed text, but within that text too lurk watchers. In *Julie*, the protagonists obsessively watch one another, standing in for others ever imagined in the background. In *A Sentimental Journey*, Yorick watches himself as he performs himself, constantly aware of the likelihood of external judgment. Apparently existing outside the realm of social sanctions, these characters still dramatize the power of social expectations as they lavishly display their sensibility, yet conceal from the reader, from one another, perhaps even from themselves, the ultimate dimensions of their feeling.

The point is even clearer in relation to characters who more obviously consider themselves part of a social world. In a crucial episode of *A Simple Story*, Matilda, forbidden to see her father, accidentally encounters him on the stairs and faints in his arms. Lord Elmwood, moved by the meeting, seems inclined to draw her closer. Then he notices that a servant is passing by; the fact appears to change his mind, and he performs his rejection of his daughter. The servant's presence is in one sense utterly trivial; in another, momentous. The appearance of a witness compels the nobleman to carry out a mandate now clearly beyond usefulness. For all his power, he feels unable to do what he feels like doing. Because of the witness, he must conceal his true feeling and enact a false one. Like Yorick, he imagines the community of judgment. Burney's Camilla, unlike Lord Elmwood almost devoid of social power, similarly feels herself watched—and she is literally correct in the feeling: watchers exist everywhere. So she alternately dramatizes and conceals sensibility, having not even the choice of privacy within her own power. Both sensibility and privacy can serve social interests. Sensibility as spectacle may allow its watchers to posit the compassionate humanitarianism of the society at large; the recourse to privacy protects the society from having to recognize inconvenient or assertive individual emotion. Eighteenth-century novels that explore the relation between the two often ground the construction of their plots on the possibilities of tension and paradox and illustrate the difficulties—perhaps the true impossibility—of "individualism."

It is perhaps no accident that the two works here treated that reflect the most vivid consciousness of how social pressures impinge on individual possibilities both have female authors. *David Simple* and *The Female Quixote*, novels by women discussed in the previous chapter, also demonstrate sharp consciousness of how social forces shape women in particular, but men as well. If privacy was, as I have already pointed out, an especially vexed matter for women, its treatment by woman writers typically demonstrates cogent awareness of why, exactly, this should be the case. Burney focuses most often on the anguish generated by social demands, but Lennox in her fanciful tale, Sarah Fielding in her sentimental one, and Inchbald in her exploration of psychological complexities all make privacy an emblem of both social conformity and social evasion. Although, as we will see more fully in subsequent chapters, men too discuss privacy, they more rarely investigate its social, as opposed to its personal, meanings.

The subject of manners, the concern of the next chapter, provides an obvious focus of awareness about the nature of social pressure. In the eighteenth century, women wrote "novels of manners." They also in other contexts contemplated the costs of social compliance. Men, typically, articulated the rules of proper behavior for women. Although a number of women also produced conduct books, their voices often sound ventriloquized: they echo the pronouncements of their male predecessors. Women, it seems, paid the largest costs, although men too, those who belonged or aspired to the gentry or to even higher ranks, behaved themselves in accord with established rules. Still, the subject of manners in relation to privacy is predominantly a matter for females.

4

Privacy, Dissimulation, and Propriety

Good manners constitute a tax paid by individuals to society, a widely condoned form of hypocrisy. Late in Frances Burney's second novel, *Cecilia*, a male character articulates this view by means of examples still perhaps morally disturbing in their very familiarity:

> are we not kept silent when we wish to reprove by the fear of offending? and made speak where we wish to be silent by the desire of obliging? do we not bow to the scoundrel as low as to the man of honour? are we not by mere forms kept standing when tired? made give place to those we despise? and smiles to those we hate? or if we refuse these attentions, are we not regarded as savages, and shut out of society? (735)

Appropriate manners, by this interpretation, entail elisions of individual judgment and feeling. Socially conforming behavior depends on suppressed utterance.

The so-called novel of manners, however, in its late-eighteenth-century refinement, explored personal uses of social convention that hint a further meaning for conformity. Like their contemporaries, Burney and Jane Austen investigate in their fiction the ambiguities of privacy. For women seeking privacy, they suggest—at any rate, for upper-class women—flawless manners provide concealment.

Manners, which register submission to social convention in its most stereotypical form, might seem to flourish in an environment sharply different from that of sensibility, which appears to dramatize individual emotional response. Yet sensibility, as we have seen, also declares conventionality and also provides concealment. The social world of late-eighteenth-century England, encouraging the cultivation of sensibility, assumed also a universal equation between social rank and manners. As

Paul Langford points out, "The pursuit of genteel status and the acquisition of polite manners in some measure united [the middle class,] which in other respects appeared diverse and divided" (59). A gentleman or lady attested position by flawless performance of social rituals; by comparable performance, would-be ladies and gentlemen strove to achieve the same level. Although those aspiring to rise in rank might (and did) study social requirements in an effort to acquire the kind of manners that might appropriately accompany higher status, the ease of thoroughly internalized rules of decorum was not readily come by. That ease, when possessed, might supply a useful screen. In the guise of social conformity, novels suggest, women guarded their difference, their specialness, their privacy: officially unacceptable personal opinions, desires, and feelings. Several of the social impositions adduced by Burney's Mr. Monckton—silence in lieu of reproach, bows to scoundrels, smiles for the hated—in fact comprise forms of concealment. Mr. Monckton does not acknowledge their personal value, except in negative terms; nor, in general, do other fictional characters. Yet the narrative renditions of compliance often reveal such value.

The concept of privacy in its nature raises questions about the proper balance between responsibility to oneself and to other people. Given a society that values social relations as potential moral discipline, privacy embodies danger. The person who claims the right to be alone, or even to keep things to herself, might meditate bad deeds or entertain bad thoughts, and *no one would know*. Privacy may lead to delusion, as Dr. Johnson suggested in his fable of the mad astronomer, convinced of his own vast power because he has little exchange with other people. Desire for privacy might imply selfishness or irresponsibility. Such possibilities, at any rate, were alive in the minds of eighteenth-century writers.

Not that a negative view of privacy entirely displaced a positive one. On the contrary, as we have seen already, awareness of the emotional, and conceivably even the moral, value of privacy informs virtually all discussions of the issue in imaginative literature. To focus on the specific situation of upper-class British women, as conveyed by such discussions, illuminates perplexities of privacy—a luxury, of course, largely confined to the upper classes. For such women, novels, diaries, letters, and conduct manuals indicate, physical privacy was hard to come by. Even if they slept alone, without the company of a sister, cousin, aunt, friend, or servant (and relatively few did), women did not customarily retreat to their bedrooms except to sleep. Virginia Woolf's vision of personal space that makes female creativity possible seems inconceivable in this period for women of the privileged classes whose lives have left records literal or fictional.

Lacking rooms of their own, needing psychic and social strategies for self-protection, such women could rely on the elaborate structures of social convention as one significant resource. Going through motions prescribed by etiquette might free a paragon of good behavior to think her own thoughts, feel her own feelings, and reveal nothing except her excellent social training. Barrington Moore Jr., writing about Eskimo culture, defines privacy in illuminating social terms: "The need for privacy amounts to a desire for socially approved protection against painful social obligations" (6). One would not expect to find similarities between the lives of Eskimos and of eighteenth-century English ladies, but the formulation works quite exactly for many novels. "Socially approved protection" from painful human obligations is precisely what good manners offer.

But early woman writers, as well as their male counterparts, grasped the inevitable corollary to the fact that one might hide behind a façade of social compliance. If one person could hide, so could another, so could everyone. Awareness of the dangers of social hypocrisy attended consciousness of its useful possibilities. A central aspect of privacy, according to a recent book by Jeffrey Rosen, "is the ability to control the face we present to the world" (46). Other people can also regulate their faces, though, so we risk universal falsity, unable to trust the messages conveyed by countenances literal or metaphorical.

Eighteenth-century writers at once celebrated and deplored consequences of the human ability to control the face offered to the world. Moralists and mentors of conduct for women brooded over the dangers of false appearance. Lady Sophia Pennington, for instance, warns her daughter:

> You are just entering, my dear girl, into a world full of deceit and falshood, where few persons or things appear in their true character. Vice hides her deformity with the borrowed garb of virtue; and, though discernible to an intelligent and careful observer, by the unbecoming awkwardness of her deportment under it, she passes on thousands undetected. . . . Thus one general mask disguises the whole face of things, and it requires a long experience, and a penetrating judgment, to discover the truth. (64)

The mother's view about governing one's face differs according to who does the governing. She worries about the "general mask," yet she consistently advises her daughters to discipline the appearance they themselves present—in effect, to hide behind their own masks. Thus: "The great art of pleasing is to appear pleased with others; suffer not then an ill-bred absence of thought, or a contemptuous sneer, ever to betray a conscious superiority of understanding, always productive of ill-nature and dislike" (92). The girl should *appear*, not necessarily *feel*, pleased with others; she should not "betray" the sense of superiority she may actually, and justifiably, experience. Behind the disguise of mandated social behavior, her emotions remain her private preserve. Her awareness that others operate the same way, however, may generate anxiety, presumably in her as well as in her guide.

Given the concern about false appearances shared by many didactic writers, it is hardly surprising that they should on occasion oppose "virtue" to social conformity. Virtue subsists, it sometimes appears, only in privacy. "The virtues that make a figure in the world do not fall to the women's share; their virtues are of a simple and peaceable nature: Fame will have nothing to do with us. . . . I think it best to avoid the world, and making a figure, which always strike at modesty, and be contented with being one's own spectator" (Lambert 141). "The world" one should avoid constitutes a realm of social performance and falsity: this view is familiar to all readers of eighteenth-century texts. With no spectators but the self, the young woman will feel no temptation to manipulate appearances; she can rest secure in her "modesty." But the recommendation to avoid the world resonates with poignancy stemming not only from the resigned relinquishment of "fame" (which has apparently rejected women before they can reject it) but from the renunciation of even the possibility of an external spectator. The really good woman, according to this prescription, has no one to look at her. No one to look—but also, it may follow, no one to share, support, participate. The privacy that insures modesty seems to entail isolation. It implies the root meaning of the word *privacy*, hinting deprivation as well as safety.

Moreover, as Adam Smith understood, the spectatorship of the self depends on knowledge of others. One watches oneself by in effect imagining someone else watching. The young woman who assesses her own virtue in isolation from the world presumably brings to bear the values embedded in writings by just such moralists as the one making the recommendation. For a twenty-first-century reader, to encounter the minute prescriptions of eighteenth-century conduct books entails a suffocating sense of surveillance. Hardly a trivial component of a woman's conduct or appearance escapes commentary. The eyes that focus on her belong to men who are constantly judging. In the world, they estimate her value in the marriage market. If she rejects the world, the eye of the moralist will yet rest upon her, if only within her own imagination. Not only do women find it hard to attain physical privacy; the many eighteenth-century conduct books indicate one reason that they also face difficulties in winning its psychic equivalent.

But good manners can help. Their value to women depends on their double valence, both social and individual. In addition to providing opportunity for self-concealment, thus for separation, manners help one fulfill the moral responsibility of relating properly to others. A 1735 treatise begins by defining good manners as "a Science in instructing how to dispose all our Words and Actions in their proper and true places." It then equates "the Rules of Good Breeding and Civility" with "the Rules of true Generosity" (*Man of Manners*, preface). Going through the motions of polite behavior—guarding against bad breath, cutting one's food into small pieces, avoiding monologue and boisterous speech—will somehow generate moral excellence: true generosity.

Yet the procedures advocated in this detailed and exhaustive manual often approach dissimulation. One characteristic instance involves table manners:

> The Man of Manners picks not the best, but rather takes the worst out of the Dish, and gets of every thing, unless it be forced upon him, always the most indifferent Share. By this Civility, the best remains for others; which being a Compliment to all that are present, every body is pleased with it; the more they love themselves, the more they are forc'd to approve of his Behaviour; and Gratitude stepping in, they are obliged almost, whether they will or not, to think favourably of him. After this, it is that the well-bred Man insinuates himself in the Esteem of all the Companies he comes in; and if he gets nothing else by it, the Pleasure he receives in reflecting on the Applause, which he knows is secretly given him, is, to a proud Man, more than an Equivalent for his former Self-denial, and over-pays Self-love with Interest, the Loss it sustained in his Complaisance to others. (9)

The prescription for proper behavior relies not on moral principles but on an economics of self-love organized by a pseudocommercial transaction in which the "well-bred Man" (read: the man wishing to appear well-bred) gives food, gets pleasure, and calculates equivalences and interest on the exchange.

Conduct books as a group delineate the paradoxical relation between distaste for and practice of dissimulation, a relation providing a frequent subject also for novelistic treatment. The anonymous author of the manual on manners clearly remains unaware of any contradiction between insistence on politeness as a moral manifestation and calculations of gain and loss based largely on "Applause." Eighteenth-century novelists, on the other hand, often investigate, directly or indirectly, just such contradictions, at least tacitly acknowledging the personal value of social hypocrisy. Novels of manners delineate a complex dynamic of concealment and revelation. Burney, for instance, in her series of fictional investigations into the lives of young women shows herself recurrently concerned with the problem of privacy as a peculiarly female issue to be considered in the context of social imperatives. If conduct books emphasize the moralist as watcher, Burney depicts in excruciating detail the experience of feeling forever watched by men and women already well established in society. The young woman in particular will be constantly assessed for deviations from the social norms of the upper classes. In *The Wanderer*, not published until 1814, but largely written long before, Burney links social conformity to questions of literal economic survival, demonstrates that privacy in some of its forms serves both social and personal ends, and conveys the urgency of dissimulation.

The explicit association of privacy with personal integrity belongs to a period later than Burney's. But if the word has for Burney less complicated resonance than it would later develop, she shares preoccupations that we now condense into the notion of privacy. This fact, hinted in the earlier novels, becomes emphatic in *The Wanderer*, which reveals how dramatically a woman's scanty resources diminish if she lacks obvious markers of high social class. In the world as it is, the poor have no right to privacy, Burney tells us, describing the encroachments that steadily threaten the "female Robinson Crusoe" whose efforts at survival provide the novel's subject.

Juliet, the hero of *The Wanderer*, in the end turns out to be well-born and well off, and she, like her fictional predecessors, makes a good marriage. But most of the novel explores the young woman's predicament during a prolonged period when her birth, her wealth, and her marital situation remain unknown. A refugee from France during the Revolution, she arrives in England not only anonymous and penniless but disguised in blackface, eloquent emblem of her condition as social outcast. Although she soon washes her face and turns into a beauty, she remains a helpless outsider until the saving revelations at the novel's end.

By conventional literary standards, *The Wanderer* is not a very good novel. Lapsing often into wooden verbosity, it abounds in extravagances of plot and in cardboard characters. But it is nonetheless a full and passionate novel of ideas, exploring the practical politics of women's lives in a way unusual, perhaps unique, among writers not overtly committed to revolutionary doctrines. Unlike her contemporary Mary Wollstonecraft, Burney claims her concern merely to recommend propriety. In a letter to her father prefixed to *The Wanderer*, she emphatically denies political interest or intention. She professes to focus, rather, on individual conduct, pointing out that "an exteriour the most frivolous may enwrap illustrations of conduct, that the most rigid preceptor need not deem dangerous to entrust to his pupils," and claiming as an aim, "to make pleasant the path of propriety" (9). But her narrative reveals the writer's interest also in making delicate discriminations about the actualities of women's lives, discriminations apparent despite the plot's implausibilities. She concerns herself substantially with the ways that the public realm impinges on all constructions of privacy: indeed, with what might appropriately be called the politics of privacy.

A twentieth-century political scientist, Ferdinand David Schoeman, articulates by analogy the nature of such a politics: "privacy norms serve the same function vis-à-vis social coercion that constitutional principles serve vis-à-vis legal coercion, protecting individuals from the overreaching control of others" (22). This characterization precisely describes the reasons for privacy in *The Wanderer*. In the context of inquiry into the female situation, privacy becomes especially crucial. Juliet's acknowledged right to privacy varies according to her perceived social status, which itself varies with the vicissitudes of plot. Her initial destitution and isolation, together with the mystery about her name, give everyone the right to ask her intimate questions. Throughout her struggle, she finds herself subject to onslaughts of inquiry. Although she attempts to protect herself with the vague locutions of polite society, her persecutors challenge every evasion.

At its most ambitious, *The Wanderer* attempts to construct a coherent graph of female possibility. Social standing, based on wealth and rank, generates one axis; the other follows the course of personal effort. *Female possibility* is quite specifically the issue (the novel's subtitle is *Female Difficulties*). Virtually every woman in *The Wanderer* needs to work for what she has not or to defend what she has. Juliet has especially complicated problems, often articulated through her efforts at privacy. Her journey to England begins as it continues, with a verbal assault by her fellow passengers in a boat escaping revolutionary France. "Why does she not say who she is at once?" irascible Mrs. Maple cries, adding, "I give nothing to people that I know nothing of" (29). Mrs. Ireton, whose "companion" the incognita briefly becomes, makes a concerted effort to get information, but the stranger's "birth, her name, her connexions, her actual situation, and her object in making the voyage, resisted enquiry, eluded insinuation, and baffled conjecture" (41). Mrs. Ireton nonetheless takes her as companion because "her manners were so strikingly elevated above her attire" (41). The "elevation" of manners suggests elevation of class: Mrs. Ireton imagines gaining social prestige by employing in a quasi-menial capacity a woman conceivably of high rank.

Juliet's manners, then, help from the beginning to protect her against the various forms of inquiry, insinuation, and conjecture, first of all because they serve as a possible class marker. Providing a socially acceptable mask, they continue to repel the interrogations of everyone with whom she comes in contact—a statement by no means implying that they cause such interrogations to cease. The right to privacy, understood as control over personal information, does not pertain to the socially powerless.

A major narrative crisis, difficult in its nature for twenty-first-century readers to take with full seriousness, elucidates the complex and crucial nexus of manners and privacy in the novel's world. It is worth examining at length, for it clarifies the social functions of privacy for upper-class women. If the poor are considered to have no right to personal privacy, those higher on the social scale may find themselves restricted by commitment to quite a different kind of privacy, socially constructed and ordained for social ends. Privacy itself, in other words, may amount to a trap—a point Burney suggests in *Camilla* and elaborates here.

In this crucial episode, Juliet, desperate for money, has been persuaded and bullied into consenting to give a public musical performance. She has previously appeared with great success on the stage, but only in amateur theatricals—and even then, she was compelled to perform. She feels many qualms; she resists the possibility as long as she can. Finally she agrees to offer herself thus to public view. At this juncture, shortly before the scheduled concert, she receives a long letter from Harleigh, who loves her and whom she loves, although circumstances prevent her from revealing the fact explicitly. The letter strongly urges her to "deliberate, before you finally adopt a measure to which you confess your repugnance." He does not know her actual "situation," Harleigh acknowledges, "but where information is with-held, conjecture is active; and while I see your accomplishments, while I am fascinated by your manners, I judge your education, and, thence, your connections, and original style of life" (343). In short, Juliet's manners and accomplishments lead Harleigh to assign her to a high social class. He pleads with her on the basis of the class to which her family of origin putatively belongs:

> Wound not the customs of their ancestors, the received notions of the world, the hitherto acknowledged boundaries of elegant life! Or, if your tenderness for the feelings—say the failings, if you please,—the prejudices,

the weaknesses of others, has no weight, let, at least, your own ideas of personal propriety, your just pride, your conscious worth, point out to you the path in society which you are so eminently formed to tread. . . . Remember . . . that your example may be pleaded by those who are not gifted, like you, with extraordinary powers for sustaining its consequences; by those who have neither your virtues to bear them through the trials and vicissitudes of public enterprise; nor your motives for encountering dangers so manifest; nor your apologies—pardon the word!—for deviating, alone and unsupported as you appear, from the long-beaten track of female timidity. (343)

Harleigh conveys forcefully a sense of extraordinary danger attending Juliet's projected endeavor: danger to her social standing; to her "female timidity," a locution that Juliet herself promptly translates as "delicacy," one of the most highly valued attributes of her sex; and to her position as moral exemplar.

The danger comes from exposure and from the decisive crossing of gender boundaries implicit in assuming a public position, deviating from proper female privacy. *Delicacy*, in the sense that Juliet intends, means, according to the *OED*, "A refined sense of what is becoming, modest, or proper; sensitiveness to the feelings of modesty, shame, etc.; delicate regard for the feelings of others." It registers an internalized sense of propriety, the quality that separates Juliet's kind of good manners from the variety practiced by those for whom manners constitute only artifice—a distinction the narrator explicitly makes. Delicacy, the basis of the good manners derived from sympathy, is an intuitive quality marking the genuine lady. The slightly covert reproach that she may abandon it in giving a concert devastates Juliet.

The distinction between the good manners "formed by the habits of high life" and the spontaneous manners inspired by "benevolence of mind," to use the narrator's language (135), occurs frequently in eighteenth-century moral discourse, reflecting anxiety about the aspect of hypocrisy hinted by such courtesy manuals as the one recommending a performance of generosity at table for the sake of self-love. The narrator wants the reader to understand Juliet's manners as conveying not only her good breeding but her good heart: emotional self-revelation as well as social mask.

If this is the case, though, Juliet runs great risks in any deviation from conventional propriety. Harleigh's letter says, in effect, that surely she already knows, by the power of her delicate intuition of propriety, the wrongness of what she proposes to do. If she does not know this, she must lack the intuitive quality itself. "Delicacy" keeps a woman from violating important boundaries. Harleigh makes it clear, through his discussion of family, that a woman's marital possibilities depend on her perceived propriety. Juliet risks unsexing herself if she compromises her delicacy—and the identification between delicacy and "female timidity" is precisely to the point. To give a public concert implies courage and self-determination, willingness to expose oneself, quite at odds with the standard of delicacy.

Obviously, in a society where appearances are everything, willingness to offer oneself to public view, to perform before an audience, openly to accept payment—all this abrogates the principles of proper female self-representation. Thomas Gisborne specifies the dangers, for women, of even private performances: "To encourage vanity; to excite a thirst of applause and admiration on account of attainments which, if they are to be thus exhibited, it would commonly have been far better for the individual not to possess; to destroy diffidence" (2:175). Exhibition before an audience transgresses female privacy, the privacy declared by a consistent socially ordained practice of concealment, the privacy that Juliet has so steadfastly preserved in her undeviating performance of propriety—the one kind of performance consistently sanctioned for women.

Reacting intensely to Harleigh's warnings, Juliet acknowledges the importance, for a woman, of controlling appearances and hints that such control becomes more difficult without the protection of a male. But circumstances rescue her. Juliet need not, after all, compromise her delicacy by performing in public; she can continue to acknowledge no interest in spectators and to preserve her psychological privacy by means of her flawless propriety. (She resembles in this respect her creator, who notoriously disclaimed all desire for public recognition and acclaim.) The novel reiterates the value of this most urgent kind of female privacy partly by the negative example of Elinor Joddrell, a revolutionary spirit whose willing relinquishment of privacy declares her advanced ideas but also predicts the madness that will overtake her. An enthusiast for the principles of the French Revolution, Elinor believes in openness. When she decides that she loves Harleigh, she says so—only to be promptly overcome by "native shame" (154), assumed to be the natural possession of females, who find it hard to cast off commitment to the privacy of the heart. Elinor calls loud attention to genuine social inequity, but she pays a high price. The distressing outcome of her attempts at freedom implies that to hide and subdue emotion, thus preserving emotional privacy, is a woman's safest course. Elinor's feelings, her body, and finally her mind, reduced to utter incoherence, testify that the cost of violating such privacy is too high to pay.

As for Juliet, after her resolute course of concealment she ultimately achieves the freedom to acknowledge her love for Harleigh and to marry him, rewarded for self-repression and for undeviating "delicacy." In a final scene of attempted encroachment, a rich and nasty old woman accuses her of theft and demands to search her workbag. Juliet refuses. Her unaffected "self-possession" abashes her accuser and reminds the reader once more about the connection of privacy, propriety, and integrity. In some sense, the logic of the narrative would suggest, Elinor Joddrell violates *herself* in violating convention.

That is to say that *The Wanderer* firmly supports social as well as moral propriety, understanding both as not only a form of restriction but also a form of protection for women. In calling it a "novel of ideas," I alluded not only to its apparent attempt to engage with large issues about the social limitation of women, but to its serious investigation of this matter of propriety. "Conservative" in her firm commitment to established principles of behavior, Burney dares a good deal in her willingness to ask questions about them. She uses her concern with female privacy to focus an inquiry into the experiential relation between women and the restrictions that control them. She gives to Elinor's inveighing against conventional limits eloquence, force, and even truth. But Juliet's history elucidates the distance of Elinor's view from the whole truth. By the nature of her propriety, Juliet reveals to discriminating watchers not only her commitment to guarding the privacy of her heart and mind but the value of what she guards. Propriety conceals, but social convention maintains that it can also indirectly reveal the emotional integrity and sensitivity constituting the foundation of female virtue. By refusing to display her heart, a woman testifies to her sense of its worth.

In conjunction with the dynamic of sensibility explored in the previous chapter, the dynamic of propriety reminds us how integral to the eighteenth-century female ethos were strategies of indirection and concealment. Refusing to display the heart provides a means of revealing it; dramatizing the heart through the manifestations of sensibility serves to conceal it. Hiding in order to display, displaying in order to hide, a woman did not need to allow herself consciousness of the ambiguities of her behavior. Elaborate social arrangements themselves insured and preserved such ambiguities.

Burney's awareness of the social—indeed, the political—implications of personal decorum or of deviations from it supplies rich texture to her narratives. In her treatment of manners in *The Wanderer*, she insists on the interdependence of society and its individual members. The intricate rules of propriety work, particularly on women, as an instrument of control, generating a culture of minute surveillance and censure. They in effect mandate hypocrisy, prescribing obsessive attention to appearances. Yet a woman can paradoxically evade the policing function of convention by demonstrating that her conformity is actually a "natural" emanation of her benevolent heart that attests sympathetic awareness of others and their needs. If Juliet employs for her own purposes the forms of polite society, she does so, the text insists, not as dissimulation, not as mere conformity, but as an expression of her native goodness. Virtue resides not in seclusion, as some conduct manuals suggested, but in conventional good behavior.

Observers in the world, then, can assess virtue by social performance. Yet Juliet demonstrates how a woman may turn even so oppressive a system to her own ends. In using the forms of propriety to protect the privacy of her feelings, she partly follows the social imperative of concealing at least the erotic impulses of a woman's heart. But she guards more than romantic feelings, assigned a range of emotional responses including discouragement, anxiety, contempt, anger, and mockery—all of which she hides from view, preserving selfhood by holding on to her own reactions. Thus she maintains herself as an individual even while conforming to the dictates of her social order.

Like the conduct manuals, *The Wanderer* conveys an ambivalent view of privacy's possible uses. But it suppresses concern about hypocrisy. Burney claims the urgency for women of preserving some intact inner realm as a vital preliminary to any sense of control or autonomy. Presumably recognizing that physical privacy for well-bred women was hardly conceivable, she explores instead the degree to which perfect social conformity, the triumphant practice of good manners, can provide its psychological equivalent. But her view is not altogether optimistic. Social convention may protect a woman's inner life, but its policing can entail a compelled privacy of decorum that forbids any expression of feelings and demands of the proper female the "delicacy" willingly to forgo public appearance. Although personally willed privacy constitutes freedom, its socially ordained equivalent epitomizes the demands that generate "female difficulties," guaranteeing the futility of Juliet's quest for financial independence and the personal autonomy that would accompany it. Juliet's manners may involve no dissimulation, but society forces on her a self-suppression that reflects the established pretense that women flourish only in relative confinement.

To posit a connection between good manners and virtuous feeling is not the only satisfactory solution to the problem of dissimulation. Burney herself, in *Cecilia*, imagining a response to Mr. Monckton's speech about social hypocrisy (with which this chapter opened), suggested the view that such hypocrisy really carries no moral weight.

"All these," answered Belfield, "are so merely matters of ceremony, that the concession can neither cost pain to the proud, nor give pleasure to the vain. The bow is to the coat, the attention is to the rank, and the fear of offending ought to extend to all mankind. Homage such as this infringes not our sincerity, since it is as much a matter of course as the dress that we wear." (735)

In other words, one must distinguish between the kind of self-disguise that serves immediate self-interest—the kind that Fielding, in *Joseph Andrews*, terms "affectation"—and the kind that belongs to accepted social ritual, which can be imagined as irrelevant to claims of virtue.

Despite sequences like the exchange between Monckton and Belfield, *Cecilia* as a whole dwells less explicitly than its successor on broad social patterns. It concentrates, rather, on the difficulties of privacy for a woman: difficulties in preserving it, but also the vulnerability implicit in its loss. Cecilia faces an unusual set of problems. Rich, cultivated, beautiful, and orphaned, she might seem to possess a high degree of freedom. Social pressures, though, bear as heavily on her as they do on other women. Despite her manifest attractions, she finds the course of true love running anything but smoothly. She has been consigned to the care of three guardians, sharply different from one another. They have in common only the fact that all impede her attainment of her objectives, however she defines those objectives. And if *The Wanderer* demonstrates the deprivation of privacy for persons perceived as of low social class, *Cecilia* shows that the well-born as well may have little recourse against the prying or even the idle curiosity of others.

Like Evelina, Cecilia becomes aware of her own love before she has any basis for confidence in its object's reciprocal feeling. Like her real-life counterparts, she has obviously been instructed in the importance of concealing her emotions until they comprise appropriate responses to a man's declaration. She has no one to confide in. Prey to uncertainty nourished by her beloved's ambiguous and contradictory behavior, she resorts, in two scenes teetering dangerously on the edge of the comic, to pouring out her feelings to a little dog belonging to Mortimer Delvile, the object of her passion.

On the first of these occasions, she deliberately seeks privacy, directing "her steps to a thick and unfrequented wood," and not pausing until she is more than two miles from the Delvile home, where she is a guest. When she thinks herself "sufficiently distant and private to be safe," she sits under a tree and soothes herself by lamenting to Fidel "that *he* had lost his master" (because Delvile is about to leave; the italics are Burney's). Then she bursts into tears, free to do so because she has "now no part to act, and no dignity to support, no observation to fear, and no inference to guard against" (520). This revealing series of negatives calls attention both to the kind of performance necessary for the preservation of privacy in a social context and to the constant obstacles to privacy: the "observation" and "inference" of others. The text reiterates the word *private* before narrating Cecilia's return to the house: "Cecilia continued in this private spot, happy at least to be alone" (521). It then reports her reentry into the social realm, where the impertinent Lady Honoria immediately begins teasing her about the signs of her tears.

Far more consequential, the second episode of nominally dog-centered emotion involves Cecilia's pouring out to Fidel her love for and doubts about Delvile—who, as the plot would have it, accidentally overhears this revelation. The manifest improbabilities of this situation (Delvile's convenient appearance is only slightly more plausible than Cecilia's complaining to a dog about his master's pride) emphasize the difficulty, for a novelist herself committed to eighteenth-century standards of female propriety, of finding a way for an irreproachable heroine to reveal what needs to be revealed. Irreproachability entails keeping everything important to oneself. And the use of manners as a device to insure privacy involves the possibility of misleading the object of one's affections as well as everyone else. As Delvile reacts rapturously to what he has heard, he discloses both his misinterpretation and his reinterpretation of Cecilia's verbal behavior. "I see what I took for indifference, was dignity; I perceive what I imagined the most rigid insensibility, was nobleness, was propriety, was true greatness of mind!" (549).

These abstract nouns carry a heavy weight of meaning. The alternatives to indifference and insensibility, both terms connoting absence of emotion, do not emphasize the contrasting presence of strong feeling. One might expect Delvile to say, "Now I realize that you really love me." Exactly this realization delights him, and Cecilia's enabling it shames her. But instead of talking about Cecilia's feelings, Delvile stresses the importance to him of her good behavior, now that he understands it as exactly that: understands his beloved as possessing propriety apparently equivalent to nobleness and reflecting "true greatness of mind." Greatness of mind declares itself through flawless conduct: that is, conduct flawless by the standards of a society decrying emotional self-revelation. But only Delvile's inadvertent violation of Cecilia's privacy permits the fulfillment of their love—and that only after further difficulties, increasingly momentous, that also turn on the problems of privacy.

Dissimulation alone guarantees privacy, yet dissimulation by its very nature can guarantee nothing. Cecilia, a moral paragon by nature and by upbringing, has, according to the good (if also crazed) old man Albany, a transparent face. But her transparency, as Albany makes clear, remains always at risk: "how long will that ingenuous countenance, wearing, because wanting no disguise, look responsive of the whiteness of the region within?" (292). Cecilia feels "confusion . . . at this public address" (292). Thus the episode in which someone attests to the value of transparency, that openness of countenance revealing all that lies within, also calls attention to the terror of publicity to the modest woman. She must be willing to make everything known, because she has nothing to hide; she must hide everything, because decorum demands that virtue subsist in private.

Such contradictory demands insure that even paragons can be suspected of deception. Many encounters between Cecilia and Delvile, before the open revelation of their mutual love, turn on Delvile's accusations of hypocrisy, which he assumes as part of the decorum of "young ladies." Appearances suggest to him Cecilia's romantic interest in Belfield; he takes her incomprehension and denials as merely formal. "Whence is it," he inquires—"half gayly, half reproachfully"—"that young ladies, even such whose principles are most strict, seem universally, in those affairs where their affections are concerned, to think hypocrisy necessary, and deceit amiable? and hold it graceful to disavow to-day, what they may perhaps mean publicly to acknowledge to-morrow?" (183). The word "graceful" suggests the degree to which the concealment that can be characterized either as hypocrisy or as the preservation of privacy belongs to the category of social graces.

A masquerade, that public ritual of disguise and self-protection, early declares the importance to *Cecilia* of the set of conflicting social demands that must be satisfied in female self-representation. Because the masquerade takes place at the home where she is staying, Cecilia herself, by convention, wears no disguise. The various men who persecute her camouflage themselves in ways appropriate to their natures: Mr. Monckton as devil, Delvile dressed all in white, and so on. More significant than such obvious specific equivalencies is the fact that equivalency is always at issue. The question of what appearances mean looms large in the plot, concerning women in more intricate ways than men. Sir Robert Floyer can indulge in manners that reveal rather than conceal his arrogance; Cecilia, if she feels distaste for her company, feels also the obligation to hide her feeling.

Burney could hardly be more emphatic about the perception that social self-presentation, almost always for women, sometimes for men as well, constitutes disguise. At rather tedious length she calls attention to such characters as Miss Larolles, always engaged in meaningless chatter, and her counterpart Miss Leeson, rigidly silent despite all provocation. Both, a persuasive interpreter explains, have adopted patterns of behavior because they think them fashionable—not because they bear any necessary relation to what they actually think and feel. Similarly, we encounter repeatedly the man whose public stance is boredom and an utter incapacity to interest himself in anything going on around him (he claims not to remember that a soi-disant friend committed suicide in a public setting), and the one who intersperses all conversation with meaningless French phrases. Both resemble Miss Larolles and Miss Leeson in having assumed public personae solely for the sake of appearing fashionable. The reiterated textual presence of such characters makes it impossible to forget the intricate question of what and how social manners disguise.

The comic foil Mr. Hobson, another tedious character because he so insistently makes a point of his presence, sees self-evident solutions for every problem of behavior—sees, in fact, no problems.

> "Let every man speak to be understood," cried Mr. Hobson, "that's my notion of things: for as to all those fine words that nobody can make out, I hold them to be of no use. Suppose a man was to talk in that manner when he's doing business, what would be the upshot? who'd understand what he meant? Well, that's the proof; what i'n't fit for business, i'n't of no value: that's my way of judging, and that's what I go upon." (409)

Captain Aresby, the man whose conversation consists entirely of fashionable jargon, much of it French, provides the immediate provocation for Mr. Hobson's remarks, but the issue of speaking "to be understood"—or not—reverberates throughout the novel. "Business," of course, does not supply a standard of conduct for most of the characters here, who commit themselves, rather, for the most part to pleasure. Cecilia and Delvile, with their more serious concerns, constitute obvious exceptions to this generalization, but for them too, "business" remains irrelevant.

Burney's undeniable social snobbery does not preclude—indeed, it may stem from—recognition that commerce provides the underpinning for idle society. The point emerges most emphatically from *The Wanderer*, but *Cecilia* implies it as well. Idleness, experienced as a burden by such upright characters as Cecilia, is also a luxury. The moral distortions it entails derive partly from efforts by those who enjoy it to disguise its burdensome aspects. Many kinds of pressure, in other words, urge the rich and well-born toward the practice of hypocrisy, codified in their systems of manners. Cecilia differs from her less worthy companions in the aims of her dissimulation. Her associates distort themselves in order to present, they think, more attractive self-images. Cecilia conceals her true thoughts and feelings in order not to offend, or (to return to the main point) in order to guard her vulnerabilities.

The kind of privacy that Cecilia seeks to attain carries no negative weight in itself, although her efforts to attain it, Delvile's suspicion of her "hypocrisy" suggests, may lead to false judgments of her. Conduct books, as we have seen, recommend disguise to young women, even while deploring the world's false faces. But Burney in *Cecilia* investigates also the negative implications of privacy, implications going far beyond the ludicrous disproportions of Miss Leeson's or Miss Larolle's self-disguising. The word *privacy*, with its cognates, recurs with particular emphasis in the final third of the novel, and its darker meanings emerge, inextricably intertwined with its urgencies.

Privacy becomes a vivid issue when Delvile suggests, for the best of reasons, that Cecilia join him in a private marriage: a marriage performed by a clergyman but not sanctioned by the community through the customary social rituals of visiting and display. Shocked by the idea, Cecilia yet finally consents to the wedding, but an unknown woman interrupts the ceremony. Her inexplicable declaration of an obstacle horrifies the participants, who do not resume their vows when she departs. Afterward Cecilia, depressed and angry, comments that "none of our proceedings have prospered, and since their privacy has always been contrary both to my judgment and my principles, I know not how to repine at a failure I cannot think unmerited" (630).

Judgment and principle both oppose privacy. Cecilia's generic objection to it stems from privacy's opposition to community and the room it consequently allows for deviant behavior and assumptions. A woman of insistently asserted "delicacy," Cecilia believes in the value of decorum, convention, and the kind of good behavior they foster—believes thus despite the facts that she thinks for herself, demonstrates her capacity to value also the unconventional and even the eccentric, and shows a marked capability to act forcefully and independently when occasion demands.

Privacy becomes reprehensible when it involves functions traditionally social, marriage providing an archetypal example. To protect one's purely personal privacy—and love, unlike marriage, is "purely personal"—does not in the same way threaten the strength of the social fabric. Of course definitions vary. Mrs. Harrel, widowed but undiminished in frivolous impulse, fatigues "Cecilia with wonder at the privacy of her life, and torment[s] her with proposals of parties and entertainments. She was eternally in amazement that with powers so large, she had wishes so confined" (792). From Mrs. Harrel's point of view, "functions traditionally social" include "parties and entertainments"; she considers it virtually a matter of duty for a woman with the capacity to create them to do so.

What Mrs. Harrel considers reprehensible privacy, the narrator clearly approves of. Nor is it altogether apparent, despite Cecilia's angry comment, that the privacy of the young couple's proceedings has caused the trouble that pursues them. On the contrary, one might plausibly argue that the impossibility of privacy generates the difficulties. Far more striking in the action of *Cecilia* than the danger of privacy is its virtual unattainability. The danger, in fact, may consist in the unattainability. Planning a private trip to London, in advance of the private marriage, Cecilia finds herself watched and interpreted at every turn. In one of Burney's characteristic nightmarish sequences, resembling in its phantasmagoric quality Camilla's descent into madness, in *Camilla*, or the scene when Camilla and another women are understood as shoplifters or madwomen, Cecilia encounters on the road to London most of the people she has previously met in the Harrels' social milieu—everyone from bored Mr. Meadows to talkative Miss Larolles. They interrupt her, change her plans, want to know where she's going and why. The most officious of them recognizes Delvile, who follows Cecilia in disguise, and actually confronts him. The more is at stake in privacy, the less it can be achieved. Cecilia's pallor and blushes betray her at Delvile Castle, and Lady Honoria listens attentively for every verbal slip. The social world comprises a network of watchers.

Whether this vision of the social universe represents a fear or a perception, it suggests the extreme precariousness of privacy as even a temporary goal. The nature of privacy implies that other people, given will and opportunity (sometimes just opportunity without will), can always violate it. Perhaps the inadvisability of private marriages depends on their sheer unlikelihood: obstacles exist everywhere. So, at any rate, the plot of *Cecilia* indicates. A single plotter within the narrative proves responsible for all the interferences, but they could happen, individually, without purposeful agency. Burney's narrative structures all register a sense of dense and potentially sinister population. The world is simply too full to allow privacy.

Cecilia, at any rate, finds less and less of it. Despite her capacity for self-reliance, she is driven to madness by the excessive difficulty of clear communication in this society crammed with individual self-interest. Not only do unknown spectators gather to witness her ravings, but her plight is subsequently literally advertised in the newspaper, all right to privacy at an end. The benevolences of literary plot redeem her at the end, but not until the novel has made an emphatic statement about the relative powerlessness of even the most forceful woman. That powerlessness registers most clearly, in Cecilia's case, in her inability effectively to control her self-representation: in our terms, if not in hers, the failure of privacy. When it matters most to her, she cannot dependably achieve privacy in her own terms either; intrusion appears to be a fundamental fact of her life. Mr. Monckton, the novel's villain, operates by making himself master of all knowledge about Cecilia. Knowledge is, in the most literal sense, power. The difficulty of interdicting other people's knowledge of her (sometimes their false knowledge, no less intrusive for its falsity) causes Cecilia much anguish.

Inasmuch as manners represent the operations of convention as social and personal pressure, they may direct attention also to the sometimes parallel workings of literary convention. Like manners, literary conventions can serve to protect privacy: the of course imaginary privacy of fictional characters; the perhaps more urgent, if equally imaginary, privacy of narrators. An ostentatious instance occurs at the end of Frances Sheridan's remarkable sentimental novel, *Memoirs of Miss Sidney Bidulph*. The eponymous protagonist begins to recede as the conclusion approaches— that conclusion in which, notoriously, nothing is concluded, the narrative ending in midsentence. Until a few pages before the end, *Memoirs* assumes the form of a vaguely epistolary novel, consisting of Sidney's long, self-revelatory journal-letters to her friend Cecilia. But that form suddenly changes. First Cecilia takes up the narrative, in a far more generalized mode than Sidney's. Then the unnamed male whose visit to a friend's mother first elicited the manuscript of Sidney's letters summarizes what he knows of the heroine's later life. Finally the story trails off into silence. No more can be known by any reading audience; only hints of further disaster remain.

In other words, the technique of the novel's conclusion calls attention to the issue of narrative privacy and to its connection with conventions of narrative decorum. Epistolary fictions typically rely on the excitement entailed by the reader's privileged violation of a letter writer's privacy. To move from epistolary convention to third-person storytelling to fragmentary summary rapidly shifts readers' expectations, compelling their awareness of authorial manipulation, flaunting the author's power to move at will from one convention to another, and asserting the final privacy of the fictional character whose inner and outer lives have previously been so fully exposed.

These shifts of convention in their connection with privacy also reiterate the novel's most important—or at least most conspicuously announced—thematic issue. The frame narrative has a man accompanying a male friend on a visit to the latter's mother. The mother, who turns out to be Cecilia, in the course of conversation comments on the theological dubiousness of "poetic justice" as a literary convention. God does not see as man sees, she insists; rewards on earth do not necessarily correspond to those in heaven. Experience tells us that good people may suffer atrociously. The story of Sidney, whose letters she possesses, illustrates the apparent injustice of life's dispensations and reminds us that God disposes differently from man.

The disjunctions of the novel's conclusion remind us, more precisely, how much depends on point of view. Cecilia has pointed out the discrepancy between divine and human viewpoints; the series of narrators calls attention to the way that point of view, that fundamental convention of fiction, determines degree of revelation. The manipulation of point of view forces the reader to experience directly the frustration of being cut off from knowledge, reminding us that different vantage points constitute different ways of knowing, echoing Cecilia's wisdom about the fact that never can we see it all, no matter what "it" refers to. Every human being possesses an ultimate degree of privacy that only God penetrates. The form as well as the substance of Sheridan's novel insists on that perception.

The apparently arbitrary shifts of convention as *Memoirs of Miss Sidney Bidulph* draws to a close, with the corresponding movement from exposure to reticence, recall patterns of the plot preceding this ending. The issue of privacy assumes considerable importance in the unfolding of Sidney's intricate misadventures. Sidney herself, socialized into the dignity of extreme verbal and psychological self-suppression, tells the world—tells her relatives, friends, and lovers; tells even herself—little about her thoughts and feelings, although a saving aspect of her socialization allows her to reveal all she knows in letters to Cecilia, hence to the reader looking over her shoulder. Her mother, in contrast, reveals just about everything to just about everyone, a trait that manifestly irritates Sidney, despite the fact that she attributes it, rather mysteriously, to her mother's "goodness." If this judgment is not entirely disingenuous, perhaps it registers a new version of the double bind that women endure. Lady Bidulph rests in her innocence, needing no concealment or deception, able and willing to pour out every fact about herself and her family. Sidney, in contrast, has been rigidly educated into judicious, and often painful, concealments. She can therefore no longer experience her innocence, always in danger of deviating from the repressive norm that her mother has apparently avoided.

In conjunction, the two habits of mind and behavior that mother and daughter embody account for many permutations. Thus, for instance,

Mrs. Bidulph tells her friend Lady Grimston all about Sidney's failed romance. Lady Grimston as a consequence arranges and precipitates Sidney's marriage to a man for whom she, the bride, cares little. Conversely, Sidney's refusal to reveal to her husband her knowledge of his infidelity enables his betrayal to continue to the point of financial and emotional disaster.

Decorum, propriety, good breeding: these concepts are matters of central concern for Sidney, and they entangle themselves with all questions of privacy. The distinction alive in *The Wanderer*, and in many other eighteenth-century works, between the decorum derived from "delicacy" and that amounting only to hypocrisy, operates importantly in this novel as well, dramatized especially in the contrast between Sidney and Miss Burchell, the beautiful young woman whom Faulkland has allegedly seduced and whom Sidney compels him to marry. Faulkland has indeed slept with Miss Burchell, but he has not seduced her: she is, it turns out, that scandalous figure, a "female rake." She doesn't *seem* like a female rake, though. She seems, rather, a young woman of good breeding whose behavior always appears appropriate. Sidney, a close watcher of other people, despite her own extreme decorum feels occasional suspicion of Miss Burchell's, of her way of assuming exactly the right emotional posture and altering it instantly at the suggestion that it might not suit the watcher. Sidney's own standards keep her, of course, from inappropriate behavior, but they do not adjust so readily to others' desires. But her suspicion does not allow her to penetrate false appearances: she insists that Faulkland marry the woman he has wronged, despite—or because of—her manifest desire to marry him herself. The reasons she offers against her own marriage turn on propriety: she would not wish to marry a rich, attractive man when she herself is beyond her first beauty and in financial need; or she would not marry the man her first husband believed to have cuckolded him. Such proclamations of flawless conduct protect her inner life from external knowledge and drive the plot toward disaster.

Investigation of *The Wanderer* called attention to the social impositions implicit in the female decorum of privacy. Burney's language and plot make it apparent yet again that women's privacy serves public purposes. Her novel illustrates the double bind of social expectations for women, without providing overt criticism. *Memoirs of Miss Sidney Bidulph* adumbrates the "public purposes" of privacy by implicating the reader in privacy's dramas. The narrative retreat from knowledge calls attention to the constructed nature of the text and to the ways that personal concealment serves social ends. Sidney conceals the horrors of her domestic situation, thus obviating the necessity and even the possibility of outside intervention. Her construction of apparent placidity protects her husband by guarding her own emotional experience. The contriver of the novel finally conceals all the hinted horrors of her character's later life, arbitrarily truncating the reader's knowledge, arbitrarily "protecting" that reader, and reminding us that nothing need be, nothing can be, done by anyone outside the text (except, of course, the writer) about a fictional figure's suffering. Sheridan may be taken to hint a parallel between the concealments that protect society and those that protect the reader. Privacy, she suggests more mordantly than Burney, exists for the sake of other people.

If Sidney operates largely on the basis of social convention, the writer of an eighteenth-century novel typically works by means of its literary equivalent. Although certain elements in the plot of *Memoirs* mark a new departure for fiction, the manipulations of point of view, the employment of a frame narrative, even the fragmentary form of the narrative as a whole—all partake of conventions already established by the sentimental novel. The rapidity with which point of view changes at the end and the gradual distancing of perspective are unusual, but the device of a new point of view as a way of bringing closure was well established. Behind such conventions the author conceals her intentions, preserving a privacy of meaning. That is, she relies finally on the reader's imagination to fill out the narrative and its import.

For readers now, possibly for at least some earlier readers as well, the "import" of *Memoirs of Miss Sidney Bidulph* may include subversive implications. Sidney herself, encouraged by her brother, calls attention to the fact that her efforts always to do the right thing have brought disaster to others as well as herself. Should we conclude the inadvisability of trying so hard to be good? The novel allows precisely such a conclusion: a perception that female socialization into selflessness constitutes a universally destructive force. But it does not enforce this reading, and its trailing away into vagueness followed by silence permits other interpretations, including the theological one suggested by Cecilia: God works in mysterious ways; human beings cannot fathom them. This deliberate ambiguity functions as a courtesy to the reader, a refusal to impose. If the narrative allows itself to be read as indictment of the social system, it does not demand such reading. Similarly, it draws back from inflicting excessive suffering on its reader. The detailed narrative ends with the shocking revelation that Faulkland, who married Sidney in the belief that he had killed his unfaithful previous wife, has committed bigamy and then, probably, suicide. At any rate, he is dead. But Sidney still has her supportive, benevolent, rich uncle, her thriving children, her rich friend. One can imagine at least bright spots in her life. To be sure, Cecilia's general summary declares Sidney's subsequent course of misery, but it offers no details. Readers can fancy what they will about the precise actualities of her experience. The decorum of Sheridan's text, then, contains the energies of her plot in the interests of the community of readers. Containment takes place by means of what might seem the novel's most disorderly aspects, its apparently arbitrary final movements among narrators. As manners, however arbitrary themselves, serve the interests of social class, literary conventions protect readers as well as writers. Containment controls the tumult of revelation, hinting the generic value of the privacy it guards.

Sidney's privacy—her concealment for the sake of herself and others—involves dissimulation, but the novel does not call attention to this fact, although the narrator's retreat into privacy depends on a series of artifices that call attention to themselves. Jane Austen explores more fully than Sheridan or Burney a possibility implicit in their fiction: that deliberate, personally chosen dissimulation, far from marking moral weakness, may play a fundamental part in the maintenance of ethical responsibility. In *Sense and Sensibility*, that novel of secrets (its first version written in the 1790s), Austen discriminates the precise social importance of privacy. She also demonstrates that women find a carefully constructed realm of personal privacy, heavily dependent on artifices of disguise, essential to preserving an equally constructed individuality.

An exemplary instance of the irreproachable dissimulation of good manners, enlisted for a personal end, occurs when Elinor Dashwood—consistently mocked by her sister Marianne for her adherence to social forms—manages successfully to arrange a private conversation with Lucy Steele, the self-professed fiancée of Edward Ferrars, whom Elinor herself loves. Attending a tedious social gathering at the Middletons', Elinor makes for herself the opportunity of conversation by politely offering to help Lucy in the work of making a filigree basket for Lady Middleton's daughter. Marianne has previously announced her detestation of card playing and has walked off to the pianoforte, leaving Lady Middleton to look "as if she thanked heaven that *she* had never made so rude a speech" (Austen, *Sense* 145). The narrator explicitly comments on the superior expediency of Elinor's methods: "thus by a little of that address, which Marianne could never condescend to practise, [she] gained her own end, and pleased Lady Middleton at the same time" (145). The forms of politeness conceal her private purposes, protect her private feelings, and enable her to enlarge her store of information by talking with Lucy. There is no suggestion that these forms emanate from her sympathy or concern for others, as good manners, according to moralists, do. The employment of manners for dissimulation and disguise illustrates their practical, not their moral, value.

The subsequent conversation, partly comic in narrative effect precisely because of its reiterated efforts at deception, underlines the point. Neither Lucy nor Elinor speaks her mind or her feelings. Both rely heavily on social forms to achieve personal ends. If they remain relatively transparent to one another, at least their disguise of propriety protects them from any need openly to confront distressing feelings or to engage in obvious conflict. Lucy's purpose is to hurt and to triumph; Elinor wishes only to gain information and to guard herself. She therefore has the moral advantage, but her means resemble her opponent's.

Through almost two-thirds of *Sense and Sensibility*, Elinor unfailingly preserves social forms, employs behavior that rarely expresses her feelings openly, and sustains her emotional life behind a psychic screen largely constructed by good manners. Marianne, open about her every impulse and emotion, is perceived by the narrator as reprehensible precisely in her openness. Her failure to preserve privacy entails her many lapses of decorum. She must learn to reform in both respects: to keep things to herself and to behave in socially mandated fashion.

More than any other of Austen's novels, *Sense and Sensibility* creates an elaborate structure of distinctions. Its somewhat schematic disposition of characters can be mapped in terms of often slight disparities of value. Those with a highly developed sense of privacy among the cast of characters include Elinor, Colonel Brandon, and Edward. Lady Middleton provides an ambiguous case that furthers Austen's project of subtle differentiation. She neither pries into others' affairs nor gratuitously reveals her own; she accepts but does not share her husband's need for constant company. Yet her lack of inner life implies that personal privacy would have little real meaning for her. Willoughby uses his ostensible openness for strategic purposes, while preserving the secrets of his sexual career. Apparently quite devoid of any developed sense of privacy (though not necessarily of capacity for secrecy) are Marianne, Mrs. Jennings, and Sir John Middleton, but they differ from one another in significant respects even on the matter of privacy.

Yet another conduct book may help to illuminate the situation of the Dashwood family. In 1743, a "Gentleman of Cambridge," adapting a French conduct manual "to the Religion, Customs, and Manners of the English Nation," wrote,

There are Rules for all our Actions, even down to *Sleeping with a good Grace*. Life is a continual Series of Operations, both of Body and Mind, which ought to be regulated and performed with the utmost Care, and of which the Success frequently depends upon those with whom we live and converse; who are too apt to put a good or bad Construction upon them, agreeable to their own way of thinking, or to the Disposition or Affection they have toward us. (Ancourt 8–9)

The world the Dashwoods inhabit still resembles that evoked in this statement—a world in which rules exist to govern all behavior, but in which judgment depends less on those rules than on individual interpretation. In such a social environment, deviation from the rules does not bring automatic condemnation: there is room for a Marianne, whose friends and relatives will "put a good . . . Construction" on her actions. Yet the moralist's account implies a more threatening large context: those beyond the immediate social circle may arrive at quite a different construction. The safe course is to follow the rules.

Marianne understands the discrepancy between her behavior and her sister's as stemming from different attitudes toward the system of social rules. She scorns Elinor's conformity and concern with the opinions of others. Like Burney's Elinor Joddrell, she assesses her own deviations from norms of social conduct as evidence of a free spirit. Her fundamental objection to the idea of social compliance stems from her conviction that such compliance would subordinate her will to the desires, assumptions, and standards of others. A true Romantic, not only in her passion for dead leaves but in her passionate individualism, she accepts her own sense of rightness as sufficient guide to conduct.

Elinor, following a different path with no support from her family, finds strength in social responsibility. Like the most serious eighteenth-century conduct book writers, she assumes an identity between politeness and morality connected with the imperative of self-knowledge. Elinor's better behavior than Marianne's accompanies a higher degree of self-understanding. Moreover, her effort to take account of the needs and feelings of others reveals exactly that "complaisance" and "delicacy" so highly valued in the eighteenth century. Yet, as the conversation with Lucy shows, she also understands manners as pure artifice, means to a personal end. "Good girl" though she is, she possesses a healthy sense of self-preservation.

As many readers have realized, Austen does not in fact endorse Elinor's position entirely at the expense of Marianne's. She makes Marianne an engaging figure, even if sober judgment cannot sanction her behavior. Her openness comprises part of her attractiveness. By comparison, Elinor can seem almost prudish, excessively controlled. Marianne expresses what she feels—not only her erotic response to Willoughby but her irritation with the Middletons, her annoyance when someone fails to admire her sister's handiwork, her boredom at trivial conversation. Apparently abandoning personal privacy, accepting risks that Elinor could not bear, she demonstrates another kind of moral courage.

The social environment of *Sense and Sensibility* lacks the human density of Burney's evoked world. No crowds beset Elinor and Marianne in Devonshire, but Austen makes it clear that even a tiny society can threaten privacy. Mrs. Jennings wants to know everything about everyone; Sir John assumes the availability to view of every romance and all desire. For Marianne, other people's prying impulses hardly matter while her relationship with Willoughby proceeds as she would have it. Everyone can see, everyone is free to know. If some—notably her sister—disapprove of her behavior, that fact does not matter either. Locked in her solipsistic love (Willoughby, she believes, duplicates her every thought and feeling), Marianne finds the rest of the world irrelevant. She neither conforms to established social standards nor cares about conformist social judgments. Her risk-taking denies the force and relevance of community.

Elinor, in contrast, possesses not only a highly developed sense of privacy but marked sensitivity to social norms. She accepts the responsibility of covering up Marianne's violations of decorum, conducting gracious exchanges with vulgar Mrs. Jennings while Marianne remains tangled in her own fantasies, creating conversations with the Steele sisters while Marianne ignores them, trying to atone to Colonel Brandon for Marianne's neglect. But she never reveals more than she should, about herself or her family. She respects other people's privacy as well as her own, understanding, for instance, what it costs Colonel Brandon to reveal his early disastrous romance and preventing herself from making any effort to pry into the nature of Marianne's commitment to Willoughby.

Most notable, however, is Elinor's preservation of her own privacy as she grieves over Edward's defection, persuaded by Lucy Steele that the man who has appeared to court Elinor is in fact already committed to Lucy. As she explains after the fact, her failure to reveal her own suffering derives from her obligation to keep Lucy's secret, but it also protects her family from grief and anxiety. Elinor upholds the established system of courtesy in keeping her suffering to herself, and she demonstrates the kind of social responsibility implicit in scrupulous preservation of one's own as well as others' privacy. If Elinor and her kind refuse to gratify the curiosity of such as Mrs. Jennings, they also avoid inflicting their own anxieties on others. To keep one's troubles to oneself is an act of graciousness as well as self-protection.

Much in *Sense and Sensibility* buttresses this interpretation of Elinor's relative taciturnity, beginning with the Dashwood women's arrival at Barton Cottage, when "each for the sake of the others resolved to appear happy" (28). The kind of privacy that consists in reserving feelings functions for the sake of others as much as for the self. Marianne learns this truth as a result of her emotional and physical suffering and makes herself worthy of reticent Colonel Brandon by trying not to inflict her pain on her family. The corresponding truth that Elinor must learn dramatizes the other side of the equation between privacy and courtesy. It acknowledges the danger of keeping feeling within, the danger of apparent vapidity, of seeming like Lady Middleton, who feels only about her children and cares for no one, who therefore accepts no social responsibility. Unimportant in the plot, Lady Middleton fills an important place in the moral scheme of *Sense and Sensibility.* The fundamental principle of politeness (and of the kind of privacy I have been describing) is, according to Hester Chapone, the "universal duty in society to consider others more than yourself" (178). But to follow this mandate literally risks the suppression of the kind of self-love that grounds the command to love one's neighbor as oneself. As the character of Fanny Price in *Mansfield Park* demonstrates, Austen was fully alert to this risk. The union of social and moral propriety demands a fine balance between the claims of the self and of others, the balance that Elinor and Marianne variously learn to achieve. Convention can be employed for self-interest, yet the interests of the community, expressed in its conventions, also threaten the fullness of the self.

According to Austen, then, preserving one's privacy, like other manifestations of good manners, helps to fulfill the individual's responsibility toward others but may entail dangerous self-suppression. This novelist does not appear to worry much about social hypocrisy, that obsessive concern of earlier eighteenth-century writers. Rendering the superlatively hypocritical character of Lucy Steele, the narrator expresses a casual contempt suggesting that Lucy embodies not common practices but a rare and reprehensible extreme. The moral anxiety of *Sense and Sensibility* focuses, rather, on the danger of social irresponsibility, particularly as a result of romantic solipsism, and the opposed danger of personal repression.

The kind of privacy these novelists explore does not necessarily make itself recognizable to the observer, as retreating to a room of one's own does. It consists in urgent inner retreat, in subtle forms of self-protection, in finding ways to be alone in company. Austen's insistence that such psychic retirement serves social as well as personal ends coexists with the consciousness she shares with Burney: that the claims of the social must accompany rather than replace those of the feeling individual. Both novelists, and Sheridan as well, demonstrate the tension between subordinating oneself to the will of the community, as expressed in its social conventions, and using those conventions for personal purposes

5

Private Conversations

Conversation is a form of relationship, not just a form of speech. Although its bearing on privacy may seem obscure, like other social conventions it can lend itself to self-disguise, thus cutting its participants off from one another rather than connecting them. Like the subject of privacy, that of conversation raises issues about the relation between interests of a community at large and those of the individuals it includes. I propose to engage the relation between the two subjects by way of a preliminary survey of conversational standards; this will prepare for an investigation of novelistic renditions of conversation and of how the patterns of conversation can function for self-protection.

The shift in English representations of conversation between the eighteenth and the nineteenth century suggests a general change in understanding of the realm of discourse and of relationship to which conversation belongs. For Samuel Johnson, in the mid-eighteenth century, and for his biographer, James Boswell, writing at the century's end, conversation constituted a mode of public display. Boswell defined his own literary enterprise in terms of Johnson's conversation: "But his conversation alone, or what led to it, or was interwoven with it, is the business of this work [the *Life*]" (Boswell 531). The biographer accepts as his central responsibility evocation of Johnson's conversation, which will enable him to define the figure who looms as epic hero for his age.

Less than three-quarters of a century after Boswell, when Elizabeth Gaskell published *The Life of Charlotte Brontë* (1857), conversation clearly belonged to the sphere of private relationship, with the act of writing rather than that of speaking epitomizing the public personage. Early in her narrative, Gaskell characterizes Charlotte Brontë and her father as "cherishing and valuing privacy themselves," therefore "perhaps over-delicate in not intruding upon the privacy of others" (42). Much later, depicting her subject as a public personage, she praises her skills as a conversationalist: "a person with clear judgment and fine sense; and though reserved, possessing unconsciously the power of drawing out others in conversation" (284). No "power" could seem more different from Johnson's "talking for victory." Moreover, the scanty examples of Brontë's conversation that Gaskell supplies typically concern intimate matters and suggest feelings, while yet retaining the speaker's dignity.

Representations of conversation in fiction, by and large, reveal aspects of the art elided by the polarity between public performance and private exchange. The conversations invented by eighteenth-century novelists often have to twenty-first-century ears a "public" ring, in their elaboration and formality, but the issues they raise bear on the matter of privacy. Sometimes they reflect the same kind of anxiety we have seen elsewhere: anxiety over what it means for another person to preserve privacy by means of concealment. But novelists use conversation to register not only the possible danger but the putative value of privacy. To examine a range of literary functions that representations of conversation serve complicates one's understanding of privacy as well as of the human relations that it fosters and impedes.

Conversation as a social mode lends itself readily to hypocrisy—that by now familiar issue profoundly implicated with privacy. Indeed, early manuals of conversation suggest the possibility that conversation in its very nature constitutes a codified species of hypocrisy. Such manuals, which flourished from the sixteenth to the nineteenth century, tacitly or explicitly emphasize artifice. They understand conversation as one among many social activities, governed like the others by endlessly elaborated rules, rules that in this instance bear at least as heavily on men as on women. Peter Burke suggests an analogy between the rules for conversation and the norms established by Johnson's dictionary, seeing both as "attempts to regulate expression" (113). Rules of this kind belong to what Norbert Elias calls "the civilizing process," which includes "the moderation of spontaneous emotions" and "the tempering of affects" (236). That process, as exemplified in the manuals, emphasizes concealment as well as moderation. But the issue of privacy, as dramatized in fictional renditions of conversation, involves kinds of concealment hardly foreseen in the rule books.

The rules essentially locate the art of conversation as a subcategory of the art of pleasing, that important attribute of the gentleman—and even more emphatically of the lady. Pleasing requires self-suppression, self-manipulation, the assumption that effects matter more than their causes.

It encourages its practitioner toward self-disguise, often in the guise of self-expression.

The self that functions in conversation, the manuals indicate, has been composed—*should* have been composed—to make social interaction as smooth as possible. And the idea of social interaction might carry heavy moral weight. An especially important guide to conversation, frequently republished for more than two centuries, was an Italian work by Stephen Guazzo, translated into English in the late sixteenth century. Entitled *The civile Conversation*, this work elucidated not only the set of rules that soon became familiar, but also the rules' moral foundation. It begins by establishing the situation of the author's brother William, who, seriously ailing, explains to the doctor how much he loves to be alone. Although he works among other men, he speaks ardently for the value of privacy. When he withdraws into his lodging to read, write, or rest, he explains, "then I recover my libertie" (Guazzo 3r). The doctor, unswayed, insists that solitude has caused his mysterious ailment. "Account solitarinesse for poison," he demands, "and companie, for an Antidote, & the foundation of life" (4v). After an essentially theological discussion of the comparative virtues of solitude and company (William argues that Jesus recommended solitary prayer; the doctor points out that Christ founded the Church), the doctor summarizes, making "conversation" synonymous with "company." "Conversation," he concludes, "is not onlie profitable, but moreover necessarie to the perfection of man, who must confesse that hee is lyke the Bee which cannot live alone" (12r).

I know of no more powerful statement of the moral dubiety of privacy as opposed to the urgency of the social life. Of course Guazzo wrote more than a century before the period that interests me most, before abundant textual evidence existed for a widespread desire for privacy. But his book continued to be read, and its fundamental argument, about basic human gregariousness, continued to be reiterated.

Efforts to suggest an equation between the rules of conversation and principles of morality continued into the eighteenth century. Benjamin Stillingfleet's 1737 *Essay on Conversation*, obviously modeled on Pope's *Essay on Criticism*, begins,

> The Art of Converse, how to sooth the Soul
> Of haughty Man, his Passions to controul,
> His Pride at once to humble and to please,
> And joyn the Dignity of Life with Ease.

(3)

It ends, yet more portentously—and very much in Guazzo's vein—

> God with Reason joins to make us own,
> That 'tis not good for Man to be alone.
>
> (24)

The entire poem insists on conversation as a test of uprightness. Modesty, sincerity, and good nature mark the good conversationalist, as they indicate the good human being. "Self-Conceit" produces bad conversation and bad men. Social life is, explicitly, an arena in which one may hope "to gain immortal Fame" (7): implicitly, therefore, the locus for competition that Johnson perceived.

Stillingfleet, in his twenty-four-page poem, makes no attempt to offer specific rules for conversation. Writers who, like Guazzo, provide detailed advice about how to make conversation "pleasing" may begin with comparable moral emphasis, but the actual rules suggest that morality has little to do with real conversation. John Constable, who published his treatise in 1738, may be taken as representative of eighteenth-century rule makers— or rule articulators. He opens with a sweeping statement of conversation's importance: "Conversation takes up a great Part, and influences almost every Part of Life" (preface). He follows Guazzo in arguing—on intellectual rather than moral grounds—for the superiority of social to "private" life: "Private Thoughts alone, can hardly suffice to that comprehensive Enlargement of the Mind, which is attained by taking in the different Sentiments, and Notions of other Men" (14). He claims as the very foundation of good conversation the ability of the participant "to be *well with himself,* but also *to be himself*" (3). That ideal of being oneself, however, may lead the reader to speculate about what alternatives Constable has in mind.

As it turns out, concern about "Hypocrisy" and "Affectation" emerges over and over. In considerable detail, Constable outlines various possibilities of self-disguise, deprecating them all: reliance on indiscriminate reading, adopting the thoughts of other men, telling jokes, speaking only of politics, conversing on the basis of secondhand knowledge. In various ways, he reiterates warnings against conspicuous self-display. Assuming that everyone feels primarily self-interested, he advocates at least verbal suppression of egotism in favor of the appearance of interest in others. And appearance, the text gradually reveals, comprises the main tool of conversation: self-disguise is, after all, essential. Shifting back and forth from concern with the speaker to emphasis on the hearer, Constable writes, "As Vanity and Self-love are apt to fix our Minds upon ourselves, and diminish our Esteem and Love for others, it frequently happens, that Civilities are feigned Expressions of Good-will and Esteem. Yet even when we are persuaded, or at least suspect they are not very sincere, still they generally please" (187). The speaker feels less esteem and love than he expresses; the recipient of compliments suspects their falsity yet enjoys them because of his own vanity and self-love. A mutually reinforcing arrangement of hypocrisy keeps conversation running smoothly.

The way one looks often affects the acceptability of conversation. One should cultivate a look of "openness," since its converse, the look of having something in reserve, always creates a negative impression. To be sure, the kind of look that seems "the Picture of a disclosed Heart" may serve as a cover for "many concealed Thoughts" (194). It is not apparent, in this instance, whether Constable wishes to warn the speaker against concealment, to recommend plausible concealment, or to remind the listener of the possibility of deception.

Possibility, even likelihood. "Smoothness," a conversational ideal, often means superficiality. As early as 1719, when Jonathan Swift published *Polite Conversation*, the mechanical quality of social conversation could provide a central target. Eric Partridge, his modern editor, summarizes Swift's project, defining his serious purpose as "to scarify the vanity and the monopoly, the pedantry and desperate attempts to be witty, the ill-bred interruptions and the ill-mannered raillery and mockery, that disfigure so many conversations" (Swift 15). Interruptions, raillery, and mockery presumably constitute eruptions of genuine aggression, but the faults that Swift dwells on most insistently belong to the realm of pretense. The verb *polish* and its cognates recur often in Swift's satiric narrative, suggesting the degree to which attention to surfaces has come to substitute for concern with the substance of conversation. Hence the pedantry, the false wit, the mockery that goes awry: all testify to attempts to manipulate appearances. Conversation, the conversation that provides the manuals' subject, participates in a social world marked not simply by rituals of courtesy but by more compelling rituals of fashion. As Swift's persona puts it, explaining his undertaking, "I determined to spend five Mornings, to dine four Times, pass three Afternoons, and six Evenings every Week, in the Houses of the most polite Families; of which I would confine myself to fifty, only changing as the Masters or Ladies died, or left the Town, or grew out of Vogue, or sunk in their Fortunes, or (which to me was of the highest Moment) became disaffected to the Government" (22). Morning, afternoon, and evening, the "polite" gather for social exchange. The significant participants in such exchange depend on "Vogue" and politics, itself hardly more, the phrasing suggests, than a matter of fashion. And the participants matter more than the utterance.

If conversation indeed can be thought of, as Guazzo suggests, as the very "foundation of life," if it epitomizes the realm of social interaction, what goes on in conversation signifies the state of human relations within the culture. Lawrence Klein has argued persuasively that early-eighteenth-century ideas about educating an enlightened citizenry depended on the notion of heterosexual conversation as a mode of inculcating diverse values. The prevalent perception of falsity at the foundation of conversation suggests uneasiness about the nature and possibility of relationship, but also a sense of something real at stake in conversation. Yet such manuals as Constable's can take for granted falsity at the foundation (despite the advice that the conversationalist should "be himself"), assuming that a realistic understanding of human nature will enable conversationalists to deal honorably and even productively within a framework of inevitable deceptiveness.

Constable concerns himself with the conversation of "Gentlemen"; Swift expresses his concerns about conversation in his satiric account of the world of high fashion, but fashion serves as a useful metaphor for all arrangements of pretense and appearance, all contrivance. Eighteenth-century fiction insists that the same issues figured at every social level. Oliver Goldsmith's *The Vicar of Wakefield* (1766), one of the century's most widely read novels, employs formal structures of conversation to create narrative ambiguities. The novel concerns mainly poor—increasingly poor—and inconspicuous members of the social order. Its protagonist and narrator, Parson Primrose, feels suspicious of the world of fashion and tries to prevent his wife and daughters from making the slightest approach to it. He cares primarily about doing his duty to God and to his parishioners and about the welfare of his family. Yet the story Goldsmith tells epitomizes as completely as does Swift's satire the uses of conversation as self-protection and self-display. It also reveals how private conversation may serve public purposes. The inevitable falsities of human interchange, in Goldsmith's figuration of them, reflect failures of self-knowledge more often than self-protection—yet the self-protections of psychological privacy also remain powerful.

Despite its comedy, *The Vicar of Wakefield* in many respects belongs to the genre of sentimental fiction. It values right feeling and often appears to assess people on the basis of their feelings as well as, or even instead of, the actions resulting from those feelings: on causes as opposed to effects, the opposite criterion to that of the fashionable world. If emotion is a value, though, intimacy is not. As in Boswell's *Life*, reported conversation in *The Vicar of Wakefield* takes place mainly in groups of three or more.

And it rarely reveals directly the thoughts and feelings of a speaker, although it may provide much indirect information.

The abundant represented conversations have a curious ring—not because of the unfamiliar formality of their diction, but because the words spoken among men and women appear to partake more of performance than of expression, despite the fact that the conversational participants rarely concern themselves with social self-display. I open my copy of the novel at random and find this, from a conversation between Burchell and Primrose. Burchell speaks, characterizing Sir William Thornhill: "Adulation ever follows the ambitious, for such alone receive most pleasure from flattery. He was surrounded with crowds, who shewed him only one side of their character; so that he began to lose a regard for private interest in universal sympathy" (Goldsmith 47). This does not sound like one man describing another (describing himself, as we eventually learn). It sounds like public oratory, or an actor's speech: something written rather than spontaneously spoken. It neither obviously emerges from nor furthers any kind of relationship. It evokes none of the associations commonly connected with the idea of privacy.

Perhaps one should classify an utterance of this sort as exemplary of the conversation of self-display, even though this is not the discourse of "society." Yet "self" is not clearly at issue. Primrose's voice, in the same conversation, does not differ markedly from that of his interlocutor. "'What!' cried I, 'is my young landlord then the nephew of a man whose virtues, generosity, and singularities are so universally known?'" (47). We hear the same note of artificiality, have the same sense of a discourse more adapted to written than to oral communication. Rarely does Goldsmith deviate from this norm in his representations of conversation. Here, for one more case in point, is Primrose addressing his children: "'You cannot be ignorant, my children,' cried I, 'that no prudence of ours could have prevented our late misfortune; but prudence may do much in disappointing its effects. . . . Let us then, without repining, give up those splendours with which numbers are wretched, and seek in humbler circumstances that peace with which all may be happy'" (44). To be sure, Primrose is a preacher by profession. But his predilection for words that we may doubt ever got spoken in ordinary friendly intercourse appears to infect everyone he encounters.

Before leaping to the conclusion that Goldsmith just isn't very good at conversation, it might be worth speculating about what literary purposes this kind of representation may serve. I do not wish to suggest that it altogether lacks differentiation. Primrose's daughters on occasion attempt to approximate fashionable conversation. Mr. Thornhill, a contemptible character (Olivia's seducer), speaks the language of Swift's targets, as do the two "women of the town" whom he employs in the guise of fashionable ladies. But speech of the sort they exemplify plays a small part in this novel in comparison to the formal discourse of Primrose and of Burchell. So distant does the talk of these men seem from ordinary language that it is difficult even to understand it as "conversation": seldom does an interchange long sustain itself; seldom does it appear to reflect a personal relationship. This kind of conversation speaks more of role than of character.

"Role," in this instance, means not a part played on the stage but a part played in society, the world's stage. Burchell's role is that of poor-but-benevolent eccentric, Primrose's that of good pastor. Both men's speeches help to define and to lend density to their social positions (in Burchell's case, a false social position—although in fact his pronouncements suit the rich eccentric he actually is as well as the poor eccentric he pretends to be). And this social function of conversation justifies its existence in the novel.

According to this interpretation, conversation serves primarily a public function, not in the sense that Dr. Johnson's widely promulgated pronouncements have public meaning, but in the novel's designs on its audience as well as the characters' understanding of how their relationships work. The implicit emphasis on social roles in conversation enables the characters' utterances to reiterate and enforce a hierarchical structure that lies at the center of the book's concerns. God, figured, as in so many eighteenth-century novels, as Providence, provides the hierarchy's apex. Primrose, the clergyman, God's agent on earth, comes next, with Thornhill, secular representative of goodness, just below him. Despite his wealth and apparent power, Squire Thornhill emerges finally at the very bottom, with the others ranged above him according to their degree of virtue and understanding. The hierarchy, then, is in the first instance not social but theological. At the novel's end, though, social arrangements roughly correspond to the theological system, as Squire Thornhill loses his social position and money while Primrose gains unexpected prosperity.

Before Providence straightens everything out, however, conversation reveals some disturbing social facts. All eighteenth-century manuals of conduct emphasize the importance of "pleasing" in social intercourse. Raillery, contradiction, captiousness, excessive ceremony: such faults (I take the list from John Locke) exemplify ways of making others uncomfortable in conversation. Civility, Locke says, is "nothing but a care not to shew any slighting, or contempt, of any one in Conversation" (203). Conversation, in other words, provides the arena for revealing the quality of one's breeding. The central rule of good breeding, according to Locke, is

"Not to think meanly of our selves, and not to think meanly of others" (199). Elaborating this crucial point (the italics are his), Locke explains that we should assume no preference of ourselves over others, but that we should be able to say and do what is proper, "without discomposure, or disorder; in whose presence soever we are" (199). Although Locke calls attention to moral issues underlying behavior (not thinking meanly of ourselves or others, not preferring ourselves), he stresses the importance of superficial propriety: actions that do not express discomposure.

Goldsmith's novel, too, considers both surface behavior and underlying causes. Squire Thornhill, the bad guy, thinks meanly of everyone less privileged than he. Raillery and captiousness are his typical modes. But his uncle, good Mr. Thornhill, in disguise as Burchell, apparently feels equally exempt from social rules, entitled to mutter "Fudge" at every sentence spoken by the pretended ladies who attempt to lure Primrose's daughters for Squire Thornhill's nefarious purposes. His contempt directs itself toward the contemptible, but its expression unquestionably violates the principles of good breeding. So does Primrose's penchant for uttering hard truths plainly. Other standards than those of good breeding supersede the rules of civility. Locke assumes a concordance between "civility" and morality. Goldsmith dramatizes the fact that incivility can mean either genuine unconcern for others, as in Squire Thornhill's case, or equally genuine concern, as with Burchell and Primrose.

Conversation is not a meaningless index of moral quality. It is, however, an ambiguous one, because it involves not only relations with others—those relations that can be judged by Locke's standards and that provide the central subject of the manuals—but display of the self. Its function as self-display intensifies the possibility, perhaps even the likelihood, of disguise and deception. Primrose's daughters attempt to sound like fine ladies, refining their language by meretricious principles as they would refine their complexions by meretricious "washes." Primrose's son Moses tries to present himself as a young man of wisdom, cleverness, and knowledge. The professional cheat Wilkinson can sound like anything he chooses. The London whores, although they occasionally slip, need only substitute the vulgarities of the rich for those of the poor to deceive their naive audience. Only Primrose never for a moment sounds like anyone other than the man he believes himself to be.

As many generations of readers have readily perceived, some discrepancy intervenes between Primrose's self-understanding and the reader's comprehension of the clergyman's nature. Less wise, discerning, and domestically powerful than he thinks, Primrose therefore to some extent deceives himself, but he never consciously deceives others. The staginess of his speech belongs to the preacher, not the secular actor. He believes himself responsible primarily to God, not to the sensibilities of others. That overriding sense of responsibility subsumes his trivial vanity and makes him a heroic figure despite his failings.

Primrose has no apparent sense of privacy whatever: he is a good man in a traditional mode, already open to challenge in the eighteenth century. To more recent perception, privacy is the sphere of authenticity. "Privacy is linked with individuality because it offers a space in which a person might become more fully him- or herself," writes Janna Malamud Smith (11). For Primrose, and probably for Goldsmith as well, that "space" lies elsewhere. The authentic inheres not in the personal but in the social. Primrose is his "truest" self in his hortatory mode, when he functions without conscious self-regard—when, in other words, he thinks least about himself—in the service of his public, divinely ordained obligation. And he holds an ideal of transparency, believing that people should be (sometimes, to his own disadvantage, that they *are*) exactly what they seem, believing in particular that his children's minds and psyches must lie entirely open before him. Why should they need privacy, as long as they are good?

Yet privacy becomes an issue in *The Vicar of Wakefield*. It matters not only for the meretricious characters whose success depends on deception but also for essentially good characters placed under a special dispensation, in this as in other eighteenth-century novels, by love, which reveals privacy's urgency and its treachery. Daughters who may willingly make themselves transparent in other aspects preserve a prerogative of privacy in regard to love. Indeed, the advice of conduct books encourages privacy, not to say secrecy. John Gregory, in the century's most famous manual for young women, expresses doubts about whether in England girls often marry for love. More often, he says, gratitude motivates them. If a woman does in fact love, she should be careful. "If you love him, let me advise you never to discover to him the full extent of your love, no, not although you marry him. That sufficiently shews your preference, which is all he is intitled to know" (35). Secrecy and privacy are not the same, but secrecy protects privacy, and a young woman's need for privacy about her amorous inclinations was in the eighteenth century widely assumed. Primrose believes that he can discern his daughters' feelings, but he does not recognize the intensity of Olivia's erotic impulse. Opaque in at least this respect, she rushes upon disaster as a result. Privacy, in short, once more implies danger, since it removes a young person from supervision.

Supervision, both the parental variety and the pervasive social equivalent so conspicuous in this novel, begins with observation. What cannot be observed cannot be controlled: hence privacy's negative weight. Unlike the function of control, that of observation carries no hierarchical restrictions. A cat may look at a king; the Primroses' neighbors can watch and judge their activities; children can survey the behavior of their parents. Most of the novel's characters, aside from Primrose, consequently rely on disguise and deception to prevent watchers from penetrating their natures and designs. At times it is difficult to discern exactly where the disguise takes place. When Primrose asks Sophia (the "wise" daughter, as her name suggests) about Burchell, the girl replies, "His conversation with me, sir, . . . has ever been sensible, modest, and pleasing" (87). Thus she describes the man with whom she is falling in love. Does she disguise the nature of his conversation; does he by his conversation disguise the nature of his feelings to her; or is it in fact the case that the conversation between the two can be fully assessed in terms of its social virtues, the virtues Locke praises? How does love happen, in such a world of performance? Goldsmith provides hardly a clue. Consigning love to the realm of privacy, he removes its operations from observation. The kind of conversation that Gaskell attributes to Brontë, the kind involving the "power of drawing out others," does not exist in *The Vicar of Wakefield*. All the represented conversation belongs to a more public category, existing in order to influence or manipulate. As a narrative device, it functions largely in the way that it functions for Primrose: a means of instruction, thus an instrument of public purpose. The novelist seems actively to avoid the kinds of sustained continuity that a twenty-first-century reader anticipates in "conversation," as he avoids also evidence of intimacy.

But the novel that relies so heavily on conversation as public performance also uses it to reveal the necessity of privacy. The more public, the more potentially empty: the true life of *The Vicar* surges beneath the conversational surface. I use this phrase, "the true life," not to designate current interpretations of what true life might be, but to allude to the emotional facts that shape the novel's plot: Sophia's love and Olivia's, Moses's yearning for importance, Squire Thornhill's lust, Burchell's hopes. Even for Goldsmith, with his apparent commitment to public ideals of a complicated sort, the life that takes place in privacy holds compelling interest.

Such interest almost necessarily must emerge in virtually any novel that claims a degree of realism. To pursue the same inquiry in relation to Henry Mackenzie's *The Man of Feeling* (1771)—also in its own time an extraordinarily popular novel—emphasizes how the paradox works. The very type of the sentimental novel, *The Man of Feeling* is ostensibly designed to arouse the reader's tender feelings. It deliberately eschews coherent plot, establishing the donnée that the manuscript telling what passes for the story was fragmented by being torn into gun wadding. Thus avoiding all obligation to consecutive narrative, Mackenzie adopts a principle of structural repetition, conducting his protagonist, Harley, the man of feeling, through encounters of two kinds. The men and women Harley meets and talks with either tell him stories of their appalling suffering and victimization or they deceive him for the sake of their own financial interests. He experiences them, in other words, as either utterly transparent or altogether opaque.

For the "transparent," any social encounter provides the opportunity to speak of themselves. "Conversation" for them consists entirely of narrative, followed by expressions of gratitude for the benevolence that Harley typically displays. The old soldier, a representative example, reports having volunteered to go with a press gang in order to save his son the same fate. His effort to help an oppressed Indian results in his own public flogging and expulsion from military service. After Harley befriends him, the two together discover that the soldier's son has died. Harley, however, makes it possible for him to support his surviving grandchildren. The starving prostitute, another victim, tells a familiar tale of seduction and betrayal. Harley, although by no means prosperous himself, provides her with sustenance and supervises her reunion with her father. The pattern resembles that of Sarah Fielding's *David Simple*, published a quarter of a century earlier, and Henry Brooke's *The Fool of Quality:* a good man hears terrible stories and does what he can to help sufferers. The help these benevolent figures offer frequently seems like reward for narrative as much as compensation for suffering, for the narrative of misery is understood to provide pleasure for its hearer (as, presumably, for its reader). The description of Miss Walton, whom Harley loves, includes the comment that "her humanity was a feeling, not a principle" (Mackenzie, *Man* 9), and the same thing could obviously be said of Harley. Moreover, the book is designed to appeal to readers who might be characterized in comparable terms. For such readers, such listeners, the arousal of tender emotion is a self-sufficient satisfaction.

In saying so, I am describing a central principle of all sentimental writing. Moreover, such writing typically rests on the same division manifest in *The Man of Feeling*, between "good" people, whose faces and words directly communicate the truth of their emotions and their experience, and "bad" people, whose faces and words deceive. Recent critiques of eighteenth- and nineteenth-century sentimentalism often understand it as an exercise in bad faith, a disingenuous reaction to the complex heartlessness of developing industrialized capitalism (e.g., Markley). But Mackenzie's kind of sentimentalism, like Goldsmith's, can be read in more complicated ways. More a fable than a novel, *The Man of Feeling* through its renditions of distant and immediate corruption (the exploitation of India, the venality of the military, the omnipresence of cheats in Harley's encounters) acknowledges that bad motives and bad principles largely govern the society inhabited by Harley and by the reader. Indeed, the repeated stories of the corruption or abuse of innocence imply awareness of the extreme difficulty of sustaining personal integrity in such a society. Despite what may seem its easy tugging of the heartstrings, *The Man of Feeling* conveys a very dark view—a view epitomized in its treatment of privacy.

The unfortunate, it seems, have no privilege of privacy. (The same point emerges in many other novels of the period.) In order to attract sympathy and help, they must reveal details of their intimate experience—the humiliation of flogging, the futility of self-sacrifice, the folly of faith, the degradation of seduction. In recompense, they get Harley's tears and some small financial assistance. (In recompense for his imagining of them—for his "conversation" with the reader—Mackenzie wins that reader's tears.) As for the venal, seductive, and self-seeking, they manipulate falsities to achieve their ends, thus concealing their natures. In this sense, they preserve their privacy—but since they appear able to function only in a social context, reliant on a constant supply of people who don't know them, the concept has little meaning in relation to them. A pressing need for society, in this novel, seems to signal corruption: Mackenzie's view is far from Guazzo's. The novel's representations of conversation convey the differentiation between the virtuous and the evil. Innocent victims converse by self-narration; corrupt victimizers converse by deception. Harley finds infrequent alternatives to these patterns, the main one being occasional discourse in the vein of Burchell or Primrose by a rare good man who remains essentially intact.

For Harley himself, a tiny sphere of privacy precariously exists. As in *The Vicar of Wakefield*, the realm of privacy is that of love. Harley's unspoken love for Miss Walton remains his personal secret until the novel's end, when, ill and feeble, he expresses it to her, in a unique fragment of what twenty-first-century readers would recognize as "private conversation," learns that she reciprocates his love, and promptly dies. Although the effect is faintly comic, partly because of the extreme narrative condensation of this dramatic event, this constitutes a dark ending to a dark book. No providential order governs Harley's world. He himself must stand in for Providence. His excursions into a larger society than that of his home village instruct him in corruption and lead to his retreat. At home, however, he has no supportive community. Unlike Primrose, he lacks even a family of his own. Capable of dimly imagining an erotic connection, he proves incapable of realizing it. Although the novel rests on a faint fantasy that good individuals may survive even in bad societies, its emotional weight lies on the opposite side. The impossibility of Harley's personal fulfillment suggest little hope. And it emphasizes the perception that the confined space of privacy provides almost nothing in the way of opportunity. If the novel represents the ambiguity of social intercourse, it does not celebrate privacy. On the contrary, it offers another tacit eighteenth-century argument against the value of privacy: privacy's sphere is one of limitation, unlike the social realm that provides a man with room to test and expand himself— and supplies even for a woman the possibility of achieving the kind of success conceivable for her.

In the space of privacy, to be sure, one can shed tears—which gets me back to the heartstring-tugging. Feeling defines humanity, the characterization of Miss Walton suggests. It also, the novel implicitly argues, fosters perception. Stephen Cox, discussing the word *sensibility*, abundantly used in the eighteenth century to designate the capacity for responsive feeling, suggests that what he calls "the argument of sensibility" often turns on discrimination. He explicates the word *sensibility* itself as implying "awareness of fine distinctions, . . . the importance of seeing beyond rules and formulas and of seeing into states of individual consciousness" (80). Mackenzie's novel aspires to such discrimination, and one mark of discrimination may be the shedding of tears. Weeping has further serious meanings, for readers as well as for characters. Although crying over words on a page often occurs only in privacy, tears link the reader (as Harley's tears link him) to an imagined wider community of those who feel and who learn by feeling, adumbrated within the novel by the nameless narrator who declares himself moved by the fragmentary story he has found. Eighteenth-century commentators, including Mackenzie himself, some years after the publication of *The Man of Feeling* (Mackenzie, *Lounger* 330), sometimes worried lest sentimental fiction enable its readers to substitute benevolent feelings for meaningful action in the world. The danger seems real enough, but the more positive possibility remains: sentimental fiction, by generating an imaginative sense of community, can diminish the isolation of privacy and heighten awareness of other people's suffering and of the dangers implicit in a society governed by money-lust.

For Mackenzie as for Goldsmith, privacy holds little positive value. Both novelists find the fantasy of transparency appealing, clinging to a vision of people who willingly make accessible the totality of their feelings and experience. Both have a dream of community, in Mackenzie attenuated to an imagined community of readers. Both employ their characters'

conversation didactically, to convey specific ideas and insights and to provide positive or negative models. The importance of the narrator's conversation with the reader emerges clearly in this configuration, but the
wistful, harsh fables set forth for the reader's contemplation raise implicit
questions even about the dependability of that community of readers that
such earlier writers as Henry Fielding could more firmly trust.

The sentimental novel, of course, does not provide the only model for
conversation or the only view of how privacy figures in interpersonal talk.
Moll Flanders epitomizes another set of possibilities. With Defoe's novel,
we enter a rendered social sphere so far below the one imagined in the conversation manuals that we might expect a different moral universe. On the
contrary, the colloquial, plausible conversation among the novel's characters embodies as fully as possible the pattern suggested by Constable:
invariable self-interest underlying every social posture. Defoe appears
to concur with what Constable implies, the utter necessity of such self-
interest, and he richly demonstrates how completely the fulfillment of
the self's interests, in a world of limited financial resources, depends on
persuasive talk. Moreover, he posits his readers as a body of people open
to persuasion by an engaging narrative and narrator. Narrative and narrator alike demonstrate that privacy can guard the crassest forms of self-
concern. Moll takes for granted, takes as a truism, the perception that in
conversation, as in writing the story of one's life, a speaker always protects
a core of knowledge and desire. It requires no skill at exegesis to observe
that Moll frequently conceals important facts about herself in order to
achieve her own ends. Indeed, Moll explicitly informs the reader of precisely this point.

At the same time that it assumes the necessity of this kind of privacy,
Defoe's novel vividly dramatizes its sinister possibilities. Dialogue in *Moll
Flanders* frequently consists of interchanges between two characters, neither of whom says what he—or, especially, she—means. Writing half a
century before Goldsmith, Defoe imagines verbal conversation (the novel
uses the term *conversation* for sexual congress as well) as possibly providing
the illusion but rarely the substance of intimacy. The extended early sequence about Moll's relations with two brothers (one makes her his mistress, the other wants to marry her) epitomizes the technique.

In her state of (relative) innocence, before her seduction by the elder
brother, Moll expresses her feelings naively and openly, and she assumes
comparable straightforwardness in other speakers. By the time Robin, the
younger brother, begins courting her, she realizes the need for dissimulation in order not to lose both men. She presents herself to the elder brother
(the one she prefers and wishes to hang on to) as open and trusting as ever,

but her purposes are hidden. To be sure, this time she doesn't win. She notes how dexterously her interlocutor "changed his style immediately" (55) in response to his perception of her emotional state. His self-concealments work better than hers: he marries her off to his brother and has no further sexual connection with her.

Moll's need to preserve the privacy of her feelings now becomes pressing, and it is not registered mainly in conversation. In bed with the younger brother, she fantasizes about his sibling. Her entire life is a lie, and she tells it effectively until her unloved husband dies and she inaugurates her fully independent career—"fully independent" because now she has at least a little money at her disposal and therefore more room to maneuver. Her maneuvering, of course, centers in the effort to find a man to support and protect her (which is not to say that she proposes to give up her "independence": characteristically, she keeps money secreted during most of her marriages), and she often succeeds in the endeavor. With virtually all the men she finds, she guards substantial portions of her inner life. She reveals to the reader but not to her husband (until revelation becomes convenient) the fact of her incest; to the reader but not her husband, the birth of a premarital child by another man. Such secrets constitute much of her privacy, but her capacity for privacy holds importance for her beyond the individual secrets: it marks her continuing preservation of a measure of autonomy.

"Oh, what a felicity is it to mankind, said I to myself, that they cannot see into the hearts of one another!" (181). The immediate context is Moll's marriage to a decent and prosperous man, who has long courted her; she has, or claims to have, a spasm of regret for her previous misspent life. Although she professes, or almost professes, repentance ("If ever I had a grain of true repentance for a vicious and abominable life for twenty-four years past, it was then" [181]), her repentance mingles easily with self-congratulation that her husband cannot know about that "vicious and abominable life." Men and women do not have windows in their bosoms; they therefore can guard themselves. Moll's conversation with this husband, as with the others, represents her as the woman he wants, concealing the woman she is.

Moll's conversation conveys who she is in a sense quite different from that implied by the conversation manuals. Ideally, a person's talk expresses personality and character: the true wit speaks wittily. Moll's personality and character depend on disguise and deception. Her conversation embodies rather than "expresses" deception: her interlocutors do not recognize it as what it is. The reader knows only because Moll seems to have revealed what lies beneath the surface. To the reader, then, but not to the immediate hearer, Moll's represented conversation conveys her capacity to deceive.

Moll has in fact revealed only some of what lies beneath. Arguably, the reader provides the most telling evidence of Moll's capacity to dupe. She tells us at the outset that she will not disclose her name; she does not tell us what else she refrains from disclosing. The long debate about how much and what kind of irony informs *Moll Flanders* essentially depends on the reader's estimate of what remains hidden. In relation to the fact that the midwife with whom she stays "had no less than twelve ladies of pleasure brought to bed" in her house, she observes, "This was a strange testimony of the growing vice of the age, and such a one, that as bad as I had been myself, it shocked my very senses. I began to nauseate the place I was in and, above all, the wicked practice" (170). When she makes such an observation as this, are we to take it as an honest report of an honest reaction, or is Moll playing the hypocrite with us too? Such questions abound as one reads. It turns out that Moll conceals herself even from "Jemmy," the husband she really loves: "I gave him a direction how to write to me, though still I reserved the grand secret, and never broke my resolution, which was not to let him ever know my true name, who I was, or where to be found" (162). If she won't let this treasured husband know who she is, why should we believe that she lets us know, really know, anything at all?

The novel's tone encourages such a question, establishing a verbal environment that might aptly be described as "conversational." Moll addresses her readers as though she spoke to them, a note familiar (although Moll's specific idiom is different) from other novels of the period. The narrator's addresses to his readers in *Tom Jones* often strikes the note of familiar conversation, as do Tristram's words in *Tristram Shandy*. The illusion of intimacy readily reveals itself as just that in the light of the many contemporaneous discussions of conversation that reveal how it is always already compromised at the outset. Much to the point here is John Constable's reminder, in his conversation manual, that civilities generally please "even when we are persuaded, or at least suspect they are not very sincere." Moll, for instance, gives us ample reason to distrust her, both by her acknowledgments of information withheld ("It is enough to tell you, that as some of my worst comrades . . . knew me by the name of Moll Flanders, so you may give me leave to speak of myself under that name" [33]) and by her accounts of her dissembling conversations with others. Yet her conversational tone creates that pleasing simulacrum of intimacy, and although we have abundant cause for suspicion, we—at any rate, many readers—enjoy the sense of ease it establishes. Suspicion feels uncomfortable as a protracted state; the comfort of trust feels better.

Familiar conversation resembles familiar letters, or so much eighteenth-century discussion suggests. Both genres more or less deliberately establish an atmosphere of self-revelation and open communication; both can hide a great deal. Both may suggest that between friends or lovers, privacy is not a desideratum—suggest this even while establishing strategies of self-protection. In every situation that we know about, Moll has urgent reasons for hiding and pretending. Privacy becomes for her a matter of economic survival. The elaborate system of physical disguises that she adopts during her time as a beggar only gives concrete form to her characteristic strategies. The notion of privacy as self-protection assumes new depth of meaning in Moll's socioeconomic circumstances.

So readers may find themselves sympathizing with Moll's guarded self-presentations, especially because her "conversation" with the reader seems more revelatory than her exchanges with characters within the narrative. Despite the fact that she provides abundant evidence of her need for concealment, we may want to believe that she tells *us* everything—though she manifestly does not. Her penchant for verbal reserve reflects her view of society as a war of each against each. Indeed, *Moll Flanders* illustrates as clearly as any eighteenth-century text the widely perceived connection between desire/need for privacy and rejection of social bonds. Early in life, Moll wishes to function as an accepted member of society: to be a "gentlewoman." This role proves elusive. She finds multiplying and ingenious ways to substitute appearance for actuality, but her commitment to the established social order diminishes to the vanishing point. (One might observe with equal accuracy that the established social order has no commitment to her.) Society as an exclusionary system, society as other people: in both senses, according to Moll's perception, society works against her. Hence her need to protect herself, always. Hence her unwillingness ever to reveal everything. Hence her ultimate determination to depend only on herself, keeping that self intact in any way she can.

At the novel's end, Moll rediscovers the husband she likes best, and she treats him, she says, with "sincerity," her sincerity and affection overcoming him (284). It is presumably not accidental that by this time she has proclaimed her repentance and professed her conversion to Christianity: she is, in effect, now reconciled to, if not precisely integrated into, society. Even now, though, she keeps to herself the fact of her earlier incest until "the old wretch my brother (husband) was dead" (316). The withholding of information has served her well; it has become a habit as well as a tactic. In relation to the reader, it appears more conspicuous than ever, as she increasingly abandons the conversational tone in favor of more formal, more obviously *written*, language. The final paragraph begins, "It must be observed, that . . ." and ends, "at first I had intended to go back to him, but at his desire I altered that resolution, and he is come over to England also, where we resolve to spend the remainder of our years in sincere penitence for the wicked lives we have lived" (317). This falling into stock diction signals Moll's new conformity—and perhaps a new kind of self-concealment, that of conventionality. The skepticism many readers have felt about the genuineness and completeness of that "sincere penitence" derives at least partly from the lack of conviction carried by the suddenly flat language.

If I am right about this, the fact emphasizes the persuasive power of the conversational tone. The "editor," in his preface to the narrative, claims that he has controlled the language: "The pen employed in finishing her story, and making it what you now see it to be, has had no little difficulty to put it into a dress fit to be seen, and to make it speak language fit to be read" (28). Nonetheless, the language assigned to Moll helps to create the illusion of her immediate presence. It thus functions as conversation does, constructing an impression of direct communication that persists in spite of all evidence of how Moll consistently protects the integrity of her self by withholding information from her readers as well as from interlocutors within the text. Such withholding only becomes more apparent as the language becomes more distant. It is demonstrated to be an urgent necessity for someone at the bottom of the social hierarchy, a resource at least as important for Moll as it is for inhabitants of social circles far above hers. The rules of the manuals have no bearing on Moll's principles of conversation, but the system of disguise built into those rules transmogrifies for such as Moll.

A final instance of how conversation, as rendered in fiction, can help to create and enforce privacy comes from Sarah Scott's remarkable novel *Millenium Hall*. Sentimental novels like *David Simple* and *The Man of Feeling* heavily utilized first-person narratives of victimization as the substance of conversation. In such novels, mistreated individuals with few financial or psychological resources tell their stories to the more fortunate, receiving help in return. The "conversations" thus generated involve little real verbal exchange and entail what might be called systematic violations of privacy. (Although these are self-violations, in that the victims expose themselves, they are in effect enforced by social and financial inequalities: the storytellers tell because only thus can they win assistance.) Scott varies this scheme, to considerable dramatic effect. She too reports "conversations" that consist mainly of narration, but the narratives are third-person stories, told in the service of large and rather subtle didactic purposes.

Millenium Hall, published in 1765, tells of a utopian community of women, who have come together for mutual support, but also for the purpose of doing good to others in more complicated ways than those pursued by such as David Simple. David, too, forms a community, but it essentially turns inward: the group of family and friends live in ideal harmony, but they do not function significantly in a larger world. The women of Millenium Hall exist happily together. They also educate large numbers of girls; instruct the elderly and establish gratifying living conditions for them; provide a haven for dwarves, giants, and others who deviate physically from established norms, as well as for physically impaired servants; pursue animal husbandry and landscape architecture; and establish satellite communities. Moreover, by showing what they have done and telling why, they effectively reeducate two men who happen upon their idyllic household. One of these men serves as narrator. What he mainly reports is conversation with the Hall's women.

"Society," according to Mrs. Mancel, one of the Hall's founders, holds great importance for the community. She distinguishes sharply between society and crowd:

> I know not two things more opposite. How little society is there to be found in what you call the world? It might more properly be compared to that state of war, which Hobbes supposes the first condition of mankind. The same vanities, the same passions, the same ambition, reign in almost every breast; a constant desire to supplant, and a continual fear of being supplanted, keep the minds of those who have any views at all in a state of unremitted tumult and envy; and those who have no aim in their actions are too irrational to have a notion of social comforts. The love, as well as the pleasures of society, is founded in reason. (Scott 111)

By the logic of *Moll Flanders*, commitment to society might be thought to preclude concern for privacy, but matters are more complicated at Millenium Hall. Not only do the women here believe profoundly in the importance of society, they understand conversation as a socializing instrument. Their conversation consistently promulgates the values they uphold, and the unnamed male narrator repeatedly praises the quality of the conversation he hears and in which he nominally participates (the women do most of the talking). Much of the text consists of his reports (allegedly direct quotation) of Mrs. Maynard's conversation as she narrates her principal associates' histories.

Mrs. Maynard's narrations adumbrate novelistic plots—not ever, quite, seduction, but approaches to it, unhappy marriages, unhappy love affairs, unhappy lives. Yet the flavor of the stories differs sharply from that of the victimization narratives in *David Simple* or *The Man of Feeling*, partly because of the happy endings achieved by all the women who end up at Millenium Hall, but more importantly because each of these women, no matter how dire her circumstances, is represented as having significant power of choice—if not about her immediate situation, about the moral decisions she makes in confronting that situation. Thus Miss Melvyn, a close girlhood friend of Miss Mancel, finds herself caught between the prospect of an intolerable marriage, to an old, ugly, parsimonious, ill-tempered man, and the equally uninviting option of being expelled from her father's house in undeserved disgrace. Although she sees both possibilities as horrifying, she contemplates them in relation to her sense of Christian responsibility and chooses, with full understanding of the prospective misery inherent in the choice, to embark on the marriage. Conducting herself impeccably thereafter, she nonetheless encounters an even worse situation than she had anticipated: her husband forbids her to see or help her friend; his angry, bitter, envious sister manages the household; the wife has insufficient financial resources for benevolent action. After her husband's lengthy illness (through which she nurses him devotedly) and eventual death, she rejoins the friend of her youth and participates in the founding of Millenium Hall as an institution.

The overt didactic message conveys familiar doctrine for women: be good, preserve your reputation, accept your husband's dominance, and Providence will provide, here or hereafter. Miss Melvyn is scantily characterized, except for her virtues. Her story has few details, its potential psychological drama largely submerged by the summary style. Consideration of that style returns us to the issue of privacy.

The difference between the first-person narratives of *The Man of Feeling* and the third-person accounts of *Millenium Hall* turns on their divergent attention to privacy. For a reader far distant in time from the date of original publication, such confessions as the prostitute's to Harley may feel uncomfortable in their extorted quality. Although the prostitute's story, like that of Miss Melvyn, lacks lavish detail, its direct association with the starving, destitute, miserable woman who tells it gives it urgency, pathos, immediacy—and a sense of intrusiveness. Miss Melvyn, like the subjects of the other stories in *Millenium Hall*, has progressed from unhappiness to an idyllic situation. More important, someone else tells her story—someone for whom the main interests in that story are the happy ending and the didactic message.

Before beginning the sequence of stories, told in response to the visitors' expressed and reiterated "curiosity," Mrs. Maynard explicitly evokes principles of privacy, saying that she sees no good reason for not complying with the men's request for information, "as my friends are above wishing to conceal any part of their lives, though themselves are never the subject of their own conversation" (Scott 76). A possible reason for wishing to conceal, the speaker suggests, is to avoid censure, but the women of Millenium Hall are too innocent to fear any severe criticisms. Their lives are an open book—but their thoughts and feelings remain largely hidden, except inasmuch as they contribute to an exemplary record of moral conflict and decision and of ethical action. Mrs. Maynard violates no privacy in reporting events that her subjects would willingly report themselves, were they not inhibited by fear of egotism. The device of secondhand narration (Mrs. Maynard can only report what she has been told) insures protection for individual psyches. Listeners can learn from stories in this form without violating anyone's privacy. Such stories have been shaped for public transmission.

The fact that good women will not make themselves the subject of conversation reiterates the principle of privacy as decorum, an established mode of protecting society from demanding forms of intimacy. If such decorum also protects the self, that meaning is elided. The corollary fact that a single good woman happily uses others as her main conversational subject suggests that knowledge of others, at a regulated distance, reinforces social norms. The knowledge transmitted by Mrs. Maynard's narratives skirts intimacy but pokes at the bounds of privacy: the stories involve such matters as attempted seduction, near rape, an illegitimate child. Firm moral constraints, however, control the representation of such potentially scandalous subjects. Their ethical meaning, not their psychological revelation, justifies them.

In such "conversation" as Mrs. Maynard's (I put the noun in quotation marks because of the absence of full verbal response to her oral transmissions), generalization protects privacy. Although the men hear, and readers read, the life stories of individual women, these stories become exempla in the process of their telling. One woman goes to bed with her fiancé on a single occasion, shortly before their planned marriage, then steadfastly refuses to marry him, on the ground that he cannot possibly respect her after her revelation of uncontrolled passion. Even after she finds herself pregnant, she resists her lover's passionate, determined, prolonged pleas. Her daughter survives and grows to lovely young womanhood; the mother reveals herself only on her deathbed. The protagonist of another story narrowly escapes rape by the man who has been responsible for her upbringing. Another, encouraged to various forms of frivolity by the older women in her life, avoids seduction only because of the intervention of a wiser woman her own age. Each tale enforces conventional norms; each invites admiration of a heroine heroic precisely in her determined adherence to established rules.

The concept of generalization as a narrative mode may seem pretty conventional itself in the eighteenth century. *Millenium Hall*, however, appeared in the same decade as *Tristram Shandy* and *A Sentimental Journey*, almost two decades after *Clarissa*. Narrative techniques of psychological particularity were available to Scott—but they would not have suited her purposes. A quarter-century after *Pamela*, at least one novel shows itself hardly interested in the matter of individualism. Despite the presence of many named characters, the psychological distinctions among them simply do not matter to the novel's enterprise.

If no individualism, one might think, no privacy. But Mrs. Maynard's explicit comment, her insistence that she tells only what each of her subjects would be willing to tell of herself, calls attention to the fact that privacy exists as possibility. It also raises a question about what, specifically, those subjects might *not* be willing to tell. And it provides at least room for an answer to that question, an answer not dependent on individual psychology so much as on what these women share—what, in fact, from one point of view makes them generalizable.

The conversations (or "conversations") in the novel that do not consist in narration emphasize didacticism even more strongly. The unnamed narrator clearly understands his conversations with the residents of Millenium Hall—conversations about which he repeatedly attests his enjoyment—as educative experiences. Most often, one woman or another will explain details of what goes on in the Hall and its environs, and why. The men learn of the establishment's economy, how and why it is self-supporting. They learn of how lavishly the upper-class women who founded the Hall support the marriages of their social inferiors. One of the men comments on the apparent inconsistency of conduct in encouraging marriage while personally eschewing it. Mrs. Melvyn insists, in response, that "We consider matrimony as absolutely necessary to the good of society; it is a general duty" (163). Like knights of old who send deputies to fight in their stead, these women substitute others for themselves "and certainly much more promote wedlock," Mrs. Melvyn continues, "than we could do by entering into ourselves." The defensiveness of this position becomes clear when she adds, "This may wear the appearance of some devout persons of a certain religion, who equally indolent and timorous, when they do not chuse to say so many prayers as they think their duty, pay others for supplying their deficiencies" (163).

Sequences like this leave room to perceive a radical subtext to this novel full of ostensibly conservative doctrine. *Millenium Hall* parades its conformities. The women who have chosen to establish and inhabit a female commune have conscientiously put themselves in the way of courtship, although in only a single instance, that of Miss Melvyn's desperately unhappy union with Mr. Morgan, has one of them actually embarked on marriage. Their lovers die, or no one sufficiently virtuous to meet their approval presents himself, or they lose their beauty by smallpox and therefore no longer consider marriage an obligation. The novel contains a number of admirable men, although also perhaps an unusually high quotient of obtuse or corrupt males. In their benevolent roles, the women employ, assist, and show hospitality to men—they do not exclude them from their environs. The virtues they encourage in those of lower rank conform to conventional expectation: the serving girls they train are industrious, honest, and clean. The virtues they demand of themselves are likewise conventional; their emphasis on benevolence situates them in the most orthodox tradition of the good woman. They are almost comically unthreatening. Scott's choice of a male narrator, who has nothing but praise for everything he sees, emphasizes the fact that these women, despite their unconventional style of life, are altogether recognizable. When Lamont, the dissipated traveler who arrives at the Hall with the narrator, takes to Bible reading as a result of his contact with its inhabitants, he underlines the point.

Nonetheless, that "unconventional style of life" implicitly criticizes a male-organized and male-dominated social structure. In the world of Millenium Hall, all is harmony. Everyone gets along with everyone else, partly as a result of conscious effort, which includes recognition that everyone has failings: one forgives others because of his or her own need to be forgiven. The carefully worked out economic arrangements of the institution allow for expansion, charity, and enduring prosperity. In this community, everyone, at every social level, thrives, as a result of constant awareness and effort.

The radical aspect of this admirable system for living resides, of course, in its being the work of women and only of women. Marriage may be a duty to society, but women do better on their own: that's what the book says. Not only do they do better; they also find far more happiness. They have high capacities of intellection and execution. They do not merely know how to please themselves, they know how to make others happy and successful.

Here is what the residents of Millenium Hall keep to themselves. Anyone can know about their lives; they lay claim to no personal distinction. Converted by one another, for purposes of communication with the outside world, into generalized and exemplary figures, they protect the knowledge of what their collective accomplishment means. The novel in which they are imagined and contained deploys a rather bland mode of didactic discourse in the service of a revolutionary secret: a secret making part of the privacy of each individual who participates. Like *The Female Quixote*, *Millenium Hall* allows readers to understand it either as reinforcing or as challenging the established order.

The conversations of eighteenth-century novels—those among characters, those implied between narrators and readers—imply diverse understandings of relationship, of personality, and of privacy. At every social level, in every circumstance, people communicate with one another. Their acts of communication as rendered in fiction confirm the implications of conversation manuals: apparent openness may hide purposes and attitudes that a speaker would wish to preserve in privacy. The most "public" forms of utterance often assist in just that preservation.

6 | *Exposures: Sex, Privacy, and Sensibility*

In eighteenth-century England, the middling and upper classes were preoccupied with sex—or so, at any rate, a number of recent social historians claim. The generalization implies no assessment of the amount of sexual activity that actually took place during the period (how could it?); rather, it registers the publicity that attended sex: the eighteenth-century efflorescence of print material alluding to or discussing sexual matters. Proliferating newspaper advertisements of sexual services, elaborate published reports of lurid divorce trials, pornographic and semipornographic fiction and verse attest to widespread interest in sexual possibility and in the sexual activities of real or imaginary others. Such interest remains vivid, of course, in the early twenty-first century, yet it may come as something of a shock to know that our predecessors revealed it as openly as we.

The abundant discussion of sexual matters in the earlier period seems at first glance incongruous in relation to the perception—I put the familiar point this time in the words of the architectural historian Witold Rybczynski—that "A desire for greater privacy characterized the eighteenth century" (86). Rybczynski concerns himself with the physical manifestations of this desire, "in the bourgeois home no less than in the palace" (86). Architectural privacy, however, need not imply any certainty of solitude on demand. Much less does it insure psychological privacy.

The apparently conflicting principles of eighteenth-century architectural and journalistic developments are perhaps inherent in the very concept of privacy. The sociologist Arnold Simmel asserts that "we live in a continual competition with society over the ownership of our selves" (72). "We think of privacy as a situation of calm and security from strife," he adds. "But it exists only by virtue of a temporary settlement of a conflict" (87). Simmel's vision of an undying competition over "ownership," of privacy as a condition wrested with difficulty and precariousness from an ever-encroaching society, bears directly on the eighteenth-century situation. Newly conscious of the desirability of private space, literal and metaphorical, eighteenth-century men and women simultaneously experienced heightened eagerness to penetrate the privacy of others. As soon as privacy exists, it challenges the desire for knowledge, as the will to know about others in turn challenges their inclination to secrecy. Secrets invite unraveling; privacy stimulates encroachment.

We have seen already that the yearning for privacy took many forms in the eighteenth century, manifesting itself in widespread concern for the personal integrity of individuals and in various forms of self-concealment and self-protection. To ponder the relation between the increasing circulation of sexual material and the intensifying attention to privacy reveals new modes of self-disguise. One eighteenth-century literary response to the general interest in sexual matters was an abundance of scandalous first-person narratives, most of them ostensibly authentic, although some clearly fictional. The conventions of such narratives demand that the narrator deliberately violate his or her own privacy; their interest derives largely from the reader's capacity to believe that the text provides an opportunity to penetrate the privacies of others. Of course, interest in other people's privacies does not logically preclude protection of one's own, and desire to remain personally inviolate, as I have already hinted, may only intensify the urge to penetrate, vicariously, the normal secrecy of others. But what about the writer's side of the equation? How do the narrators of first-person scandal preserve privacy while trafficking in revelation?

The mediating term between sexual revelation and privacy, I propose, is *sensibility*. I have claimed the relevance of sensibility to other aspects of eighteenth-century attempts at privacy, but the connection between stories of sex, performances of sensibility, and desire for privacy may seem less than obvious. To be sure, the nexus of sensibility and sexuality has long been apparent, exemplified, for instance, in Austen's figure of Marianne. (See Hagstrum for the most extensive treatment of the relation between sex and sensibility.) James Boswell, an indefatigable self-narrator, provides another case in point. His journals demonstrate as well the narrative use of sensibility as an instrument of self-protection.

When, in 1762, Boswell comes to London, twenty-two years old, supported by a skimpy allowance from his father, determined to win a commission in the Guards, his plans include copulation. He indulges his sexual needs through casual encounters with prostitutes and other working-class young women. On one occasion, he meets a young whore named Alice Gibbs, takes her to a "snug place," and prepares to have intercourse, using a sheath to guard against venereal disease. She, claiming good health, begs him to employ no protection, and he complies, having what he calls in his *London Journal* "a very agreeable congress." The next day, though, he feels worried. His reflections articulate a characteristic conflict:

> Much concern was I in from the apprehension of being again reduced to misery, and in so silly a way too. My benevolence indeed suggested to me to put confidence in the poor girl; but then said cool reason, "What abandoned, deceitful wretches are these girls, and even supposing her honest, how could she know with any certainty that she was well?" Temple was much vexed and dreaded the worst. (263)

Boswell in fact acquired no disease from Alice Gibbs, although he was less fortunate in other sexual encounters. My interest in the episode, though, is literary and psychological rather than biographical, focusing on the question of how a man manages such revelations about himself.

Those revelations occur, to be sure, only in a journal, a form we may think of as belonging to the realm of privacy. But Habermas's reflections on the eighteenth-century popularity of journal- and letter-writing seem apposite here. "Subjectivity," Habermas writes, "as the innermost core of the private, was always already oriented to an audience." He has observed a bit earlier that during this period "the diary became a letter addressed to the sender" (49). Boswell's journal has from the beginning another addressee as well, since he sends it in weekly installments to his friend John Johnston, who on occasion shows parts of the journal to others, as does Boswell himself. Moreover, the writer of the journal records his fantasy of having the manuscript he has produced laid up in the archives of Auchinleck, his family seat, presumably for future publication. Consciousness of an audience is never far from Boswell's mind. He deliberately chooses to violate his own privacy, while simultaneously devising strategies for protecting it.

Despite the apparent forthrightness with which he narrates the encounter with Alice Gibbs, Boswell relies on a self-serving interpretive structure to explain himself and to direct attention away from his self-indulgence. Neither the "benevolence" nor the "cool reason" that Boswell attributes to himself in fact precisely applies to the situation. One can readily imagine other explanations than benevolence for a man's putting faith in a whore's health, and "cool reason" hardly generates the judgment that "these girls"—in a period when young girls from the country, trying to support themselves in the city, often turned to prostitution as their only resource—are invariably "abandoned, deceitful wretches."

What Boswell calls cool reason and what he calls benevolence alike help to organize and to interpret his sensibility. The notion of benevolence that encourages him to believe the prostitute's claim rationalizes Boswell's hope of escaping infection; the reason assuring him that all prostitutes are degraded wretches covers his fear of physical damage. Desire and fear, the self's wants and its aversions, comprise the bulk of Boswell's autobiographical material. His ingenious interpretations of them as forms of virtue help supply the comedy and the pathos of his journals.

They also guard him from opprobrium. Writing a journal, especially a journal to be read by others, entails the stresses implicit in every conscious performance of self-representation. Boswell deals with these stresses not by attempting to appear entirely upright but by explaining himself in highly personal ways. Like Rousseau (whom he met in 1764, and with whose longtime mistress he soon embarked on a brief but intense sexual liaison), Boswell employs analysis of his own feelings as justification and disguise. He may not act as irreproachably as his father would have him, or even as he would have himself, but behind his actions, he claims, lie sensitive and subtle emotions.

Sensibility means to Boswell the capacity for intense feeling and for intense consciousness of feeling. He differentiates himself from other men on the basis of his emotional capacity, whether he emphasizes his susceptibility to depression or what he sometimes calls his "great soul." This emotionality provides material both for pride and for self-castigation. In moments of melancholy, Boswell understands his own intensity as weakness. The men he admires most—Dr. Johnson and General Paoli, the liberator of Corsica—he characterizes as "manly." In the penultimate sentence of the *London Journal*, he admonishes himself, not for the first time, or the last, "Let me be manly" (333). The word echoes through his journals, and through the *Life of Johnson*, designating those with a firm sense of identity, with sensibility under control. His need to prove his manhood in the most literal physical terms, as well as in the moral sense—to prove it to himself but also, through representation, to others—helps to account for his insistent narration of sexual encounters. But he manifests an equally compelling need to assert the delicacy and profundity of his feelings.

The most brilliant of Boswell's reports on his sex life is probably the extended episode in the *London Journal* about his seduction of "Louisa," an actress from whom he expects "a winter's safe copulation" (161). Both comic and pathetic, the story begins as triumph and ends as defeat, when the writer realizes that Louisa has given him gonorrhea. All the details are delicious, although the manifest scorn for women that Boswell displays, his failure to acknowledge any consciousness in Louisa, and his obsession with multiplying conquests will feel distasteful to many readers of a later era. But Boswell's attitudes and his activities typify his period.

In the world the young man inhabited, his dalliance with Louisa, his apparent contempt for her and for other women, his venereal infection, and his full account of these facts and attitudes would have seemed unremarkable. Prostitutes, in this period, swarmed the streets of London and "commonly offered their services in the pages of the popular press" (McKendrick 150). Roy Porter observes that "perhaps the most marked feature about Georgian sexuality was its public nature, its openness and visibility." He points out that "sex was a prominent part of the written and printed culture," with pornographic works addressed to every social level, with abundant sexually and scatologically explicit prints, "engraved by leading artists," and with newspapers advertising not only prostitution but "sexual services of all kinds" (8). Male members of the upper classes—and Boswell, despite his relative poverty during the year recounted in the *London Journal*, belonged to a distinguished family—routinely assumed the sexual willingness of working-class women, patronized prostitutes, and boasted of their seductions.

Recent social history, as well as evidence from the eighteenth century itself, suggests an atmosphere of intense publicity around the sexual arrangements of the upper classes. Never before, and not afterward until the late twentieth century, have equivalent amounts of journalistic attention been accorded to sexual activities of the rich and famous. If Boswell publicizes his own seductions, attempts, and commercial sexual encounters, he only reports, for modest circulation, the kind of news more flamboyantly circulated elsewhere. The realm of privacy seems far removed from the subject of sexuality in eighteenth-century England.

Yet the exemplary account of the liaison with Louisa suggests ways in which someone writing about himself, ostensibly telling all, can in fact create an equivalent for reticence even while narrating his experiences in intimate detail. At once textual encroacher on and protector of his intimate life, Boswell devises ways to report his indiscretions, his vanities, and his follies, while yet maintaining his integrity. For this complicated enterprise he possesses two main resources, both of which I have alluded to already: his narrative skill and his commitment to sensibility. Both protect him from the total self-exposure he appears to traffic in.

The story of Louisa, as he tells it, involves confronting a comic series of obstacles before he can consummate his passion—his state of being "really in love," as he sometimes puts it. He finds himself unexpectedly impotent; Louisa's period arrives inconveniently; the landlady shows up at just the wrong moment. Finally, though, he and Louisa go to an inn, under false names, equipped with a bag of macaroons, and they make love five times during the night. Boswell's delight, as he reports it, derives as much from pride in his own physical performance as from anything resembling love. Even in narrating this first sexual encounter with Louisa, he describes himself as imagining other women while copulating with her. "I could not help roving in fancy to the embraces of some other ladies which my lively imagination strongly pictured. I don't know if that was altogether fair" (139–40). He subsequently bolsters his self-esteem at a social gathering of the nobility by fantasizing how interested in him all the ladies would be if they knew he could achieve five orgasms in a single night. Louisa comes to bore him well before he discovers that she has infected him.

Boswell's narrative skill reveals itself in small details and in large structures. My favorite sentence from the *London Journal* exemplifies his rhetorical deftness. It occurs during a detailed account of events leading up to Boswell's seduction of Louisa, at the stage when he first allows himself physical liberties. "Upon this," he writes, "I advanced to the greatest freedom by a sweet elevation of the charming petticoat" (115).

Eighteenth-century women, although they wore layer upon layer of clothing, did not wear underpants or the equivalent. The elevation of the petticoat would expose Louisa's nakedness. Boswell indeed advances to "the greatest freedom" when he lifts that petticoat. But his formulation of the event de-emphasizes its carnality by adopting the language of romance and sentiment ("sweet," "charming") and by reporting the action without an actor: the sweet elevation appears to take place all by itself. Boswell tells in detail the physical progress of a seduction, but he tells it with constant stress on his own feelings: his concern about Louisa's assessment of him, his self-persuasion of being in love, his vacillation over whether lending his inamorata money should be perceived as a sensitive or a foolish act. His way of telling implicitly acknowledges an audience that may smile at the discrepancy between diction and happening while being lured into complicity with the character in his highly stylized role.

Boswell becomes, makes himself into, a "character": a personage linguistically created before our eyes, partly as a man of sensibility. His selection of an alias for the night at the inn, his anxieties about the display of his "powers," his bringing along the little bag of macaroons, his standing in the inn's cold courtyard in order to intensify the physical comfort that awaits him—this collection of disparate details, with many others, aligns his account with the contemporary fictions it strongly resembles. One might say (it has often been said) that Boswell has a novelistic sense of detail. That novelistic detail, along with the novelistic technique apparent in every aspect of the storytelling skill the journal-writer brings to his account of Louisa, fictionalizes both central characters in the story. Louisa never seems altogether real because Boswell fails to imagine her as a consciousness. She exists for him as an instrument of pleasure, interchangeable with the other women he fantasizes about even in the act of making love to her. He is, of course, immensely real to himself, and he provides for the reader much data of his own consciousness. Yet he presents himself too as a character—an almost Sternean hero of lust and sensibility, subject alike to comic mishap and to bursts of feeling, so consciously *rendered* that he seems quite removed from the vulnerability of an actual man.

This is not to say that the *London Journal* is anything but realistic in its evocations of experience, or that Boswell apparently fails to reveal anything he knows about himself. He seems to reveal as much as he can, without concealment, and he conveys the texture of his life with exemplary fidelity. But the literary consciousness he brings to the act of writing and the sheer skill with which he makes experience into narrative have the paradoxical effect of emphasizing his textuality rather than his actuality. And, oddly, his emphasis on himself as a man of sensibility intensifies the sense that we are reading about a literary character.

If we have read many eighteenth-century novels, we have learned about many other such characters—and so, of course, has Boswell. In his stress on his own "benevolence," "imagination," "great soul," he deliberately allies himself with heroes of novel and romance. If one extracts from the *London Journal* the facts it reports, trying to separate them from Boswell's interpretation of them, one might, for instance, conclude that the protagonist of this journal is a weak and vacillating young man. Boswell, who reports in rich detail his own vacillations, does not offer them as evidence of weakness but of sensitivity. One can analyze him like a fictional character. Just as we may say about Richardson's Lovelace, in *Clarissa*, that he believes himself to have all the power in his relationship with Clarissa but in fact becomes increasingly weak, we can say about Boswell, for instance, that the *London Journal* reveals a young man's struggle to determine his own identity and his need to ally himself with "Great Men." Or we might comment about his insecurity in his "manliness." Boswell would not say the same things about himself, although he provides the raw material that justifies them. We reconstruct the realm of his privacy, in other words, as we question the adequacy of the truth he tells—but Boswell himself has guarded his privacy by his dexterous production of the language that fictionalizes his narrative even as it reports his life.

Many autobiographies lend themselves to comparable interpretations, protecting the privacy of their creators by the deftness of their linguistic and narrative manipulations. But scandalous autobiographies may compensate for the impression of violated privacy they create by other means as well. For a woman (an actual woman, as opposed to a fantasy-creation like Fanny Hill) to expose her own sexual adventures means something quite different from a man's comparable exposure. Scholars disagree about dominant attitudes toward female sexuality in eighteenth-century Britain. A. D. Harvey, for instance, claims that "sexuality, which was something that men and women had been perceived to share and have in common before the 1700s, became increasingly a male territory thereafter" (168), as women were increasingly considered to lack sexual feeling. In contrast, Roy Porter maintains that the attribution of "overwhelming and grotesque sexuality to women" remained common throughout the eighteenth century (15). Women writing about their own sexual experience, however, often avoid the issue of their sexuality in order to emphasize their victimization. A complicated instance is *Memoirs of Laetitia Pilkington*, published in three volumes in the mid-eighteenth century (the first two volumes a few months apart in 1748, the third volume posthumously in 1754) and enormously popular in its own time. Pilkington lacks Boswell's storytelling skill, and her narrative becomes increasingly incoherent as it continues. Yet it displays great energy and gusto, and it delineates a new and perplexed relation to privacy. The common distinction between memoir and autobiography in the eighteenth century turns on the memoir's emphasis on the public rather than the private. As Goulemot puts it, "In a sense the memoir ends where private life begins. Anything not pertinent to public life was excluded" (381). But Pilkington's *Memoirs*, concerned almost entirely with domestic and sexual matters, implicitly claim that the dark underside of public appearances deserves primary attention.

Pilkington tells a long story of marital and postmarital distress. Descended from a family of some distinction, she was courted by an impecunious young clergyman, Matthew Pilkington. By her account, she remained entirely "passive" during the courtship and accepted Pilkington at last because she thought herself doing her parents' will. Soon after the marriage, the couple became friendly with Jonathan Swift, who encouraged Mrs. Pilkington in her poetry writing and, she says, aroused her husband's jealousy by praising her intelligence and her poetic gifts. At any rate, after several children the marriage went sour. Pilkington took a mistress and openly lavished gifts on her, even while his family lived in poverty. According to Mrs. Pilkington's account, he tried to lure or trick his wife into committing adultery. Finally, he claimed (and found witnesses to attest), he caught her in the act (she claims she was only looking at a book in the company of a young man). In 1738, he divorced her in consistory court in Dublin on grounds of adultery. Mrs. Pilkington, pregnant, remained in Ireland for a few months, giving birth to a daughter, then fled to London.

The precariousness of her economic position (her husband refused to pay the support authorized by the court) led to hard times in London. At one point, she was imprisoned for debt. She published proposals for a volume of poetry, but attracted no great support. A proposal for a memoir proved more successful, and the first volume won considerable popular interest, mainly, it seems, on two grounds: it provided much intimate information about Swift, and it offered many scandalous or near-scandalous stories, almost entirely about the two Pilkingtons. (The subsequent volumes increasingly present scandalous episodes about other people; in the third volume, the author claims that many have offered her money for a promise *not* to tell stories about them.)

Matthew Pilkington, his wife maintains, was sexually loose. She herself was not. Her typical story about herself belongs to the genre, made familiar by *Pamela*, of the narrow escape tale: she finds herself in a sexual situation of great danger but in the nick of time manages to preserve her honor. Thus she provides titillation without self-condemnation. She never actually acknowledges sleeping with anyone, although she certainly arouses the reader's suspicions. But the intimate details that she reports appear to violate her privacy in fundamental ways.

A sample passage, which I shall quote at some length, will suggest the kinds of questions raised by Pilkington's account:

> I could reckon up numberless Instances of Mr. *Pilkington's* Aversion to me; one in particular I cannot pass over. One Day, at Dinner, the Pin in the Robing of my Gown, prick'd my Breast; as there was no body but my Husband and Children present, I made no Scruple of uncovering my Bosom, to examine what had hurt me; upon which Mr. *Pilkington* rose from Table, and said, I had turn'd his Stomach. As I really had a fine Skin, and was then a most remarkably neat Person, I thought he only jested; and merrily told him, he should kiss my Breast, and make it well: But, alas! It was not like *Prior's Lover's Anger*. . . . [Here Pilkington quotes a poem about a woman's hurting her breast and exposing it to a man who sees it as a "Seat of Delight" that makes him forget what he was going to say.] For he told me, he was sure he should faint if I came near him; and either pretended to throw up his Dinner, or did it in reality. After which polite Compliment, he drank a large Glass of Cherry-brandy, to settle his Stomach; and repair'd to his usual Haunt, *i.e.* to buxom *Joan* [his mistress]. (1:85)

This episode strikes me as shocking in its intimacy and in the humiliation it reports—more shocking, in fact, than most of the sexual stories. It belongs emphatically to the sphere of privacy. The narrator stresses the fact that only because she was alone with her husband and children did she expose herself physically. The question remains why she chooses to expose herself verbally.

The stories Laetitia Pilkington tells of her life with her husband encourage the view that privacy holds different meanings and different values for women and for men. Boswell in company with Louisa at the inn exists within a context of valued privacy. Pilkington at the breakfast table with her husband and children does not: for her, privacy can sustain itself only in solitude. Yves Castan summarizes the views of a woman identified only as Mme. de Maintenon, a schoolmistress, writing about the situation of women in eighteenth-century France: "A married woman could count on no rest, no secrecy, no privacy of her own, for her services were continually and urgently in demand by husband, children, dependents, and servants. She had no more private life than 'a sergeant traveling from skirmish to skirmish' in the thick of battle—and battles were relatively infrequent, whereas the married woman was constantly under fire" (61). A comparable situation existed in eighteenth-century Britain, where Pilkington reports herself constantly at her husband's disposal.

Privacy, domestic privacy, entails danger for this autobiographer. So does privacy with another man. She tells of weeping in the summerhouse over the death of one of her children. A "fine Spark" opens the door and comes in, saying that Mr. Pilkington has sent him. They return to the house and drink coffee; the man forcibly attempts to make love to her. When she says she will tell her husband, he laughs and explains that Mr. Pilkington "describ'd you to me, as a Lady very liberal of your Favours, and begg'd I would be so kind as to make him a Cuckold" (1:80, 81). Similar episodes abound, both before and after she leaves her husband. The privilege of solitude seems rarely attainable to her, and a privacy of two implies threat. Pilkington illustrates the historical point that "Women have inhabited the 'private realm' but lacked the benefits of privacy" (Janna Smith 206).

This fact, abundantly substantiated in the text of the *Memoirs*, suggests a reason for Pilkington's deliberate self-exposure and helps to account for its literary energy. Self-exposure constitutes defense and expresses anger. A married woman in the mid-eighteenth century might have abundant reason for anger. A divorced woman would undoubtedly have more. Lawrence Stone summarizes the situation of a woman separated from her husband:

a separated wife faced exceptionally severe penalties. Unless she was protected by a private deed of separation, she was in practice virtually an outlaw. All the income from her real estate was retained by her husband, as well as all future legacies which might come to her. All her personal property, including her future earnings from a trade and her business stock and tools, were liable to seizure by her husband at any moment. She was unable to enter into a legal contract, to use credit to borrow money, or to buy or sell property. All her savings belonged to her husband. And finally all her children were controlled entirely by their father, who was free to dispose of them as he wished, and to deprive their mother of any opportunity ever to speak to them again. (4–5)

Laetitia Pilkington had to leave four children behind when her husband rejected her. According to her, he insisted that all were bastards and severely mistreated them. (Two of them eventually made their way to London and joined her.) Having experienced the powerlessness of the married woman, she was forced to suffer the greater powerlessness of the divorcée. To uncover the actualities of domestic privacy and of the privacy of the unprotected woman provided her only opportunity for revenge.

I spoke earlier of the emphasis on victimization over sexuality in scandalous autobiographies by women. It is true that Pilkington tells mainly of the ways in which others—her parents, her husband, the men and women she meets—take advantage of her. Yet her stance is not that of victim: anger emerges more strongly than self-pity. She stresses her economic difficulties more even than her sexual ones—they too provide cause for rage. But she tacitly and explicitly emphasizes also the wonder of her self-sufficiency. The act of writing such a book as this is one of extraordinary self-assertion. By it, Pilkington acquires both money and revenge. The self-exposure of her privacy constitutes an aggressive tactic. When she tells of her husband's vomiting, or pretending to vomit, at the sight of her bare and beautiful breast, she tells of her own intimate humiliation, but she also exposes his brutality. To reveal his efforts to have himself cuckolded degrades him more than her. To report her sexual and economic danger in London reproaches the man who left her destitute, childless, and unprotected. She restores her self-ownership by taking public possession of her story. Only her violations of her own privacy, in other words, protect her privacy in the deepest sense.

One does not ordinarily think of anger as a product of "sensibility," which associates itself more readily with softer emotions. But sensibility, given its connotations of intense emotional responsiveness, can express itself not only in sympathy but in rage at inequity and injustice. One need only think of the diatribes of Smollett's Matthew Bramble in *Humphry Clinker*, or Yorick's meditations on the Bastille in *A Sentimental Journey*. If anger impels Pilkington to ignore the conventional limits of her own privacy, it also authoritatively justifies her self-violation.

Pilkington relies on deliberate self-exposure as an aggressive and defensive tactic. Her jaunty prose suggests that she has risen above her painful experience, describing it from the distance of a journalist or a sociologist and with the hard-won perspective of a woman sufficiently wise not to take herself too seriously. On the other hand, like Boswell, she alludes to a literally unspeakable stratum of feeling that makes her what she is and makes her unique. In an atypically abstract formulation, she summarizes: "I am, in short, an Heteroclite, or irregular Verb, which can never be declined, or conjugated" (1:273). A heteroclite, according to the dictionary, is a word that does not operate by established rules. Pilkington's metaphor suggests that she remains finally uninterpretable, that more exists than she can reveal. She reports her experience in lavish detail, probably fictionalizing it in the process, and uses her sensibility in the form of anger to justify her self-revelation. Yet her power to signify depends, rather, on what she refrains from reporting, on another aspect of sensibility—what cannot be declined, conjugated, or known.

Pilkington's narrative proceeds often by a kind of stream of consciousness. She tells anecdotes as they occur to her, lapsing into complaints about the hypocrisy and lechery of the women who disapprove of her, changing the subject by having recourse to such phrases as "But enough of that." Yet an atmosphere of fictionalizing clings around her memoir. The scrupulous scholarship of her recent editor, A. C. Elias Jr., has uncovered some deviations from fact, and Elias surmises others. Any reader is likely to do the same. One may, for instance, well have difficulty crediting Pilkington's total passivity during her courtship. The story of reading a book with a young man (Robin Adair, the other participant in her alleged adultery) sounds implausible in the extreme. So do the multiplied accounts of her resistance to all sexual overtures. For purposes of aggression and defense, the literal truth may not prove altogether adequate—although Pilkington explicitly prides herself on dealing candidly with her readers, "when I not only acquaint them with my Actions, but reveal to them even the inmost Recesses of my Soul as freely as to Heaven" (1:181). Presumably she partly remembers, partly manufactures her narrative of herself as more sinned against than sinning. In this sense, she, like Boswell, creates herself as a character. But the character lacks the kind of continuity, consistency, and complexity that Boswell achieves for his autobiographical version of himself. The woman-on-the-page serves the purposes of the woman-with-the-pen but may prove rather less satisfactory to the reader.

The reader's relation to Pilkington's text is likely to reflect some of the text's ambiguities. The wealth of scandalous detail it provides surely engages the interest of even the high-minded. Most of the scanty body of critical material on Pilkington considers her *Memoirs* in the context of other scandalous works by women (e.g., Nussbaum, Thompson). The original audience read these volumes avidly for the sake of the gossip, slander, innuendo, and juicy stories they contain. Even centuries after the deaths of the cast of characters, the fascination with such material remains. Surely twentieth-century readers' interest in Boswell (the *London Journal* achieved a place on the *New York Times* best-seller list in 1950, the year of its first publication) was not altogether unconnected to the sexual detail he offers, the direct firsthand account of what it felt like, more than two hundred years ago, to be the kind of young man who wants to get virtually every woman he sees into bed.

Pilkington has acquired many fewer readers since her own time. Her memoir becomes increasingly disorganized and repetitive, even a trifle paranoid. Yet her record of herself and her social world holds its own power, the power of intimate revelation. Can one fail to relish stories of Jonathan Swift going into a rage over an overcooked roast and demanding of the bewildered cook that she take it back and undercook it to his liking, or Swift pinching Mrs. Pilkington black and blue in order to correct her verse, or Swift rubbing her face with rosin and pitch to present her to the company as a dwarf? Then there is the account of the young woman Pilkington meets who has declined to prosecute her husband for bigamy, since his life would be forfeit, and who therefore ends up "in the oddest Situation imaginable, even a kept Mistress to my own Husband" (1:167). And the story of Pilkington's almost falling victim to a procuress. And the alleged member of Parliament who shows up at seven o'clock one morning, pulls off his clothes, and leaps into bed with the narrator. Feeling interested in such events partly because they evoke a vivid sense of eighteenth-century life, we as readers in effect endorse the position that an authentic view from the underside clarifies meanings of public life and public persons, that Swift as domestic tyrant and Swift as brilliant satirist demand intellectual reconciliation—or at least that one wants to know both sides.

The issue of privacy comes up now in a new way. Boswell and Pilkington may, as I have argued, protect their privacy even in the act of exposing it, but their literary enterprises depend on putting the reader into the position of voyeur. In other words, although they guard against unacceptable

violation (Pilkington, for instance, never mentions the illegitimate pregnancy of her sixteen-year-old daughter, who returned to her during this
personal crisis), they construct their accounts as invitations to forbidden
knowledge. The promise and the appearance of intimate revelation keep
the reader reading. It is the highest achievement of this literary mode to
conceal its own concealments.

So the reader may feel somewhat uncomfortably complicit in a morally
dubious enterprise. Reading Boswell or Pilkington is not quite equivalent
to reading the *National Enquirer*, since the autobiographers talk about
themselves, consciously choosing to uncover themselves to public view. If
they can write what they do, surely one can legitimately read it. The moral
dubiety perhaps stems from readers' uneasiness about their own motives
and impulses. Why should we want to know how many orgasms Boswell
had or how Matthew Pilkington felt about his wife's breasts? Even more
emphatically, why should we eagerly read scandal about public figures long
dead? The appeal of a peek into other people's privacy remains peculiarly
compelling.

Such peeks, into the privacy of fictional rather than actual characters,
provide the fundamental material of pornographic fiction. Connecting
"the development of a whole new realm of privacy" with the rise of industrialization, Steven Marcus links both with the growth of the novel, which,
he points out, "depicts, as no other kind of art had before, the inmost
private experience of human beings; and it is generally read in conditions
of silence and solitude." Pornography, he goes on to say, demands yet a
higher level of privacy. Speaking of pornographic novels, Marcus writes,
"In a world of private experiences, they represent a further withdrawal into
the arcane, and the only thing more secluded and secret than they is the inside of one's head" (247). Despite the incontestable truth of these comments, I would argue that pornographic fiction may in fact entail a rather
more complicated relation to privacy than such formulations suggest.

"Privacy is the exclusive access of a person . . . to a realm of his own,"
Ernest Van Den Haag writes. "The right to privacy entitles one to exclude
others from (a) watching, (b) utilizing, (c) invading (intruding upon, or in
other ways affecting) his private realm" (149). In Van Den Haag's view, privacy remains "largely a moral norm," despite the fact that it has become a
matter for legislation (151). Another essay published in the same collection
as Van Den Haag's, by Hyman Gross, answers the question, "Why is privacy of the person important?" with reference to the requirements for
maintaining "an integrated personality in a social setting. Although we are
largely unaware of what influences us at the time, we are constantly concerned to control how we appear to others" (173).

I juxtapose these quotations because in conjunction they suggest a way of thinking about the complexities of a book like *Fanny Hill* in relation to privacy. Certainly the most famous pornographic novel of the eighteenth century, John Cleland's book allegedly earned more than ten thousand pounds for its publisher. Successfully defended against prosecution for obscenity on the ground that it contained not a single indecent word, it won a large readership. Its diction indeed belongs to sentimental fiction, although much of its substance would conform to virtually any definition of the pornographic.

Fanny Hill, published in the same year that saw the appearance of the first volumes of Pilkington's *Memoirs*, tells the story of a young woman from the country who, like Pilkington, successfully makes her way in London—by rather different means. The account belongs in a sense to the same fictional subgenre as *Pamela*: poor girl makes good and rises in the world. It might even adopt, with some irony, the subtitle of *Pamela: Virtue Rewarded*. Fanny Hill's chief virtue is fidelity (of heart, not body), but she has other admirable qualities as well, including almost unfailing cheerfulness and adaptability, willingness to try anything, and an amiable desire to make others happy. Of course, she is by profession a whore.

Fanny is represented as having, in Van Den Haag's sense, no awareness of a right to privacy. Watching and being watched compose much of her most pleasurable activity, and her narrative invites the reader into comparable functioning. We in effect watch her watching and being watched and are implicitly urged to share her guilt-free enjoyment. The notion of privacy as freedom from being watched, intruded upon, or used by another is quite meaningless here, in a context where people seem to exist for one another's use. (Fanny uses her customers for her own purposes; they use her for theirs.) Indeed, the utter abandonment of such a standard supplies the prerequisite for Fanny's pleasure and perhaps for the reader's as well.

But the implications of Gross's observations have considerable bearing on Fanny's moral position. If privacy defines the conditions for maintaining an integrated personality in a social setting, Fanny, whose sense of herself remains firm through all her vicissitudes, quite consistently sustains her privacy. Gross suggests that control of appearances is the basis for privacy. Cleland's fantasy of Fanny Hill reveals just how subversive an idea this is—and how incompatible with the more conventional notion of privacy advanced by Van Den Haag.

The vision of the integrated personality as dependent on control of appearances allows the interpretation that only hypocrisy guarantees integrity. *Hypocrisy* derives from a Greek root whose first meaning is "the acting of a part on the stage." Its connection with the deliberate adoption

of a role has emerged earlier in this study, in discussion of patterns of conversation and the uses of manners. The link between a whore's hypocrisy
and stage acting is yet more apparent: after all, a whore's professional
success depends on her acting of an offstage part. Fanny, after her first
naive and straightforward pleasure in lesbian exchanges, in watching
heterosexual intercourse, and in her defloration by young, handsome,
charming Charles (the object of her undying love), becomes a consummate actress—with everyone but Charles. Reunited with him at last, after
a long separation, Fanny repeatedly invokes the word *sincerity,* most significantly, perhaps, in her allusion to "that sincerity which, from me to
him, was so much a nature in me" (222). When she goes to bed with
Charles, she appears to have regained her psychological virginity: "a sweet
sensibility, a tender timidity, love-sick yearnings, tempered with diffidence
and modesty, all held me in a subjection of soul incomparably dearer to
me than the liberty of heart which I had been long, too long! the mistress
of" (218). Sincerity is her nature, but only with Charles. Sensibility, timidity, and the rest characterize her now but have not characterized her before, except in her first sexual encounter. The integrity of her personality
has survived, as it were, beneath a thick carapace of pretense and of kinds
of feeling that she now disowns.

Now Fanny has her privacy, despite the openness of her confession—
a confession "open" because of the "confidence, without reserve, with
which I engaged to recount to you the most striking circumstances of my
youthful disorders" (217)—to the particular reader for whom she writes
and to the succeeding generations by whom she has been read. It is the privacy of her inwardness, the feelings that can be named but not fully communicated. Her account of the physical lovemaking breaks off: "oh!—my
pen drops from here in the ecstasy now present to my faithful memory!
Description, too, deserts me and delivers over a task, above the strength of
wing, to the imagination; but it must be an imagination exalted by such
a flame as mine, that can do justice to that sweetest, noblest of all sensations" (220). The incommunicability of her sensations, despite her efforts at
unreserved confidence, declares her unviolated and inviolable privacy. She
can tell us everything about her encounter with a sadomasochist or (more
daringly) her watching of a pair of homosexual men, but she cannot tell all
when it comes to her relationship to Charles.

Unlike Boswell or Pilkington, the fictional character Fanny Hill openly
acknowledges both that her "sincerity" depends on her interlocutor and
that there are crucial facts about herself that she does not, because she cannot, communicate. Reminding us of the necessary limits of revelation, she
thereby alleviates the reader's potential discomfort at knowing, "seeing,"

entirely too much. What we vicariously see is less important than what we cannot see. Fanny's extended career of hypocrisy has enabled her to preserve herself, it seems, morally and psychologically intact. Her "vice" doesn't matter even to Charles, who readily excuses it on the basis of economic necessity. What matters more, and is clearly intended to matter to the reader, is her capacity for that metaphorical new virginity: the integrity she has miraculously sustained.

The fantasy aspect of *Fanny Hill* as a novel emerges vividly in all its aspects, from its rhapsodies over the size and wonder and power of various male "machines" to its depiction of the prostitute's life as quite free from essential degradation, from Fanny's lack of any real sense of guilt to her constant encounters with equally cheerful, equally beautiful, equally forthcoming (verbally as well as physically) fellow prostitutes. Cleland's fantasy about privacy may be most important of all. It justifies the pornographer's activity by declaring it nonessential. One can watch, utilize, and intrude upon others (to return to Van Den Haag's terms) by reporting in lavish physical detail the actions and the appearances of sexual activity, which we conventionally consider to epitomize the material of privacy. Still, the pornographer interferes with no privacy because he defines it as existing elsewhere. He imagines his central character as reporting on herself, as well as on others, and as untouched by the reportage because mere action and appearance have no bearing on real privacy, inherent in the uninvadable sensibility.

Sensibility, one of the eighteenth century's most crucial literary and psychological terms, provided an important basis for Boswell's self-satisfaction (if also for his suffering). Laetitia Pilkington's self-description as "Heteroclite," her claim of uniqueness, also depends on sensibility, her awareness of unrecognized emotional complexities in herself, her incommunicable, uncontestable capacity for feeling. When Fanny Hill reminds us of her "sweet sensibility" along with her lovesick yearnings, she alludes to the emotional depth that can justify her despite a misspent life. The two autobiographers and the fictional character all implicitly insist on a personal essence quite independent of behavior, an essence incapable of being watched or invaded, a locus of integrity and therefore of privacy.

Fanny Hill marks an important moment in the history of the novel because it makes more explicit suggestions already lurking in *Pamela* and certainly in *Clarissa* (published just a year or two before Cleland's novel). *Pamela*'s long tenure on the Catholic Index of prohibited books indicates unmistakably that Henry Fielding was not alone in seeing its heroine as determined to find the best market for her virginity and in understanding the pornographic implications of the action. Pamela does not lose her virginity until she wants to, but she comes close. The memorable scene in which she finds herself undressed and in bed between the would-be rapist Mr. B. and his wicked housekeeper ends, like other memorable scenes in the book, with her fainting. When she comes to consciousness, she remains intact. But the reader has received the titillation of a rape scene without the full horror, and without the concomitant guilt. The voyeuristic position has enabled us metaphorically to violate Pamela's physical privacy, as Mr. B. does literally, but no more than Mr. B. can we violate the privacy of her soul. Our position is the same with Boswell and Pilkington, although they don't themselves make the point so clear.

Fanny Hill makes both the physical and the psychological data more extreme. Steven Marcus, particularly concerned with nineteenth-century England, describes the world of pornography as "without psychology" (32), a world of organs and actions. Cleland's novel, although well-supplied with organs and actions, also claims its concern with the inner life. To be sure, Fanny's psychic processes are fairly uncomplicated and largely unexplained. Emotional anesthesia overtakes her, plausibly enough, when she makes the transition from sexual relations with Charles to connections with men who purchase her favors, and her subsequent responses seem fairly superficial. One might argue that her generally good spirits derive from repression, but Cleland offers so little detailed psychological data about her, and her language is so conventionalized and repetitive, that it would appear ludicrous to apply psychoanalytic terminology to the character. Yet her intermittent performances of "sensibility" (mostly elicited by sexual displays) serve as conventional signs of inner experience, reminders of the realm of privacy that the novel insists on preserving for its characters.

By "the novel" I mean to designate both this particular piece of fiction (for *Fanny Hill* is unquestionably a novel as well as a piece of pornography) and the eighteenth-century novel as genre. Richardson, before Cleland, had already made the inner life his subject; such novelists as Sterne and Mackenzie, after him, would make that life a matter of display. Fanny Hill as character oddly prefigures Sterne's Yorick and Mackenzie's Harley. For Fanny, who acts constantly (in both senses of the verb), as for the later male protagonists, who act meaningfully hardly at all, unutterable feeling provides justification, serving equally well for action or inaction. Private sensibility preserves a realm for which public judgment proves irrelevant. It serves as implicit standard in all the books of ostensible revelation that I have discussed.

Despite the success of *Fanny Hill*, original English pornography did not flourish in the Restoration or the eighteenth century until the century's very end. Peter Wagner suggests that much erotica has disappeared, but he also concurs with other commentators in observing that France supplied much of the demand for such material (*Eros* 231). Virtually all Englishmen of the educated classes read French, and translations, moreover, abounded. More common than native pornography in the second half of the century, and even more pertinent for investigation of privacy's perplexities, were works that appeared to promise pornographic revelation but delivered something quite different. Although often of dubious literary merit, such fictions expose with remarkable clarity the ways that the matter of sexual privacy implicates itself with a burgeoning capitalist economy.

If *Fanny Hill* foretells in some respects the novel of sensibility, it also emphasizes—for the most part unsentimentally—the connection of sex, love, and marriage to money. Cleland's perception of a link among these matters is of course far from new. Pamela's eye to the main chance includes vivid awareness of the power of money, which she acquires, of course, by marriage. Clarissa's troubles originate in her parents' desire to profit financially from her marriage. None of Richardson's novels has much discernible satiric edge, nor does *Fanny Hill*, but one can discern satiric potential in these works. Fanny's characteristic economic metaphors seem appropriate enough for a whore, but they remind the reader of a commercial society's pervasive concern with financial gain. Need for money drives her to prostitution in the first place; desire for money motivates her in many of her subsequent activities. Despite her sexual promiscuity, Charles happily accepts her as his wife. He says he forgives her because poverty drove her to her career, but her possession of a great deal of money at a time when he has very little obviously equalizes the two of them and compensates for previous sins.

Fanny herself takes a rosy view of her wealth and its convenience in facilitating marriage, and the reader is invited to believe that she settles promptly and happily into respectable domesticity. Later eighteenth-century novels, however, consider the relations between sex and money in a less attractive light. Three works that suppress their pornographic potential for the sake of satiric or directly polemical exploration of the sex-money nexus are the memoirs of Lady Vane, inserted in Tobias Smollett's *Peregrine Pickle* (1751); the *Genuine Memoirs of the Celebrated Miss Maria Brown*, attributed to John Cleland (1766); and Charles Johnstone's *Chrysal: or, The Adventures of a Guinea*, also published anonymously, two years earlier. All provide titillating stories as part of their episodic plots but employ them as means for social commentary and criticism. All play with violations of privacy, promising more than they deliver, in order to make, or at least to hint, public statements: at least to adumbrate general social criticism.

To the volume containing "Memoirs of a Lady of Quality," Smollett prefixed, in the second edition of *Peregrine Pickle*, a pair of letters, one from the lady herself, addressed to "Lord ——" and asking whether he thought her justified in publishing her memoir, and a long response from the unnamed lord, concurring with her decision: "If your character suffered cruelly from misrepresentations; if your foibles were magnified and multiplied with all the aggravations of envy and fiction: if the qualities of your heart were decried or traduced, and even your understanding called in question; I agree with your ladyship, that it was not only excusable, but highly necessary to publish a detail of your conduct, which would acquit you of all or most of those scandalous imputations" (3:3). The letters emphasize the anomalous position of these "memoirs," claiming truth and immediacy, but inserted into a work of fiction. The lord's argument for the "necessity" of publication turns on the need to clear a private person from public scandal: more specifically, to reveal the "qualities of . . . heart" of a woman of feeling. But his apparent uneasiness about publishing such material, like the even more pronounced uneasiness of the lady herself, concerns the generally assumed impropriety of making the private public.

Just this aspect of the memoirs, however, constitutes the main ground of their interest for readers—especially, perhaps, readers of novels. The author of the memoirs confesses to a career of sexual misconduct, as judged by conventional social standards. But the story she tells, in her view, justifies her misbehavior. Blissfully married, at the age of fifteen, to a man as devoted to her as she was to him, the lady suffered widowhood two years later. At her father's behest, she then marries a rich nobleman who, on the wedding night and thereafter, turns out to be impotent. I oversimplify only slightly in saying that her husband's impotence supplies the justification for all the lady's subsequent behavior.

The details of that behavior don't matter much. The lady takes up with various lovers, remaining faithful to each as long as possible, but finally separated from each of her men by one or another cause. Through all her adventures, her husband continues to pursue her. She sues for divorce but loses the suit. Her husband demands her presence in his house. He promises to allow her a separate bedroom (in one instance, a separate house) but always violates his promise. He makes various financial arrangements with her but never follows through for long; financial need sometimes forces her to take a lover. Like pornography, the story seems infinitely extendable. The lady's account (which occupies 160 pages of *Peregrine Pickle* in the Shakespeare Head Edition) comes to an altogether arbitrary conclusion, with yet another diatribe against her husband and the final assertion, "For my own part, I look upon him as utterly incorrigible; and as fate hath subjected me to his power, endeavour to make the bitter draught go down, by detaching myself, as much as possible, from the supposition that there is any such existence upon earth" (Smollett 3:220–21). There is no reason to think her career of successive lovers at an end.

Since the lady's self-vindication depends entirely on condemnation of her husband, details of his sexual behavior form an important part of her narrative. Like Fanny Hill, this writer relies on euphemisms, but she makes her point clear: "His attempts were like the pawings of an imp, sent from hell to teize and torment some guilty wretch, such as are exhibited in some dramatic performance, which I never see acted, without remembering my wedding-night. By such shadowy, unsubstantial, vexatious behaviour, was I tantalized, and robb'd of my repose; and early next morning I got up, with a most sovereign contempt for my bedfellow, who indulged himself in bed till eleven" (3:91). This is as sexually explicit as the account gets; a corresponding kind of detail is lavished on the happy wedding night with the first husband.

So we're a long way from pornography here—but not from sexual self-exposure. At the very beginning of her narrative, the Lady of Quality announces what she wishes to convince her hearers of: "that howsoever my head may have erred, my heart hath always been uncorrupted, and that I have been unhappy, *because I loved, and was a woman*" (3:63). Like Pilkington, then, she considers herself victimized because of her sex. Like Boswell, Pilkington, and Fanny Hill, she claims sensibility—the uncorrupted heart, the propensity to love—as the basis of her virtue. Because of her situation as a woman of sensibility, she must detail her loves in order to justify herself. Her references to her loathed second husband invariably allude to or evoke his sexual inadequacy; her account of herself focuses instead on that other locus of privacy, the feelings. As novels had already trained readers to expect, the open revelation of emotions might provide equivalent titillation to that of pornography (with less potential shame or guilt).

Both kinds of exposure—the sexual exposure of her husband, the emotional exposure of herself—serve the same polemical purpose: to expose, in a rather different sense, the inequities of a set of social arrangements that accord all power and wealth to men. Over and over, the writer of these memoirs finds herself helpless, forced to rely on a male protector, because she lacks control of the money that would allow her independence. Independence, she makes clear, is what she wants, and what remains impossible. The act of writing, for her as for Pilkington, attempts to equalize power, and it conveys rage. It can do these things only by deliberately and purposefully violating privacy.

The precise nature of that violation takes on a certain ambiguity in its fictional context. Lady Vane (Lady Frances Vane, 1715–88) and her sexual career, in its general outlines, would have been sufficiently familiar to the eighteenth-century public that readers would have recognized the putative author of the "Memoirs" as a living person; certainly contemporary letters indicate such recognition (see Thompson 173). At the time of publication, she was engaged in a lawsuit against her husband, perhaps hoping to win a legal separation and financial maintenance; the "Memoirs" supported her case (Thompson 173–74). These facts, too, were well known. Yet the presence of the justification for female promiscuity within a novel of male adventure raises the possibility that the titillating document itself constituted a fiction. Certainly it passed the conventional bounds of privacy by its allusions to impotence and sexual frustration as well as its open discussion of female need for money. But, in this period when authors, in the guise of "editors," often asserted the truth of their novels, one can hardly be certain whether those bounds are literal or imaginary, whether the Lady of Quality, like Fanny Hill, belongs to the territory of fantasy—her privacy, therefore, a figment of the imagination, violated with impunity by her imaginer—or whether, like Mrs. Pilkington, she deliberately tells the untellable in order to make a point, or to attract readers, or both.

At any rate, like Mrs. Pilkington, she claims to tell the truth and to tell it for a reason, as the introductory letters indicate. And, like Mrs. Pilkington, she may well shape the truth to her purposes. The line between fact and fiction in all these scandalous documents wavers heavily. The illusion or the actuality of violated privacy, however, serves an important function in either case: it is the real source of the scandal.

Genuine Memoirs of the Celebrated Miss Maria Brown is unquestionably not "genuine." Its social purpose, though, is apparent. The title page attributes the work to "the Author of a W** of P***"—that is, John Cleland. This dubious attribution is obviously designed to attract readers in search of the sensational. The *Memoirs* have in common with *Fanny Hill*, however, only their first-person narration (not, in this instance, disguised as letter writing) and their general subject matter, the career of a whore. They reveal no emphasis on organs and relatively little on sexual actions, considered in isolation. Although Maria Brown loses her virginity in short order (by the betrayal of the man she believes herself about to marry, who lures her to a tavern and drugs her into unconsciousness), she does not begin her real sexual career until almost two hundred pages into the narrative. Fanny Hill becomes moralistic, as she herself points out, only after some years of sexual commerce and indulgence—only when safely married. Maria, with much less apparent capacity for pleasure than her predecessor, begins moralizing much earlier, and her moralizing is integral to the novel's effect, as Fanny's is not.

Memoirs begins with insistent announcement of its own truth. The reader is not to consider it "in the light of a novel or a romance," but as "real adventures" (1:1). The subject "has nothing but plain truth and simple nature to recommend it" (1:2). The name of *Brown* may sound fictitious, but "it was certainly my family-name" (1:2). Far from Fanny Hill's emotion-filled self-presentation, Maria Brown's sounds flat and determinedly matter-of-fact. She tells the story of her rape rapidly, although with at least a brief emotional flare-up ("alas! I was brought back to life and shame by the cruel efforts of this perfidious man, to rob me of woman's most precious jewel" [1:111]). Her early pregnancy, her aunt's repudiation of her, her stay in the hospital, her infant's death—Maria relates all this with great dispatch. Then she pauses for reflection on the ways of the world, contrasting the social fates of men and women. Men can with impunity commit every variety of sin. If financially successful as a result, they will be "cherished and esteemed" by the respectable. "But, alas!" Maria continues, "if we do but once deviate from the track delineated by custom on the chart of chastity (which, if any, is but a subordinate virtue), if we attempt to pass but one barrier without paying toll, or only mistake the intended barrier, we are arraigned at the bar of *honour*, and our *reputation* is pronounced irreparable by a jury of *prudes* and *old maids*!" (1:147). The rest of the chapter consists of summary exemplifications of the contrast she has outlined.

Although—or perhaps because—this chapter stands as an interruption to the narrative (which continues, predictably, to report Maria's fall into various stages of prostitution), it articulates a set of ideas important to the novel's effect. Despite its self-serving rhetoric (the jury of prudes and old maids, for instance, sounds like special pleading), in language and in substance it conveys the energy of conviction. The metaphors of chart following, toll paying, and barrier passing aptly communicate the young woman's sense of mechanical and difficult demands; the arraignment at the bar, in contrast to the relative triviality of the preceding figures, suggests how high the stakes are. Since the sentence about a woman's situation immediately follows the description of men praised because prosperous, no matter the means of their prosperity, it emphasizes both the relative pettiness of financial possibilities for women (paying or not paying a toll) and the stringency of the formulaic demands placed upon them. And the parenthesis about chastity as a subordinate virtue, if a virtue at all, like the pattern of imagery indicates Maria's partly self-serving rage at the female situation and her potential for revolutionary thinking as a result of her state of compulsory alienation.

Such moments in the text suggest a nascent feminism, never fully developed. Rather like Pilkington, Maria Brown uses isolated feminist perceptions as a form of self-justification. The anger sounds persuasively authentic, but, despite the plural pronouns, the narrator does not sustain her sense of a common female fate. Still, she does not, like Pilkington, apparently feel the need to differentiate herself from other women on the basis of superior virtue or higher consciousness. She typically (though, as we shall see, not invariably) accepts her occupation as prostitute, despite her clear-sighted perception of its evils.

Like Fanny Hill, Maria varies her predictable account of her own career by interspersing narratives from others she meets. One young woman reports her seduction by a priest who, after her pregnancy is discovered, flees the convent with the substantial amount of money he has amassed over the years and cohabits with her in London, under the name of "Mr. Martin." Like Matthew Pilkington, Mr. Martin suggests, and finally insists, that she sleep with other men for the sake of financial return. "You know," he explains, "you must turn every thing to your advantage in this life" (1:217). He devises various plans for turning his mistress's charms to his profit, but finally accumulates so much debt that he flees to the Continent, callously abandoning the young woman who has served his ends.

The Mr. Martin episode resembles others that Maria reports in conveying a flavor of parable. The novel reiterates simple but emphatic ideas: men take advantage of women whenever and however they can; women should therefore try to take advantage of men. Introduced to professional prostitution by a bawd, Mrs. Laborde, Maria learns "to secure my health, improve my natural charms, and play them off on every occasion to the most advantage upon the men" (2:24). She willingly indulges—not without contempt—perverse male sexual tastes in order to enlarge her income. Before long, she has accumulated enough money to provide financial help for the young man she sleeps with on the side, as it were. But she experiences the misery of the prostitute's existence, although she does not share details with the reader. "Let me draw a veil over his behaviour, which was still more nauseous and disgusting than his person" (2:30): this is one of the teases about pornographic rendition. Drawing a metaphorical veil over details of her experience, Maria calls attention to the issue of privacy. In the guise of moralizing ("nauseous and disgusting"), she tacitly invites the reader to let fantasy evoke the behavior she herself declines to describe—thus equating the privacy to which Steven Marcus alludes, that of the inside of individual readers' heads, with her own. "Veiling" becomes invitation rather than deprivation.

Such practices as those she will not specify, however allusions to them may titillate the reader, also help to create the degradation of the prostitute's condition. Maria holds forth at some length about the generalized sufferings of her state: "When I reflect upon the cruel and extravagant whims which a woman of pleasure is exposed to, I cannot believe, that there is any condition, however mean, however laborious, that is half so miserable: I do not except even that of a bailif [sic], or a courtier": so she begins her lengthy diatribe on the subject (2:30). The issue, once more, is power: Maria feels acutely her utter dependence on male whim. She invites sympathy not for the situation of all women but for the particular plight of the sex worker, always at the literal disposal of men. The equation of bailiff and courtier offers a satiric flick at society's ways—not even high rank exempts even a man from dependence—but the emotional energy of this passage depends on the harsh irony in a "woman of pleasure" who gives pleasure, but receives none.

In many respects, *Genuine Memoirs* offers an intensely confused piece of narrative. Sometimes it sounds like one more cry of rage from a woman; sometimes, despite its relative lack of specificity, it sounds like male sexual fantasy. (Notably, the author offers more detail about a lesbian encounter—generated by the voyeurism of two elderly men—than about most of the heterosexual exchanges, specifying, for instance, that Maria experiences orgasm.) Its most consistently effective moments, however, all concern the dominance of money as the only real instrument of possibility. As one bawd puts it, "Every woman that is desirous of making her way into the world by her person, should imitate the tradesman, and have no other object in view but interest and gain. Her heart should always be inaccessible to any real passion: it is only necessary that she should seem to be enamoured with the man she proposes making her property" (2:157). The explicit comment that the woman of pleasure simply imitates the tradesman (in the only way open to her), like the notion of the man as the woman's property, emphasizes the satiric point: prostitution is business, the effective courtesan a businesswoman, and her hypocrisy and manipulation only duplicate the patterns of the male capitalist economy.

Nothing private about all this: the point is, rather, that thus society as a whole operates. The issue of privacy becomes part of a satiric message. Maria Brown pretends to violate her own privacy, at least gestures at such violation, but actually reveals little of what ordinarily remains hidden. To uncover scandalous privacies becomes a device for revealing more public scandals, rarely acknowledged as such.

Given the narrative confusion of the whole novel, the ending becomes particularly unsettling. On her way to a sexual assignation, Maria stops off at church. "A sensible and pathetic discourse which I heard that night, was the cause of my conversion": with no more ado than that, Maria Brown abandons her loose life (2:221). Shocked by her own past conduct, she sheds many tears, goes to no public place except church for twelve months, and feels horrified by "the reflection, that what I subsisted upon were the wages of prostitution" (2:223): not so horrified, however, that she gives them up, much though she wishes to engage in charitable activities. "I was not so enthusiastically bigoted," she comments, "as to forget my past misfortunes, or the terrible situation a woman is in, who is thus divested of the means of support (2:224). At this point, an honest and benevolent tradesman appears on the scene. Maria promptly marries him, gives birth to several children, and proposes to live happy ever after.

The miraculous conversion occurs without preparation, at an arbitrary point in the episodic and infinitely continuable action. It solves the problem of an ending neatly if not plausibly. But it is quite impossible to determine how much irony clings to such an event. Maria waits for her conversion until she has amassed enough money to live comfortably. She calls the reader's attention to this fact and to her rejection of any acts of charity that might cause her financial inconvenience—and in the process of noting her financial prudence, she also reiterates the narrative's insistence that a woman who lacks "the means of support" exists in a dreadful situation. A tradesman seems exactly the proper mate for Maria: he will appreciate her nest egg, and she knows all about trade. Trade, this novel tells us, makes the world go round. Hence, prostitution. Unencumbered by the conventional language of sensibility (except in rare moments), this fiction, despite its verbal clumsiness and primitive plot, conveys a stark awareness of what economic realities can mean for a woman and of how they function for men as well. Sensibility in the form of anger entirely replaces its softer counterpart. It turns outward rather than inward, a mode of insight, not only of internal experience or social display.

Even a cursory look—all I propose to provide—at the last of my cases in point, *Chrysal: or, The Adventures of a Guinea*, shows how readily pornographic hints lend themselves to incorporation in a clear satiric context. The novel's donnée, indicated by its subtitle, itself suggests the satiric focus and method of the work. Beginning with the extraction of gold from a Peruvian mine, we follow its minting into a guinea and its subsequent international circulation. The spirit temporarily confined in the gold possesses the power of reading the minds and feelings of those it encounters. It reports the venality and lustfulness of priests, the weakness and corruption of the nobility, the avarice of fine ladies, the hypocrisy of the benevolent—and the preoccupation with money shared by everyone. In effect literalizing the notion of a window in the bosom, the novel reveals once more what Swift had pointed out long before: insides are usually less attractive than outsides. The sexual episodes epitomize the universal pattern. A man makes sexual overtures to his daughter but appears to the public a paragon of benevolence. A young woman of good birth, alone in London, encounters an older woman who seems to be motivated by pure desire to do good. The woman is actually a bawd who has been hired as procuress by the girl's father, who of course reacts in horror when he sees his daughter's situation, and who unmasks the procuress to the innocent girl. A wealthy and dissolute young man supports an extravagant mistress, while his wife complains of his sexual neglect and attributes it to sexual incapacity. The fact of the mistress, the text suggests, only disguises the fact of his impotence. In each instance, people are not what they seem.

Privacy, in the logic of this fiction, is a social convention designed to obscure unpleasant actualities. Burney's perception that privacy can amount to a social imposition now receives fuller elaboration. Only publicity can shame corruption and protect the good. Treating sexual matters in exactly the same way as other sorts of hidden vice, Charles Johnstone's biting narrative insists that the operations of society depend on the shared assumption that desire for money motivates everyone and justifies everything. Maria Brown, telling of her sexual activities, abandons privacy for the sake of self-justification, but incidentally for social criticism as well; the Lady of Quality, and, for that matter, Mrs. Pilkington, do exactly the same thing. Violation of privacy can serve purposes of reform as well as of voyeurism. For women, given their limited legal resources in the eighteenth century, such violation must have seemed especially powerful as a means of psychological if not material remediation. Because sexual issues, in our society, generate an especially high charge of interest, they provide useful material for writers of both genders and of various agendas who share a willingness to manipulate the conventions of privacy to their own purposes.

7 | *Trivial Pursuits*

The idea of privacy has considerable dignity in our society. Even those who, riding on a bus, talk loudly about their love lives on their cell phones often revere privacy as an abstract concept. Choosing to allow others to hear them is one thing; having a stranger or an enemy read their e-mail is quite another. Most Americans would defend vigorously the notion of an inalienable right to privacy, however they may differ about what exactly that means.

Twentieth-century theorists of privacy, as we have seen, often invoke fairly elevated concepts in their discussions. Privacy, to recapitulate, "is a condition of being-apart-from others," sought for rather than dreaded like its darker counterparts, "alienation, loneliness, ostracism, and isolation" (Weinstein 88). It "is the exclusive access of a person . . . to a realm of his own" (Van Den Haag 149). "The need for privacy amounts to a desire for socially approved protection against painful social obligations" (Moore 6). In its legal meanings, privacy protects the right to abortion, to confidential health information, to not being ordered out of your car by a police officer or subjected to a strip search without due cause. In its psychological import, it is thought to protect the integrity of the individual, constantly threatened by social pressure. Morally, it provides space for meditation and insight. Privacy is where you can be yourself, we think—including your socially unacceptable self. Privacy is where no one knows about you and no one bothers you. Although the condition of privacy might include another person, a union of two against the world, might even contain two or three others in an enclosure of intimacy, it most often connotes solitude.

Despite all dignities of description and definition, though, in practice what we protect when we protect our privacy is often remarkably trivial. Reading diaries calls emphatic attention to this fact. Though a diarist like Virginia Woolf may record provocative ideas, even she also sets down banal thoughts and actions. Some diarists, at the other extreme, itemize nothing but the inconsequential. The appeal of reading trivia might not seem immediately obvious, but in fact diaries filled with altogether commonplace detail often find wide readership. With due awareness that diarists may covertly write for an audience beyond themselves, most readers yet assume that diaries expose at least certain aspects of their writers' privacy: what they might not tell their friends. It is worth investigating the appeal of revelations that uncover only humdrum.

Diaries, for readers beyond the original writer, speak to a particular kind of desire. Ronald Wardhaugh alleges that "The private lives of public figures are of interest to us not only because they show us quite different aspects of character, but also because we can try to judge how successful the individuals are in separating the two existences" (15). Such a formulation suggests a dispassionate, remote kind of interest. But surely we also want, when we have an opportunity to penetrate the "private lives of public figures," the more primitive gratification of discovering that other people, even famous people, "public" people, resemble us. Self-doubt afflicts everyone. Could others be as undisciplined, as wavering, as rebellious, as lazy, as—fill in the blanks—as we? Do others have such nasty thoughts and impulses? We read diaries partly to find out, to glimpse the shape of other people's self-doubt and their ways of triumphing over it, to see how they resolve the struggle between good and bad proclivities. We long for consoling testimony that others, like us, have something unmomentous yet personally important to conceal. Diaries allow us to investigate the gap between public persona and private actuality, not only in order to judge success but to reassure ourselves that the discrepancies we discover in ourselves exist everywhere. Freud has assured us that everyone is fundamentally the same, but we can never have too much evidence.

To read a published diary, then, does not merely constitute voyeurism. Readers may fulfill serious purposes in the reading, and they do not necessarily seek the sensational. They may discover in the pages of a diary unexpected moral and psychological insight. More even than novels, published diaries invite the reader to enter intimately into another life, imaginatively sharing someone else's inner and outer experience. More even than novels, diaries can provide reassurance about the contours of shared humanity. Nor does such reassurance depend only on revelations of a hidden, dark, unsocial or even antisocial life. Quite opposed kinds of revelation can validate other aspects of the reader's experience. To uncover the relentless triviality of a writer's everyday life may confirm the value of a reader's mundane daily career. A diary can reveal the importance of commentary unspoken. It can uncover unexpected ways of achieving personal dignity. It can redefine authenticity.

Diaries accomplish such ends—not, of course, the ends their writers have in mind; rather, those that the genre itself implies—by many means. The diaries most widely familiar to twenty-first-century readers often emphasize the inner life (Virginia Woolf, Boswell) or acquire interest by the social anatomies they provide or by their whiffs of scandal (Pepys, Anaïs Nin). They often breach their writers' privacy in rather dramatic fashion. But other diaries provide less obvious appeal. We might look first at two diaries that concern themselves particularly with external experience—what someone buys and how much he pays for it, what someone wears and how she looks—while dwelling hardly at all on the inner life. The lives they narrate seem inconsequential. Yet the records of those lives, arguably, compel the imagination. Their power stems partly from the fact that they give new imaginative contours to the idea of privacy.

As I have already suggested, we often assume that diaries by their nature belong to privacy's realm. Although Boswell's journals, like Pope's letters, show signs of having been written with awareness of ultimate readers other than their nominal addressee, although some of Burney's journals were sent to her sister, most diaries exist for the eyes of their writer, with an occasional intimate sharer. Even diarists who betray intermittent longings for readers besides themselves usually write most often for self alone. The diaries that Woolworth's sold in my youth, for the use, mainly, of teenage girls, had tiny brass locks and keys. The idea of a secret life of writing lured me into a small investment, but my diary survived only six days: it made me too self-conscious. That diary was to be my secret, but already I had become a severe critic of my own writing. The journal's scanty entries did not measure up to my standards.

I fancy I see vestiges of self-consciousness like my own in certain diaries I read. Boswell's initial posturings, Burney's invocations of "Nobody": such sequences register the writers' sense of the momentous endeavor in which they have engaged. If they provide their own audiences, they must dread themselves as critics. Diarists in effect interrupt their own privacy by their records of their lives: they forever have a witness in themselves. (That's true of all of us, as Adam Smith pointed out, but if you don't write it down, you need not acknowledge that you know.) Dividing themselves into experiencer, commentator, and audience, they can control no part of their willfully fragmented selves.

The reader of diaries, of course, is unlikely to have all this in mind. But that reader will understand the diary as in a special sense a "private" document, and the act of reading will include the expectation of sharing another's privacy. It comes as a surprise, then, if a diarist says no more to the page than he might say to the most casual visitor. Yet what he says— I use the masculine pronoun because I think of James Woodforde, whose diary I am about to discuss—means something different when he writes it down. One can arrive at an interpretation of the nature of his privacy by pondering his choices as he sets down what he presumably wishes to remember of his life.

Less renowned than Boswell, and less entertaining, the eighteenth-century clergyman James Woodforde has nonetheless attracted a steady audience since his *Diary of a Country Parson* was first published between 1924 and 1931. Even the five volumes of the original publication contained less than half the total diary, which covers forty-four years (1758–1802). A World's Classics edition, further condensed, runs to 619 closely printed pages. Its introduction, by the original editor, John Baldwyn Beresford, testifies to the diary's great popularity, its interest alike for scholars, statesmen, "and that elusive person, the common reader" (Woodforde ix). Yet the book, quite devoid of remarkable personal revelation, offers virtually no testimony about its writer's inner life, no dark secrets of soul or psyche, and no scandal of any kind, save veiled reports of the mainly financial misconduct of one visitor to the parson's household. Far from removing the screen that hides a man's inner recesses, it in effect declares that screen integral to the personality.

Woodforde never married. He proposed, sort of, and was sort of accepted, but the object of his affections subsequently married another man. His account of the "proposal"—here given in full—exemplifies his tone about intimate matters: "I went home with Betsy White and had some talk with her concerning my making her mine when an opportunity offered and she was not averse to it at all" (28 May 1774; 95–96). The cautious negative formulation ("not averse") hardly suggests passion, on either side. If Betsy's later defection caused Woodforde suffering, he does not acknowledge the fact in his diary. If he regretted his celibacy, if he felt sexual longings or indulged them, if he endured loneliness, the diary never says so. Far from telling all, this particular diary firmly declares large stretches of personal experience off limits.

Yet I for one find it unexpectedly absorbing. The question is why. The data Woodforde provides are not obviously compelling, although a reader remote in time from the writer must feel a certain awe and fascination at the lavish menus. Many menus make their appearance: recording the food he has eaten, and especially that he has offered guests or been offered while visiting, constitutes one of the diarist's favorite activities. How could he and his friends eat so much?

> We had for dinner, two fine Codds boiled with fryed Souls round them and oyster sauce, a fine sirloin of Beef roasted, some peas soup and an orange Pudding for the first course, for the second, we had a lease of Wild Ducks rosted, a fore Qu: of Lamb and sallad and mince Pies. (23 Dec. 1773; 86)

> I gave them for dinner, a Couple of Chicken boiled and a Tongue, a Leg of Mutton boiled and Capers and Batter Pudding for the first Course, Second, a couple of Ducks rosted and green Peas, some Artichokes, Tarts and Blancmange. After dinner, Almonds and Raisins, Oranges and Strawberries. Mountain and Port wines. (8 June 1781; 171)

Such summaries, sometimes less detailed, appear every few pages. In the final years of his life, Woodforde recorded every dinner he ate. If consistency of notation be the criterion, food would seem James Woodforde's primary concern in life.

In second place, a close second, by the same standard of frequent occurrence, is money. The diarist records all his spending. He details the wages he gives his servants, the amount he pays for gin and books and buttons:

> Nancy bought her a new black beaver hat with purple Cockade and band. She gave for it 1. 2. 0. She bought it of One Oxley in the Market place. I also bought a new hat of him, pd. him for it 1. 1. 0. Whilst my Niece was at Barths, Stay & Habit Maker, I walked to Bacons and paid him for Knox's Sermons lately published, one Vol. Octavo 0. 6. 6. To the Widow Studwell, at the China Shop, pd. 0. 8. 0 for Basons &c. To 4 Maccarel, pd. 0. 1. 8. Paid Sudbury for my new Cellaret &c. 4. 4. 6. To 11. Dozen of Buttons, Coat & Waistcoat, some Italian, some Clay's Paper ones, all black at Bakers pd. 0. 9. 6. (24 May 1793; 435)

Such data, like the lists of food, hold historical interest. One can, for instance, note how servants' wages slowly rise over the years and register the inexpensiveness of smuggled liquor (which this pious clergyman consistently purchased). But as the substance of a diary, the recurrent tabulations lack the resonance that readers of private records characteristically anticipate.

To dwell on small expenditures and large meals makes sense, given the apparent paucity of event in Woodforde's life. During the more than forty years covered by the diary, almost nothing happens. For twenty-six of those years, Woodforde lived in a country village that he served as pastor. His niece, Nancy, joined him there in 1779 and remained with him until his death in 1803. The deaths of siblings and parents punctuated his life. He had few intimate friends, and his most absorbing occupation beyond his pastoral duties apparently consisted in making beer. He sometimes helped his workers bring in hay; he bottled the gin he bought; he christened and married and buried his parishioners. Occasionally he journeyed to a nearby town. (The record of expenses quoted above delineates the contours of one such visit.) Yet more rarely, he visited or was visited by members of his family. He shows some concern for the madness of King George III, some awareness of war with America, but little consciousness beyond this of national or international affairs. In short, he led a quiet life.

Part of his account's fascination consists in this very quietness, which in an odd but significant sense bears centrally on the question of privacy. The forequarter of lamb one partakes of, the price one pays for buttons— these are hardly confidential matters. Yet their place in Woodforde's diary helps to define the nature of his private existence—not "private" solely in distinction to a larger "public" world, but private in that it belongs to him alone. The texture of his life, like that of most lives, derives from routine, the things he does over and over. So it is for most people: much of our time goes in paying the bills, doing the marketing, taking the dry cleaning, emptying the trash, sitting at a desk performing repetitive tasks. A diary like Woodforde's validates the aspects of life that we take for granted, or even actively resent. "Public" personae conceal the universal secret that most "interesting" lives rest on a substratum of predictable and repeated small occupations. To write with precision about the things that one does all the time, almost without noticing, declares their importance. James Woodforde paid nine shillings sixpence for eleven dozen buttons: no more, no less. The buttons would adorn coats and waistcoats. Made of different substances, all were black. What could be more trivial? Yet, knowing about those buttons, a twenty-first-century reader can feel in touch with the kind of experience that composes a man's days. The quality of "dailiness" in this diary, a genre by definition recording the passage of days, creates much of its appeal and reminds its readers that the hidden life we posit in others actually includes not only psychic upheaval but taking out the garbage.

Indeed, there is a peculiar sense of intimacy—and the sense of intimacy is one of diary reading's rewards—in sharing routine trivia, the ordinary data of every day. Husbands and wives, at the end of the day, often talk about just such matters: the price of buttons, the lunch menu. The special pleasure of conversing about "nothing" belongs primarily to those close to one another, those who share lives or live in close touch. In interpersonal writing, too, the minor detail surfaces only in frequent and close communications. What we paid for buttons does not make part, in all probability, of the yearly ritual letter to our college roommate, but it might come up in hasty daily e-mails to an intimate friend. Partaking of the trivia that compose much of Woodforde's experience, we partake also in the essence of his life.

Yet twenty-first-century readers, however charmed, are unlikely to feel satisfied with self-revelation at this level. Reading diaries, we seek evidence not only of the hidden life in the sense I have been trying to define but of an inner life of psyche or soul. *Diary of a Country Parson* provides, for the most part, clues rather than hard evidence about such matters. It creates a puzzle of meaning. This, too, comprises part of its appeal.

In this parson's diary, the spiritual life plays no overt part. The writer records the burials, christenings, and marriages over which he presides. When someone dies, he characteristically sets down a pious wish that the departed may be happier hereafter. He tells nothing, though, about his own spiritual struggles, insights, or convictions. It is as though his ordination resolved all spiritual problems forever, declaring his adherence to a body of doctrine and thereby settling everything.

Almost equally reticent about his emotional vicissitudes, Woodforde occasionally confesses to feeling "low" but rarely speculates about causes. Only infrequently does he appear to know what makes him unhappy. The acknowledged reasons for depression, though, make a suggestive sequence, allowing the reader to penetrate (or to imagine that she penetrates) more deeply into the writer's privacy—more deeply, perhaps, than he has consciously penetrated himself.

The closest thing to a dramatic event in Woodforde's record of himself is a prolonged and inconclusive series of encounters between him and three recurrent visitors who made part of his life, two of them for some eight years. The cast of characters includes Betsy Davy, eleven years old when she first appears in 1781; her mother, identified only as Mrs. Davy; and her putative fiancé, Mr. Walker, who comes on the scene in 1788, six years older than Betsy. Betsy and Woodforde's niece Nancy, who lives with him, become close friends. Mrs. Davy shows up frequently, invited or not, as, subsequently, does Mr. Walker. Woodforde early has doubts about Mrs. Davy: "Nancy by being with Mrs. Davy had learnt some of her extravagant Notions, and talked very high all day. I talked with her against such foolish Notions which made her almost angry with me" (30 June

1781; 171). By 1785, the diarist has included many comments about how "bold" and distasteful Mrs. Davy is. Nonetheless, he feels hurt when she acts cold toward him: "Mrs. Davy did not by any means behave as she used to do towards me—was scarce civil to me" (22 Jan. 1785; 241). Nancy and Mrs. Davy have forged some sort of alliance: "Nancy had two Letters from Mrs. Davy this Afternoon done up in a parcel, and with the same a little Lump of something, but what, I know not—as Nancy never mentioned a word of what it was, nor of a single word in either of the Letters—I care not for it, but shall take care to be as private myself in matters" (10 Dec. 1786). (Even privacy, it seems, can become a matter for competition.) Mr. Smith reports that Mrs. Davy is a woman of bad character, but Nancy doesn't seem to care. Mrs. Davy continues to visit, although the parson does not wish to see her. As he comments after one of their encounters (when the visitor has dined and spent the afternoon), "Mrs. Davy was not well pleased with me nor I with her. She is without exception the most bold woman I know" (20 April 1789; 348).

When Mr. Walker makes his advent, his visits follow a similar pattern. At first Woodforde seems to like him and to enjoy the liveliness he provides. Gradually, hurt feelings emerge:

> On his taking leave he went up to Nancy and wished her well shaking her by her hand, and then went to Betsy and did the same, but to me (altho' in the Room at the same time) he never said one word or took the lest notice of me (tho' I also helped him on with his great Coat) after he was mounted and just going out of the great Gates then he said good Morning and that was all—very slight return for my Civilities towards him of late and which I did not expect. It hurt me very much indeed. (19 Nov. 1788; 338–39)

Worse still: "Nancy, Betsy Davy, and Mr. Walker are all confederate against me and am never let into any of their Schemes or Intentions &c. Nancy I think ought not to be so to me" (2 Jan. 1789; 342). It comes as considerable satisfaction to Woodforde when his friend Mr. Custance tells him of Walker's profligacy and deceit. The young man, it turns out, has traded on Woodforde's name to try to raise money. He is no good. "I was astonished to hear such things," Woodforde comments, "but not so much as I should otherwise, had I not been an eye-witness in some degree of his profligacy and extravagance. I have a long time given him up, his behaviour to me last Winter made me despise him utterly. Nancys encouraging him to come to my House after such behaviour has greatly lessened my esteem for her, as she shewed no regard for me" (28 Jan. 1790; 370–71).

Woodforde begins, in his relations with all these visitors, by enjoying the novelty and excitement they provide. But he remains sensitive to slights. When he feels slighted, he confides his distress to his diary. Hurt feelings soon give way to a conviction that he is beset by conspiracy: Mrs. Davy sending a mysterious "lump" that Nancy won't tell him about, Nancy and Betsy and Walker scheming against him. The progression delineates a man eager for yet fearful of relationship.

As far as one can tell from the diary, he has few close connections. Aside from his relatives—all of whom, save Nancy, live at a distance—he appears to feel intimate with no one except, for a time, Mr. and Mrs. Custance, among their few neighbors of the gentry. Mrs. Custance's frequent pregnancies and lyings-in, with their attendant christenings, punctuate the diary's record. Mr. Custance serves as confidant, sounding board, intermittent pragmatic advisor, and relayer of local gossip. But the Custances and their many children decide to move to Bath. The day of their departure produces a disjointed record from Woodforde, beginning with a detailed account of his friends' leaving. They are, he explains, accompanied by "five of their Children with two Nurses and Rising the Butler," riding in their own coach and four with an attending post chaise (7 Oct. 1792; 423). Nancy sees them, Woodforde hears them. He emphasizes the physicality of their journey in all its details: they use their own horses, but they will change in Attleborough; servants will ride the horses back. Then, as if to transcend the reality of horses and carriages and servants, he resorts to piety, only to acknowledge bleakly the emotional cost to him of this leaving: "Pray God bless them and theirs, and may every thing turn out to their most sanguine wishes. It made us quite low all the whole Day. It is a great, very great loss to us indeed" (423).

Nowhere else in the diary does Woodforde so emphatically register emotional deprivation. When he elsewhere acknowledges feeling "low," he either treats the feeling as a weakness to be overcome or attributes it to physical causes. His emotional range seems limited—either that, or he simply fails to pay much attention to it. Just as he never mentions Betsy White after his account of his approach to her, he does not dwell on his mourning for the loss of the Custances. But his very reticence, the absence in the diary of any subsequent allusion to someone filling the departed neighbors' role in his life, underlines the magnitude of that loss.

Ill health, the diary suggests, sometimes accounts for Woodforde's low spirits. His rare bouts of irritation hint another cause, perhaps more important. On at least three occasions, he reports his niece's complaints about their shared life. (The diary never specifies Nancy's age, but she is obviously a good deal younger than its writer.) His reaction to those complaints, confided to the diary, not necessarily to Nancy herself, is always the same.

> Dinner to day, Breast of Veal rosted &c. Nancy made me very uneasy this Afternoon and does very often, by complaining of the dismal Situation of my House, nothing to be seen, and little or no visiting, or being visited &c. If we have of late lost our best Friends, by the removal of Mr. Custance's Family to Bath, and the Death of Mr. DuQuesne, must it not be affected by me as well as her? In short my Place has been too dull for her I am sorry to say for many Years.—As things are so—infœlix! (19 Jan. 1794; 451)

Nancy complains that life is dull at the parsonage; Woodforde responds that his situation duplicates hers. The reader might question this claim, recognizing that the diarist at least has regular occupation and an acknowledged role in community life, whereas his niece exists in a condition of absolute dependence on whatever social life becomes available to her. But such facts have little relevance. It matters far more that Woodforde clearly feels the monotony of his own existence. That recognition emerges only in the context of Nancy's complaints, which elicit both resentment ("I suffer as much as she does") and covert pride ("But I don't complain about it").

The year before he wrote his account of Nancy's railings, Woodforde had commented on a letter he received from another niece: "Mrs. Bidewell brought our Newspapers and likewise a Letter from my Niece Jane Pounsett in which was a great deal about nothing at all" (6 Apr. 1793; 433). An unsympathetic reader might offer the same indictment of Woodforde's diary. Perhaps the writer can put into a document intended only for himself precisely what he would exclude from a letter. For himself alone, he can report the trivia that compose his life. For himself alone, he can dignify those trivia in the setting down. He lives a life as dull as Nancy's, but instead of allowing himself habitually to resent it he enables himself to celebrate it.

So, at any rate, I read *Diary of a Country Parson:* as an insistent record of the prosaic, dignified by its recording, an account that inadvertently reveals the longing and fear of its maker as well as the heroism with which he suppresses such emotions. The recording and its choices constitute a moral achievement. Stuart Sherman describes the characteristics of secular diaries as including "the *quotidian* as series and structure, . . . time as measured but blank, . . . a field open for self-creation by self-inscription" (22). Woodforde's version of "self-creation" resolutely refuses grandiosity; the self he makes claims no more than the quotidian.

In finding heroism in confinement to such a claim, I in effect invent my own version of the diarist. Diaries provide a superficial illusion of transparency, but in fact they partake inevitably of all privacy's ambiguities. Eighteenth-century novels remind their readers in many ways of the layers of disguise that envelop the personality, hinting that the attempt to share all thoughts and feelings amounts only to a final disguise. Diaries may substantiate the point, inviting their readers to invent a personality for the voice that speaks through them. Whether they ostensibly reveal an inner life or confine themselves to external detail, they provide ambiguous material for interpretation. Lacking coherent plot to focus the reader's attention, lacking deliberate structure beyond that of sequential time and recurrent reference, they do not systematically direct the search for meaning. Yet the fantasy of intimacy they encourage makes the reader believe in the possibility of "knowing" another consciousness on the basis of its language.

A diary yet more insistently concerned with the external is that of Elizabeth, first duchess of Northumberland, separated from Woodforde by gender, class, environment, marital status, and, consequently, experience. Lady of the Bedchamber to Queen Charlotte and a close personal friend of the queen, daughter of one duke (the duke of Somerset) and wife to another, the duchess spent much of her life circulating in the highest reaches of aristocratic society. She meticulously reports such matters as banquet menus (although not, like Woodforde, the bills of fare for her daily meals) and court costumes; she comments, sometimes nastily, on the characters and appearance of those she encounters; she shows herself vividly aware of sexual actualities. Rarely, and only incidentally, does she mention either of her two sons. Her diary contains detailed descriptions of what she sees on her travels and especially of court festivities. It also includes such entries as this:

April 1757.—Number of Boys at Eton, July the 23, 1755, was 466, of wch. Noblemen 41. Number of Boys 1756, 408, whereof Noblemen, 38. My Lord [i.e., her husband] weighed, 12 st. 13 l.; I, 12 st. 9 l.; Sr. Charles Sedley, 11 st. 11 l.; Ld. Warkworth [her elder son, age 15], 5 st. 4 l. Anually Ship'd at Sunderland 180,000 Chn. Of Coal, from Newcastle 200,000. (*Diaries* 8–9)

And this, my favorite, partly because of its position in the text, printed as though it were the final paragraph of an account of the king's visit to the duke and duchess ("they afterwards all dined at a Grand Entertaint given by the Duke & Dss of Northumberland where the number of Dishes served up was 177 exclusive of the Desert" [142]). Here is the last paragraph of what has previously seemed a coherent narrative:

> An account of the salmon taken in the Tweed in the year 1770: 9000 Salmon, 33221 Live salmon trout, 43,000 Kitts of salmon sent to various parts of Great Britain, the Mediterranean & the West Indies, for the taking & curing of which 250 Familys of salmon coopers, & 250 Familys of Fishermen are employ'd besides Hawkers & others amounting to 600 familys. (22 Aug. 1770; 143)

Anomalous though such entries seem—what connection have the number of Eton schoolboys or of Tweed salmon to the daily life of a duchess?—they may provide a key to the consciousness at work here: the sense of privacy emerging from publicly available information. This diary issues from the mind and pen of a woman intensely curious about the world. A woman: therefore largely cut off from formal education. And an aristocratic woman at that: therefore destined to spend much of her time circulating in a social environment dominated by exacting conventions. She seizes on facts, devours them, writes them down. Their value to her can only be surmised, but it is not hard to connect her interest in miscellaneous facts with her concern for precise observation.

When she goes to the opera, for instance, she has this to say:

> Elisi the first Singer has lost his Voice & is grown as fat as a porpoise, Savoy the 2nd Man has a very fine Voice & is a handsome figure, Cipra a most exceeding good Tenor. The Spagnoletti was as ugly as the Devil, half her Face being burnt away, she supplys it by Pasteboard, has a Glass Eye, dresses like a Gorgon and is as hoarse as a Raven. Visconti is tolerably pretty but has not the least Idea of Music. (2 Nov. 1765; 62)

She comments also on the state of the sets and of the boxes for the audience, as though she feels an almost journalistic obligation to set down the precise condition of everything and everyone. Nothing in the diary itself hints any anticipation of readers beyond herself. The record exists as a kind of artificial memory, and she wishes to remember not how she feels but how things were.

The text available to current readers bears an uncertain relation to what the duchess actually wrote. As the title page specifies, the volume contains only "Excerpts." Nothing in the editor's introduction provides any clue to the principles guiding the choice of excerpts or even any indication of the relation in magnitude between the parts and the whole. As published, the diary begins in 1752 and ends in 1776, the year the duchess died, but it contains obvious gaps. We may believe that the duchess wrote everything here attributed to her, but we cannot know what else she wrote. For my purposes, though, such facts have relatively little importance, since my primary interest focuses on the reader's experience of reading what is given. Offered this as a diary, what can we make of it?

The quotations already offered may sufficiently suggest that we can readily make entertainment. A far more sprightly writer than Woodforde, the duchess obviously entertains herself by writing down what she thinks, however indiscreet. Of Alexander Boswell's house at Auchinleck: "the Pedimentis terribly loaded with Ornaments of Trumpets & Maces & the Deuce knows what. It is but a middling House, but justly it is a romantick Spot (16 Aug. 1760; 25). Of the king giving a speech: "The Crown like to fall, sat down upon his nose & misbecame him greatly" (18 Nov. 1760; 14). Of herself: "Went home voided a large Stone. Tired to Death. Went to Ball; tired to Death. A bad Supper. Miss Townshend drunk" (6 May 1760; 15). Of the hereditary prince of Hesse-Darmstadt: "he is exactly like a great Mastiff Puppy, tho but eighteen he is above six feet high strong & robust with a heavy Countenance, an Oval Face with large Features, his Forehead is well enough, his Hair sandy, his Mouth wide, his Lips thick the under one hanging down; tolerably good Teeth, his skin fair, a few small marks of the smallpox scattered here & there, far from handsome and very shortsighted" (5 May 1771; 150).

We may deduce from such passages a sharp observing consciousness, a woman with zest for life, someone not afraid of her own judgments. But the diary provides no evidence about whether the duchess felt free to share those judgments with others. Its reports of a largely ceremonial existence suggest otherwise. At banquets, balls, and other court events, the duchess sat in prescribed places with prescribed companions. When she traveled on the Continent, with a large entourage, her arrival in hamlet or city became an affair of state. She offers no reference to intimate companionship, no indication even of a companionate relation to her husband. (Such matters, of course, may have been excised from the published diary.) The document provided between covers suggests an existence not at all lonely but psychologically isolated nonetheless—an existence of little physical privacy but rich in its psychological equivalent.

The diary as we have it emanates from both realms, that of ceremonial public existence and that of private reflection. Its charm depends on the intersection between them, on the conjunction between a reported experience largely controlled by rigid convention and a mind meditating on that experience. Unlike Woodforde's diary, this record of a life provides no consecutive narrative over the course of years. It may linger over a single event, such as a trip to France that included the duchess's presence at the wedding of the Dauphin, its every aspect, including the appearance of all participants in the ceremony, meticulously evoked. But because of its selectivity it creates a necessarily misleading sense that the duchess's life consisted almost entirely of her public appearances. One gains no sense of progression or development from the fragmentary narrative here provided.

Yet the diary tells its own kind of story—a story of privacy. It tells of a woman's mode of creating and holding on to a sense of self by insisting on her own assessments of experience. Those assessments acquire their power not by great verbal skill or wit but by the energy of their assertion and the impression of conviction they generate. Here, for example, is the duchess reflecting on one of the many public events surrounding the Dauphin's marriage, a state banquet:

> The little Madame [the Dauphin's sister, previously described as "round as a Ball" (112)] eat with a voraciousness & eagerness I never saw equall'd & whilst she gobbled down the Meat on her Plate, her Eyes seem'd to devour all the rest that was on the Table. The Dauphin eat very little, seem'd quite pensive & hung over his Plate playing with his Knife. The Comte D'Artois on the other hand was eternally talking and doing the honours to the Dauphine. The Comte de Provence did not eat a morsel. (16 May 1770; 122)

In a scene that might be represented as pure spectacle, the duchess discovers the telling physical details of human behavior that convey character and suggest feeling. She never contents herself with life in the mass. The vision of the about-to-be-married Dauphin playing with his knife, appearing "pensive," suggests the pathos of state marriages. The behavior of the eternally talking Comte D'Artois epitomizes the role of the courtier. We can only speculate about the comte de Provence—one would like to have more on the subject from the duchess's pen.

She asserts, always, her own point of view. On occasion she even mocks herself. One final long quotation will epitomize her capacity to see clearly, steadily, and with considerable self-awareness:

> At my return home, Mr. Bruce the great Traveller [in Africa] came and drank Tea with me. He by no means answer'd the Idea which I had form'd to myself of him. I had figured to myself a figure with a vast Beard as long as Liotards [a Swiss artist], a Turban & a flowing Turkish Robe, but instead I

saw enter a fresh well looking man in a Scarlet Coat embroiderd with Gold, a White Feather in his Hat and a Chin as smooth as a Billiard Ball. He was very polite but I confess I was not so much entertained with his Conversation as I expected to have been. (25 Apr. 1774; 214)

Politeness will not suffice for this duchess; white feathers do not entertain her as flowing robes might have done. She uses detail to elaborate the comic discrepancy between expectation and actuality. Implicitly she suggests her weariness of the conventional behavior that surrounds her and that she herself practices, her desire for something new, and perhaps the inevitability of that desire's frustration.

The wistfulness detectable in this paragraph illuminates the diary as a whole. The duchess lives in a world of high decorum and showiness (here symbolized by the white feather), a world in which glossy surfaces efface what goes on behind them. Perhaps the duchess of Northumberland yearns for more authentic encounters, despite the pleasure she takes in whatever is given her. Her ability to set down the details of her existence and to comment on her own experience, to penetrate surfaces and note the signs of life beneath them discovers authenticity even where it appears not to exist. She anchors herself to facts—the literal weight of her husband and son, as well as herself; the number of salmon caught in the Tweed, but also the rotundity of the Dauphin's sister, the position of the king's crown, the significant talkativeness of a courtier. These facts in effect populate her privacy. She records only the occasional moment of isolated existence ("I came home quite Overcome with heat, settled my Accounts, play'd on my Flute, eat some pease and went to bed" [4 June 1771; 158]), but she records lavishly the contents of her mind, not in the guise of introspection but in the shape of a continuing process of knowledge and judgment. She judges with gusto: "the Gardener is the most supremely ignorant of any Man I ever saw in my life" (18 Sept. 1752; 4). She offers her judgments with confidence, perhaps partly because she offers them to herself. Those judgments affirm her selfhood, define her to herself and to her readers two centuries and a half after the fact. She attains on the page a kind of dignity unconnected with rank and social status, a dignity of active consciousness. The facts she seizes and grasps, the evaluations she achieves: these create a vivid impression of inner life even in a record almost entirely devoted to external event.

Woodforde's diary and the duchess's inhabit an extreme end of the continuum between introspection and objectivity. Both writers offer hints about the nature of their inner life, but for neither does it supply a primary subject. Most eighteenth-century diaries resemble theirs in this respect;

Boswell is unusual in the amount of attention he devotes to his own feelings. Even John Wesley, whom one might expect to concentrate on internal experience, turns increasingly toward the external, focusing attention on the size (enormous) of his impromptu congregations and dwelling on doctrinal disputes. Wesley published his own journals, in installments; his awareness of a public audience presumably helped to shape them. Moreover, he feels intensely conscious of God as audience. For him there can be no privacy: God always watches. If he confesses to unspecified "other desires" that distract him from Christ, he promptly testifies that Christ enables him to "put them all under my feet" (1:160); he need not dwell on them. He dwells, rather, on the converts he makes and the signs of salvation that they manifest.

A few diaries have come down to us that took obvious pains to conceal themselves. Like Pepys before them, some eighteenth-century diarists wrote in cipher, making their records inaccessible to the casually curious. Such writers presumably assume their privacy on the page as well as inscribe evidence of private aspects of their life. One such diarist was Dudley Ryder, born in 1692, destined to become attorney-general in 1737 and to hold the position until, in 1754, he assumed the place of chief justice in the Court of King's Bench and was made a privy councillor. His diary, however, dates from long before, when, a twenty-three-year-old law student, he worried obsessively about his relations with women, whether or not he should marry, and what chance he had for success in his chosen career. Free to confess the inmost secrets of his consciousness, he indeed sets down his anxieties and his deepest concerns—and most of them turn out to be about matters that might be objectively described as trivial. Over and over, for instance, he worries about whether he has "stinking breath." He rather thinks he does, but he cannot find out for sure. Perhaps he should ask his mother. He ponders that possibility, then decides that he cannot raise the question; he does not know how he could formulate it to avoid embarrassment; his aunt, to whom his mother tells everything, would be certain to ridicule him. He takes various remedies, just in case. Then he returns to the problem: perhaps that stinking breath accounts for the fact that women find him less attractive than other men.

The connection between women and bad breath calls attention to the true importance of the issue from Ryder's point of view. Still tentative about even the career he has chosen, he feels compelled to discover what place in the world he will inhabit—not what character he has, not, like Boswell, who he will "be," but how and where he will be accepted. Marriage makes part of the conventional pattern, but he does not feel quite sure that he wants it for himself. On the one hand, he believes in "a natural tendency, a prepossession in favour of the married state." "It is charming and moving," he continues, "it ravishes me to think of a pretty creature concerned in me, being my most intimate friend, constant companion and always ready to soothe me, take care of me and caress me" (Ryder 310). This idyllic, if one-sided, view of marriage clashes with his observations of how life goes for his father and mother: his mother always peevish and irritable, his father perversely irritating her. He will take care, he decides, not to marry a peevish woman. But how can he be perfectly sure?

Moreover, he fears, women do not like him. Possibly they scorn him because he is a "small" man—physically short, he presumably means. More probably, they feel unwilling to bother with him because he cannot seem to find exactly the tone for conversation with them. Even when whores accost him at the theater, he feels uneasy; he never knows what to say. On occasion he seeks out a whore, he claims, in order to practice conversation with her. And he does not "romp" enough: women seem to like men who romp. Even when he engages in this ambiguous activity, the women he wishes to attract do not respond as he would like. He never knows when he is supposed to "salute" a woman. When he meets a woman for the first time and kisses her, his cousin tells him she thinks that improper. Other men seem able to kiss women playfully all the time. Ryder plots and plans in order to win a kiss. Often he fails utterly.

The diary fills many pages with such matters. How does one manage to keep on the proper side of a woman when walking through a crowded place? Is it better to come constantly to see her when you feel interested in a woman, or would it be more judicious to stay away on occasion? Should one confide one's sense of attraction to others, in the hope that the news will get back to the object of one's affections? Ryder writes verses on the curling locks of Sally Marshall's hair, then struggles over whether to send them to her. And so on: the often foolish minutiae of an underconfident young man.

But the judgment of triviality, however incontrovertible it may seem, depends on the hierarchy of values held by the judge. To a country clergyman with limited resources, what he spends and how may constitute a matter of considerable importance. Dinner may be the most exciting event of his day: what he eats matters to him. The number of salmon caught in the Tweed might, to a noblewoman caught up in a ritualized social existence, provide significant reassurance of her imaginative and intellectual connection to a wider world. Dudley Ryder goes to a ball and notices how well a dancing-master dances. "I almost envied his condition and a secret wish came upon me that I had been a dancing-master to have had an opportunity of excelling in that way. It came into my head then that I was well made for dancing and had I been brought up to it should have excelled in that way, whereas in the present way of life I did not think I should make any figure" (204). The thought is ludicrous, given the British class system; a passing fancy. But almost the entire diary entry for 23 March 1716 expounds it. Its importance for the writer in all his uncertainties far exceeds its rationality.

Many people convert the trivial to the significant by incorporating it into narrative. I in effect did exactly that in my "explanations" of what James Woodforde and the duchess of Northumberland wrote down: I suggested a kind of story of their lives deducible from their diaries and assigned importance to otherwise meaningless detail on the basis of that story. The story I told, however, did not necessarily (or even probably) correspond to the stories they would have told of themselves, about which, given the nature of their diaries, one can only speculate. The fact that diaries provide raw material from which their readers can construct stories contributes to the satisfaction of reading them. Perhaps the most satisfying diaries, though, supply explicit stories of their own.

Privacy is, after all, a region of stories. In psychic realms generally concealed from observation, people construct narratives about themselves that express their fears and hopes, interpret the data of every day into a meaningful pattern, discover a trajectory for their experience. Such narratives belong only to the self, ordinarily conveyed to others inadvertently and in fragmentary fashion if at all. They do not necessarily even rise to full consciousness. Yet diaries can on occasion transmit these private chronicles, which generally depend heavily on the trivial events of every day. The records that provide such narratives generate a peculiar fascination.

That fascination, of course, belongs to the reader of diaries. For the writer, transmitting the most private of stories may appear to comprise a great danger. The extreme self-protectiveness of some diarists suggests the possibility that simply writing down the material of one's life can violate a sense of privacy. "Publication," by definition, makes the written word public, but even writing ostensibly intended only for the self endangers self-concealment. A diary like Woodforde's seems to poise between a desire to conceal and a need to record. And Woodforde's account of his life by no means constitutes an extreme example of journalizing discretion. A recent biography of Jane Austen cites the diary of Elizabeth Smith, the daughter of a member of Parliament, courted by a man named William Chute. She records his proposal thus: "Mr. Chute in the morn. Mr. Chute to dinner. Answer." The next day's entry reads "Mr. Chute to dinner. Miss Cunliffe to supper & slept with me. Final decision." This, Claire Tomalin explains, "signalled the engagement" (93). The extreme terseness of such a journal may reflect immediate practical concerns, worry about the likelihood that a sister (Elizabeth had three sisters) or a mother might read the young woman's reflections. But perhaps it conveys, more fundamentally, the same tension I have alleged in Woodforde's diary, the impulse to hide warring with the desire to claim significance for one's life.

Keeping a diary in cipher presumably reassures its writer that he has managed successfully to hide. At any rate, Dudley Ryder's diary is far more openly revealing than either of the others we have examined, and it reveals, specifically, the story he tells of himself. A reader's knowledge of Ryder's later career alleviates the sadness of the young man's self-narrative, but the record of stereotypically adolescent insecurity retains poignance. (Ryder, at twenty-three, resembles Boswell at the same age, setting down in his *London Journal* the vacillations of a young man who has not yet discovered the limits of his own nature, who he should and can "be.")

For Ryder, the problem, as I have already pointed out, centers not on who to "be" but on what he can do and, especially, what effect he has on others. He has in some ways a firm sense of identity, and he does not altogether like the identity he has discovered. He sees himself as doomed to social failure. The story he tells organizes itself around a series of unsuccessful social efforts, and his self-interpretation emphasizes his belief that others hold a negative view of him. This "story" leaves out a great deal, leaves out even much of the data that the diary includes. The reader can construct quite a different narrative by emphasizing different details. Given knowledge of the young man's subsequent career, a different story, indeed, seems far more plausible. But that is to say that public facts should determine private interpretations—and of course they do not.

The diary opens with an extensive statement of its purposes, a statement in some respects virtually identical to Boswell's comparable inaugurating paragraph:

> I intend particularly to observe my own temper and state of mind as to my fitness and disposition for study or the easiness or satisfaction it finds within itself and the particular cause of that or of the contrary uneasiness that often disturbs my mind. I will also take notice especially of what I read every day. This will be a means of helping my memory in what I read. I intend also to observe my own acts as to their goodness or badness. . . . I shall be able then to review any parts of my life, have the pleasure of it if it be well spent, if otherwise know how to mend it. It will help me to know myself better and give a better judgement of my own ability and what I am best qualified for. I shall know what best suits my own temper, what is most likely to make me

easy and contented and what the contrary. I shall know how the better to spend my time for the future. It will help me to recollect what I have read. (Ryder 29)

Two themes recur in this long paragraph: the hope of remembering what he has read, and the desire to discover what makes him "easy" and what otherwise. The entire set of reasons has a moral flavor. This sounds like a young man concerned to improve himself, interested in the goodness and badness of his acts, eager to spend his time wisely, tacitly apologetic about the possible egotism of keeping a diary. The diary itself corroborates these suggestions. Ryder indeed faithfully sets down what he has read, and he comments on the content of the books he studies, books written in Latin and French as well as in English. But the record of his reading makes no part of the story he tells about himself; if it did, the story would be quite different. He appears to know from the outset what contents him and what does not; the document records few discoveries. The introductory paragraph suggests that Ryder's interest balances between the internal (how he feels) and the external (how he behaves). In fact, his itemization of behavior serves almost entirely to explain or justify his psychological condition. He has what one might consider a remarkably modern concern with the nuances of his own inner life. Indeed, the story he tells, ostensibly an account of his performance (a significant word) in the world, actually relays the vagaries of his self-esteem.

"It is the most agreeable state of mind a man can be in to be pleased with his own performances," Ryder writes (9 June 1715; 33). He seldom enjoys this state. Consider a typical report of one of his social encounters: "I did not behave myself with that ease and freedom of carriage that is becoming. I don't know how, I am mighty apt to be uneasy in the company of strange ladies and don't know how to compose my mouth, my eyes or settle my hands or legs. Every part of me seems to be in a restless posture and I am at a loss how to dispose of myself" (6 Aug. 1715; 70). Nothing is obviously at stake in this episode: Ryder visits Mr. Smith, plays the flute with him, then converses with him, his cousin, and the cousin's recently acquired wife, who enter during the evening. Only one lady inhabits the scene, and she is safely married. Yet Ryder, by his own report, suffers exactly the kind of uneasiness that marks his exchanges with eligible young women and even with whores. He sees himself as unpleasing to women. "I don't know how, I am the worst person in the world to entertain a lady in conversation. . . . I wish I could arrive at that talent of appearing indifferent in the company of the ladies. It is this that chiefly gives that life and spirit to a conversation which is agreeable and which the women especially universally like, and indeed what enters very much into the modern character of a gentleman" (3 Sept. 1715; 90). The talent of *appearing* indifferent: Ryder understands how much appearance rather than substance figures in all social intercourse; he yearns to control the impression he gives rather than to change his nature.

Going to visit his parents precipitates another set of reflections on appearances:

> Went to Hackney on horseback. Walked the horse all the way. I had a mind to think as I went along, but did not much. It is a strange thing how vanity and love of being observed and esteemed mixes itself insensibly in our most ordinary actions. I could not help as I went along pleasing myself in hopes somebody or other that knew me would meet me in that thinking studious posture. It might give them a notion of me as a great thinker, that knows how to employ myself alone and take pleasure in retirement. This is not the only time I have had that thought in my head and it has made me put on a more fixed countenance than ordinary. (6 April 1716; 224–25)

When he arrives at his parents' house, he finds it "almost filled with ladies." This time, though, he gets along well. "I had the assurance to put on a certain air of familiarity and indifference towards them which I thought became me very well" (6 April 1716; 225).

Here and elsewhere, Ryder demonstrates his acute consciousness of the difference between appearing and being. Putting on a "countenance" or an "air" of one sort or another determines the judgments others will make of him. Although he comments on the "vanity and love of being observed" implicit in his behavior while leading the horse, he does not blame himself for indulging such emotions; his vivid self-awareness includes no self-condemnation. Vanity and love of being observed are, he knows, in the nature of things. He condemns himself, rather, for failures to manipulate appearances effectively. His self-doubt concentrates on this matter.

Roughly the final third of the diary concerns the young man's vexed relations with one Sally Marshall, with whom he believes himself in love. She does not emerge very distinctly from his account (he is far more interested in himself), but her flirtatiousness is apparent. She presents herself alternately as indifferent to Ryder and as attracted to him. A reader may suspect that the causes for her shifting attitudes reside in Sally rather than her would-be lover, but the diarist desperately seeks reasons in his own behavior—in the appearances he presents. He represents himself deliberately in different ways, sometimes believing for a time that he has mastered the proper stance, only to find Sally changing ground yet again. The diary ends indeterminately (ends, indeed, in midsentence), without resolving the relationship. The introduction reports Ryder's much later marriage to another woman, but readers receive enough data from the text itself to surmise that this particular infatuation will not result in any lasting connection.

Ryder's association with Sally Marshall never rises to the level of courtship: he does not openly declare himself her lover, although by his own account he conveys his attraction to her clearly and repeatedly. The importance of that association in the story the diary tells depends precisely on its failure to develop into an open wooing and on the meaning of that failure to Ryder. The reader may think the young man's feelings largely trumped up. He seems to talk himself into being in love; he wants others to notice his state, playing the part of lover as self-consciously as he did the role of deep thinker. At intervals he talks himself out of it as well, although only for brief periods. But being in love, courting a woman, from his point of view constitutes a significant developmental stage, a marker on the road to full manhood. At one point he reports a revealing dream. "I dreamt I was married to a young lady, bedded her, and the next morning found myself in the greatest hurry and confusion of mind in the world, longing to be unmarried, in which trouble I awaked. I fell asleep again and dreamt I was married to another young lady and enjoyed her and then repented again with the same or greater trouble and concern of mind" (24 Sep. 1716; 335–36). Ryder does not comment, except to emphasize the intensity of the "trouble and perplexity, . . . uneasiness and remorse" that he experienced (336). He has never felt these emotions more fully, he says, in his waking hours.

The diarist records these dreams immediately after a conversation with his cousin Joseph, who also professes himself in love with Sally Marshall. The two young men first vie in proclaiming their passion, then declare their love "a very foolish vain thing that proceeded from an impotency of mind and ought not to be encouraged" (335). At the very least, the diarist feels ambivalent about Sally and about the idea of marriage. But the approach to courtship constitutes a challenge, and his inability to persuade Sally even to take him seriously marks for him his inability to figure as he would wish on the social scene. When he tries to fill the role of dashing young man about town, he only registers his own insufficiency. The sense of that insufficiency dominates the year's diary and controls its story.

The raw material for a different story exists in the text, unemphasized by its writer. It consists in his notations on reading and his political commentary. The latter displays more partisan passion than wisdom. Ryder, committed to the Whig cause, applauds all severities toward Jacobite sympathizers, readily believes allegations of conspiracy, and frequently declares his allegiance to King George. The almost daily remarks on books, in contrast, reveal a remarkable degree of judicious discrimination. Not only does Ryder read widely and consistently; he thinks about what he reads. He seeks knowledge of human nature but remains sensitive to stylistic effects. He does not accept as given the merits of even classical texts. Instead, he finds for himself the distinctive virtues (and defects) of every author. The determination and the range of his reading, as well as his ability and willingness to comment on that reading, provide evidence of a strong mind capable of focusing profitably outside itself. In conjunction with the demonstrated intensity of political feeling, such qualities make Ryder's subsequent public career plausible—even, perhaps, predictable.

But twenty-first-century readers have the benefit of hindsight in interpreting an eighteenth-century text. Ryder himself, lacking supernatural foresight, glimpses the possibility of another story of himself, another aspiration than that of being a "modern gentleman." After one of his many unsuccessful encounters with "the ladies," this time at Aunt Bickley's, he feels, as usual, "very much dissatisfied" with himself. He goes on to wonder:

> Why cannot I be satisfied with the character of a man of sense and enjoy myself without the trifling inconsiderable reputation of a good tattler with a woman or a fine gentleman among the ladies? What I am now aiming at, the character of agreeable company to the women, when I have got it can be enjoyed by me but a little while, to lose the relish of it at last by matrimony. But yet I am strangely prejudiced in favor of this pleasure and I cannot tell how to exclude it out of my present ideas or prospect of happiness. (12 Apr. 1716; 228)

A different character—that of "man of sense"—would imply a different story. Ryder here implicitly acknowledges his possession of the qualities defining such a character. His question implies that he already can claim the "character" of sense; he wants a "character" he does not have. Because he does not have and cannot achieve it, he must tell the story of his own inadequacy. Or perhaps the sense of inadequacy itself dictates the need to aspire for what he cannot attain.

In any case, the story of the private, interior life here set down concentrates on self-doubt. That self-doubt implicates itself intricately with the matter of appearances. If novels of the period indicate that control of appearances protected privacy, especially for women, Ryder's diary suggests that the reflections of privacy can concentrate heavily on the matter of appearance. The writer maintains a lucid awareness of the difference between appearance and substance. He comments, for instance, that he has learned to avoid the appearance of peevishness, but that this is not enough—he must discover how to stop feeling peevish. Yet he connects "pleasure" with the successful manipulation of appearance, which he apparently considers the central operation of life in the world. His subsequent public career drew on qualities that he "really" possessed: intellectual acuity and political energy. One can only wonder whether he considered himself also to have mastered the art of appearance. In any case, the diary of his youth dramatizes the tensions that may control the realm of privacy, its narrative brilliantly evoking a dynamic of self-doubt.

Frances Burney, one of the century's best-known diarists, reveals an intense and intensifying interest in narrative—but the story her diaries most obviously tell does not focus on herself. Those diaries for the most part seem closer to memoir than to autobiography. A little unnervingly, Burney's self-rendering sounds exactly the same when she writes presumably for her own eyes alone (or, as she puts it initially, for "Nobody") and when she sends accounts of herself and her life to the father-figure Samuel Crisp or to her sister Susanna. In the introduction to volume 2 of the ongoing edition of Burney's *Early Journal and Letters*, Lars Troide notes that the diarist frequently "composed parallel accounts" of social evenings for her journals and her letters to Crisp. Since the "two versions of a given evening substantially overlap," he continues, Troide has chosen the longer or earlier version of the accounts, using notes to add supplementary details from the alternative narrative (Burney, *Early* 2:xi). Journal entries and letters thus intermix in the current edition. Aside from the salutations to letters, nothing in the text reveals whether diary or letter provides the immediate source.

The common critical assumption that the writer's sense of a specific audience shapes epistolary prose thus appears to have no bearing on Burney's literary effects. The interchangeability of genres raises questions about the implied audience of the journals, casts a new light on Burney's well-known invocation of "Nobody" as that audience (perhaps "Nobody" wears a face like Samuel Crisp's?), and may make one wonder whether the notion of privacy has any relevance at all to this particular undertaking. If a letter to "Daddy" Crisp isn't exactly "public," neither is it a spontaneous effusion. Nor is the diary that such letters often parallel.

At the beginning of her youthful journals particularly, Burney lays considerable stress on their privacy. Words like *private* and *secret* recur, as she explains her choice of "Nobody" as confidante by pointing out that "To Nobody can I be wholly unreserved—to Nobody can I reveal every thought, every wish of my Heart, with the most unlimited confidence, the most unremitting sincerity to the end of my Life!" (Burney, *Early* 1:2). When she leaves a page of the journal on a chest and her father appropriates it, the young woman expresses great alarm. She emphasizes the authenticity of her self-expression: "How truly does this Journal contain my real & undisguised thoughts—I always write in it according to the humour I am in, & if any stranger was to think it worth reading, how capricious—insolent & whimsical I must appear—one moment flighty & half mad,—the next sad & melancholy. No matter! it's truth & simplicity are it's sole recommendations" (1:61). Already, though (the entry dates from 1769; Burney was seventeen), the young writer vividly imagines the "stranger" who might read her journal and assess her on the basis of what she has written.

By 1774 and 1775, the journal has increasingly adopted a narrative structure, offering sketches of people, dialogue, and event that foretell the novels yet to come. Its writer's "real & undisguised thoughts" may emerge by indirection, but they no longer provide the primary material of her record. To entertain "Daddy" Crisp, Burney sets down the details of her social experience. If she practices her narrative in the pages of her journal, she often apparently practices for the journal in her letters. No longer can one find evidence of capriciousness on the page; no longer do "truth & simplicity" appear the primary criteria for inclusion. Truth, perhaps. But one easily detects the hand of the literary artificer in the construction of scenes and stories.

Here, for example, is a bit of Burney's long account of an evening in the company of James Bruce, the African traveler who disappointed the duchess of Northumberland by his white feather, his smooth chin, and his polite but not entertaining conversation:

> Haughty by Nature, his extraordinary Travels, & perhaps his long Residence among savages, have contributed to render him one of the most imperious of men. He is, indeed, far the most so of any that *I* ever saw.
>
> He is more than six foot high, is extremely well proportioned in shape, & has a handsome & expressive Face. If his *vanity* is half as great as his *pride*, he would certainly become more courteous if he knew how much smiles become him, for when he *is* pleased to soften the severity of his Countenance, & to suffer his Features to relax into smiling, he is quite another Creature, & looks indeed very handsome. (2:82)

Like the duchess, Burney focuses her attention mainly on Bruce's appearance. The duchess, detailing her expectations of the explorer, and her disappointment, uses her account of her visitor as a way of expressing her own feelings about social convention and social routine. Burney, in contrast, interests herself in appearance as a register of character. She invites the reader's attention to Bruce as a figure functioning in society, not someone significant only in relation to her. She renders him as she might represent a character in fiction, giving him a single strong personality trait (his "imperious" nature), then suggesting the possibility of conflict between the pride that expresses itself in imperiousness and the gentler feelings hinted when he relaxes into smiling.

The entry containing this description of Bruce is dated 4 March 1775. An editorial footnote explains that Burney repeats the same account in a letter to Crisp, written jointly with her father, in late March. She has, in short, already polished the narrative to her satisfaction. It reveals almost nothing of her feelings about Bruce: he is the most imperious man she has encountered, but she does not tell us how that fact affects her. Much earlier in her journal, writing about its authenticity, "truth & simplicity," she claims the record's function as artificial memory. "I doubt not but I shall hereafter receive great pleasure from *reviewing* and almost *renewing* my youth & my former sentiments" (1:61). But the characterization of Bruce does not directly convey any "sentiments" at all. It conveys, rather, Burney's increasingly assertive role as writer, controlling reality by setting it down. Written as a journal entry, the passage could, without change, function as well in a letter to a much older male friend—a letter also read by her father. And one can readily imagine it without change in a published essay on Bruce. Only in the sense that it emanates, as writing must, from a particular consciousness does this seem a record of privacy.

A more complicated instance of Burney's distancing through artifice concerns an event of intimate importance to her: the courtship of Thomas Barlow, apparently endorsed by her father and by various female relatives as well as by "Daddy" Crisp, but decisively rejected by Burney herself. Here, if anywhere, one might expect a view of the writer's inner reality. Instead, the young woman both reports and enacts a series of performances. Lars Troide rightly notes the "novelistic quality" of the narration (2:14). The kind of novel it evokes is quite specifically a Burney novel: a work concerned with the intricacies of social pressure and response from the point of view of a female protagonist.

As Burney reports the events, she suffers not the slightest conflict, except in relation to the possibility of contravening her father's wishes. If he wants her to marry Barlow, she will, she knows, be unable to resist a paternal injunction. But Charles Burney does not go so far. He urges his daughter not to give her suitor his final dismissal before coming to know him better, but the young woman feels no doubts. She has met Barlow on a social occasion. Almost immediately afterward, he sends her an ardent letter. She wishes unequivocally to reject his overtures, but her father insists that she leave the letter unanswered. Crisp writes an urgent warning about the dangers of preferring rakes to solid fellows like Barlow, and the yet more emphatic dangers of the single woman: "Consider the situation of an unprotected, unprovided Woman" (2:123). A second letter from Barlow succeeds the first, and an unanticipated and embarrassing visit. Burney dismisses Barlow with an unambiguous rejection of his suit, but he comes back yet once more, determined to convey his adoration. This time, the object of his affections treats him with conventional coldness. Finally he disappears for good.

From the beginning of her courtship narrative (in her "private" journal, not in letters), Burney adopts a tone and manner of high artifice. The first entry (8 May 1775) begins with a general observation:

> This month is Called a *tender* one—It has proved so *to* me—but not *in* me—
> I have not breathed one sigh,—felt one sensation,—or uttered one folly the
> more for the softness of the season.—However—I have met with a youth
> whose Heart, if he is to be Credited, has been less guarded—indeed it has
> yielded itself so suddenly, that had it been in any other month—I should not
> have known how to have accounted for so easy a Conquest. (2:115)

Her tone as well as her utterance declares her heart-whole. Mocking both her would-be lover and the very idea of love at first sight, she possibly betrays slight pride at her own resistance but no other kind of feeling.

Although Burney's tone changes, her veneer never cracks during the protracted account of the Barlow episode. The aspect of the affair that arouses emotion in her involves the pressure of her family. "They all of them are kindly interested in my welfare; but they know not so well as myself what may make me happy or miserable. To unite myself for Life to a man who is not *infinitely* dear to me, is what I can never, never Consent to" (2:120). She dramatizes her resistance and the feeling that underlies it. "I had no *argumentative* objections to make to Mr Barlow, his Character—Disposition—situation—I knew nothing against—but O!—I felt he was no Companion for my Heart!—I wept like an Infant—Eat nothing—seemed as if already married" (2:146–47). Seven years before, at the age of sixteen, she had confessed to her journal "that I scarse [*sic*] wish for any thing so truly, really & greatly, as to be in *love*" (1:10). She would be content, she elaborates, to love without return; she wants the emotion itself. At twenty-three, she appears not to have changed her mind. Her performance on the page, with its dramatic insistence, echoes the dramatic actions of rejecting food and weeping like a baby. Without doubting the genuineness of the feeling expressed, one may yet note how emphatically she uses that feeling for rhetorical effect, both orally and in her written rendition.

Her actions, like her written account, rely on the extremes of self-protecting and self-dramatizing artifice. With Barlow himself, by her report, she employs a range of social maneuvers. To his pleading, she responds, "you know there are many odd Characters in the World—& I am one of them" (2:143). Barlow replies with painful sincerity, but Burney continues to mock: "'I give you leave, Sir,' cried I, laughing, 'to think me singular—odd—Queer—nay, even whimsical, if you please'" (2:143). When he returns for another visit, she curtseys and refuses to sit down or to speak until spoken to. Even when another guest arrives, she remains standing, so that she need not ask Mr. Barlow to take a seat. She regrets her rudeness, she says, but he might "draw *Inferences*" from more friendly behavior (2:152). To her father, at the opposite extreme, she exclaims, "O Sir! . . .—*I* wish for Nothing!—only let me Live with you!" (2:147). In both instances, she achieves the desired effect. Barlow goes away, never to return, frozen by her icy social manner; and her father, persuaded by her verbal extravagance, stops urging her to entertain a suitor.

As a writer in her journal, then, Burney employs linguistic maneuvering that corresponds to the maneuvering available in the vast repertoire of decorum for social behavior. As the protagonists of her novels hide their inner being with a screen of flawless manners, so she, in the most private of literary forms, employs various kinds of convention to keep her privacy intact. Although one may deduce a good deal about Burney from reading her journals, these documents do not function as open windows on the soul. On the contrary, the windows all have, at the very least, Venetian blinds.

The vexed textual history of Burney's journals emphasizes their self-protectiveness. If the early journals were originally written only for the eye of "Nobody" (and one may note, in the context, the high artifice of that creation of Nobody), by late in her life Frances Burney D'Arblay foresaw the publication of her personal record. She went through the entire accumulation of many years, blacking out indiscreet words, phrases, and sentences (including even such expletives as "good God!" that appear abundantly in *Evelina*), rewriting or adding to portions originally written long before, and cutting away many pages. Modern textual editing has rescued a great deal, although the cut out pages have vanished. But Burney's intent to guard her interior life is manifest in the "lacquer of prudent after-thoughts" with which she overlays her private writing (*Early* 3:xv).

Stuart Sherman comments about Burney's extensive and belated self-editing, "Burney's excisions have often been read as a last instance of her fearfulness and prudery, but within the long complex history of her writing life they seem to me rather to constitute a final assertion of autonomy and authorial power" (272). Autonomy and power are concomitants of privacy; Burney claims them late in her life, although she could rarely achieve them earlier. She had from her youth, though, dramatized her own ambivalence about privacy. *Evelina* achieved instantaneous success in 1778, both critical and popular, and its author could only feel pleased. But she felt also intense alarm at the possibility that the world would know her as author. In an early episode—one of many comparable events—she reacts to a note from Samuel Johnson's friend Anna Williams that reveals Mrs. Williams's knowledge. "I instantly scrawled a hasty Letter to Town, to entreat my Father would be so good as to write to her, to acquaint her with my earnest & unaffected desire to remain unknown, & so to prevent, at least any *further* propagation of this my poor mauled to pieces secret" (3:62). The earnest and unaffected desire to remain unknown wars with the desire to make herself known. One can discern both impulses in the journal.

The four diaries here considered obviously do not exhaust the range of possibilities for the eighteenth-century diary as genre. They do, however, suggest a variety of ways for writers to use a private form to protect their privacy. One may surmise different motives for the writing of each of these self-records. Woodforde validates a repetitious, unexciting, and largely uneventful existence by setting down its details; the duchess of Northumberland asserts her own significance by holding onto her judgments and knowledge. Writing in shorthand, Dudley Ryder can afford to meditate about his thoughts and feelings. Frances Burney hones her skills as writer, rendering with increasing precision and wit the many aspects of social existence and making of herself a character in the social drama. As men and women in society manipulate conventions to guard themselves and to attain their ends, so men and women in their diaries devise rhetorics for simultaneous self-assertion and self-concealment.

8 | *Privacy as Enablement*

Much eighteenth-century writing suggests that the value of physical privacy inheres in its defensive function. Pamela and Clarissa retreat to their "closets" in order to protect themselves from physical and psychological violation. Pope begs his man John to shut the door against intruders; Anne Finch petitions for an "absolute retreat" that would evade the frivolities and corruption of the court. In this historical period marked by its official enthusiasm for the "social," many found society at least intermittently threatening. Conditions that under other circumstances might be described as isolation or alienation, figured instead as privacy provide defense and escape. Think, for instance, of Arabella's father in *The Female Quixote*, who retreats from court into pastoral seclusion, condemning his wife and daughter to dangerous separation from the social world, but glorifying for himself the value of shutting out corruption.

The defensive value of privacy is and has been, of course, apparent to others as well as to eighteenth-century British citizens. Describing twentieth-century Eskimo culture, the anthropologist Barrington Moore writes, "On the surface all is harmony and cooperation. Beneath the surface there is a considerable charge of resentment. Privacy thus appears as an escape from the demands and burdens of social interaction" (14). Eskimo society provides an example of social organization sharply different from Great Britain's, but the perception of "demands and burdens" implicit in human association can manifest itself even in a world largely controlled by the assumed value of such association.

Eighteenth-century thinkers glorified the social. Lord Shaftesbury, for instance, inquires rhetorically, "WHO is there can well or long enjoy any thing, when *alone*, and abstracted perfectly, even in his very Mind and Thought, from every thing belonging to Society?" (2.2.204; 80). Society is essential to all enjoyment, Shaftesbury concludes, and he knows that "Whoever is unsociable, and voluntarily shuns Society, or Commerce with the world, must of necessity be morose and ill-natur'd" (2.2.215; 85). Yet the impulse to shun such commerce becomes apparent both in architectural and in literary terms.

Aristocrats gained increasing privacy, in the form of increasing amounts of space assigned to the individual, but servants continued to hover around them, making genuine seclusion difficult to achieve. Most of the population enjoyed even less privacy than aristocrats found available. If "servants had been moved out of the way" in country houses (Girouard 11), that meant only that large numbers of attendants no longer inhabited every space where the family might congregate. Servants continued to preside over domestic affairs. I use deliberately ambiguous phrasing here: they "presided" in the sense that the housekeeper and butler and steward organized every large household's operations, but also because they knew everything that went on in the household—not only what was spent, what purchased, what consumed, but what the master and mistress, and probably their sons and daughters, thought and felt and did.

In the country houses, enormous staffs of servants functioned as much for conspicuous display as for actual service. They stood around; they listened. In the metropolis, "owing to the impersonality of urban society, the visible indications of social position assumed a greater consequence than in the country" (Hecht 3). As a consequence, domestic retinues in great families were typically even larger. But not only great families had servants. Peter Laslett points out, startlingly, that between 1574 and 1821, servants were "a feature of almost one-quarter of the households of a category as low as . . . tradesmen and craftsmen, in the centre of the social scale, and that some labourers . . . had servants" (153). In the developing middle classes, *everyone* had servants. When, in *Sense and Sensibility*, the utterly impoverished family of Dashwood women move their household, they take along two servants: clearly a minimum for gentility.

In small and modest households as in large and grand ones, servants watched and listened—and knew a great deal about family affairs. The consistency with which servants' manuals recommend discretion, keeping the family secrets to oneself, reveals the universal assumption that servants would know such secrets. An early-nineteenth-century example of the genre offers special warnings to the valet (who "is much about his master's person, and has the opportunity of hearing his off-at-hand opinions on many subjects" [Adams 136]) and the hall porter. The porter's "best qualities are patience and good temper, to which may be added, secrecy in regard to the affairs, connections, and intercourse of the family. A close tongue, and an inflexible countenance, are, therefore, indispensable, and he should practise the maxim of hearing and seeing all, but saying nothing" (Adams 150). Eliza Haywood, writing in 1743, is equally emphatic in warning against "discover[ing] the Affairs of the Family where you live. The smallest and most trivial Action *there* should never escape your Lips, because you cannot be a Judge what are really such, and what are the contrary. Things that may seem to you Matters of perfect Indifference, may happen to prove of great Importance to those concerned in them" (13). Anthony Heasel, in his 1773 tract, *The Servants Book of Knowledge*, invokes biblical authority for similar warnings. "When a servant keeps tattling up and down every occurrence in the family, it often brings dishonour on his master. . . . It is also a very great sin, and one of the breaches of the fifth commandment; for as we are commanded to honour our parents, so it is necessarily implied that we also honour and respect all those who have authority over us" (quoted in Hecht 75).

J. Jean Hecht draws the obvious conclusion from this kind of data: "To a certain extent the probing eyes and attentive ears of the servant . . . imposed on his master an onerous constraint" (207). At every class level above the lowest, men and women, even when technically "alone" in their homes, might well feel constrained, devoid of genuine physical privacy. In the light of such facts, the persistent convention of poems about the delight of rural solitude assumes new meaning. Milton's *Il Penseroso* provided a model for numerous subsequent poems of praise for melancholy and its solitary wandering. Equally conventional, and almost equally popular, was versified encomium of some such locale as John Dyer's "Grongar Hill," where a poet might imagine the experience of isolated contemplation. One of Pope's earliest poems (he claims to have written it at the age of twelve) is an "Ode on Solitude." It begins,

> Happy the man, whose wish and care
> A few paternal acres bound,
> Content to breathe his native air,
> In his own ground,

and concludes,

> Thus let me live, unseen, unknown;
> Thus unlamented let me dye;
> Steal from the world, and not a stone
> Tell where I lye.

It is difficult to imagine that the adolescent poet (probably several years older than twelve) actually felt such desires, but the sentiments would have been readily available to him in many printed sources.

Implicitly or explicitly, poetry of this sort suggests that the value of living unseen and unknown depends on the contrast between this state and the ordinary existence of the Englishman or -woman: seen and known by many, surrounded by more and less visible observers. Like the father in *The Female Quixote*, poets reiterated this theme. They are not, to be sure, centrally concerned with the intrusiveness of servants; yet in a more general sense they persistently suggest that privacy matters for essentially negative reasons: for what it is not, what it keeps at bay. It keeps at bay more than servants: a common version of poetic convention emphasizes the value of country privacy as an alternative to urban community and corruption. The convention probably derives ultimately from Horace, but seventeenth- and eighteenth-century English poets, recognizing its applicability to the immediate political situation, revivified it. A sonnet by William Drummond of Hawthornden condenses into fourteen lines the essential elements of many poems from his own time and later:

> Thrice happy he, who by some shady grove,
> Far from the clamorous world, doth live his own;
> Though solitary, who is not alone,
> But doth converse with that eternal love.
> Oh how more sweet is birds' harmonious moan,
> Or the hoarse sobbings of the widowed dove,
> Than those smooth whisperings near a prince's throne,
> Which good make doubtful, do the evil approve!
> Oh how more sweet is zephyr's wholesome breath,
> And sighs embalmed, which new-born flow'rs unfold,
> Than that applause vain honour doth bequeath!
> How sweet are streams to poison drunk in gold!
>   The world is full of horrors, troubles, slights,
>   Woods' harmless shades have only true delights.
>   (Sonnet 22, in Fowler)

The systematic contrasts between a world full of horrors and a seclusion that protects against those horrors, supplying instead the pleasures of a highly conventionalized nature, justify the choice of solitude. The man who "doth live his own"—who feels in possession of his own soul, unthreatened by applause, poison, or the varied forms of worldly temptation—can readily give up the pleasures of company in favor of silent communion with "eternal love." The poem makes its points elegantly and economically, but the predictability of its phrasing ("vain honour," "harmless shades") emphasizes the degree to which it draws on a preceding body of poetry for its ideas as well as its expression. Neither its evocation of the troubling world nor its account of the zephyr-filled country carries any sense of personal immediacy.

These comments imply no negative judgment of Drummond's sonnet. Its effectiveness depends precisely on its reminders of a long verse tradition, with the implicit corollary that corrupt courts and harmonious birds have existed over the centuries. One can draw on historical knowledge in making the choice of seclusion, or of writing about seclusion. But is seclusion the same as privacy? Perhaps not. Since privacy in its essence depends on personal choice and personal experience, the poetry of convention, however expert, however moving even, arguably cannot evoke it.

Robert Burton's great seventeenth-century *Anatomy of Melancholy* includes a summary poem that actually uses the word *privacy*—uses it to express extreme ambivalence:

> Friends and companions get you gone,
> 'Tis my desire to be alone,
> Ne'er well but when my thoughts and I
> Do domineer in privacy.
> No gem, no treasure like to this:
> 'Tis my delight, my crown, my bliss.
> > All my joys to this are folly,
> > Naught so sweet as melancholy.

> 'Tis my sole plague to be alone:
> I am a beast, a monster grown;
> I will no light nor company,
> I find it now my misery.
> The scene is turned, my joys are gone,
> Fear, discontent and sorrows come.
> > All my griefs to this are jolly,
> > Naught so fierce as melancholy.
> > > ("The Author's Abstract of Melancholy," in Fowler 65–80)

The association between privacy and melancholy hardly constitutes a new idea, but Burton skillfully epitomizes the ambiguity of that association. Which is cause, which effect? Melancholy seeks privacy as indulgence; privacy, though chosen, proves malignant, generating its own melancholy. Yet even the "positive" side of privacy, its gratification of desire, carries a hint of danger in the idea of "my thoughts and I" *domineering* in privacy. There is something unnatural in the rejection of community, some risk of excessive self-valuation and self-gratification. Human beings may wish to be alone but possibly should not indulge such wishes—as potentially dangerous as other forms of untrammeled desire.

Burton's rollicking meter implicitly comments on all the instances he cites as examples of human folly. Readers are not invited to take the desire to be alone or the pain of being alone with excessive seriousness, any more than they are encouraged to linger over any of the other alternating patterns of the poem. The combination of penetrating insight with faint mockery marks the intellectual brilliance of an apparently offhand poetic utterance. From the point of view of the poem, human psychology is various, complicated, inconsistent, and at once interesting and ludicrous. Although the poet speaks in the first person, he does not seem deeply involved in any of the experience he claims. He distances himself rhetorically from the self he describes.

I cite these seventeenth-century examples to suggest a broad literary context for later poetry of privacy. That context reflects psychological as well as social actualities: not the literal presence of servants so much as the broad and vague personal consequences of that presence; and not necessarily immediate experience so much as poetic tradition. Drummond evokes country isolation as conventional defense; Burton suggests emotional reasons both for choosing and for rejecting privacy. Neither conveys or endeavors to convey intense personal commitment to the existence of separation from society at large. Neither attempts to explore the value of privacy as a life choice. The great poet of privacy would not appear until late in the eighteenth century. William Cowper, in *The Task*, both specifies and investigates a range of meanings for privacy conceived as a personal choice with extensive implications. He claims for this choice positive value extending beyond either self-defense or self-indulgence, suggesting that privacy allows for kinds of experience that cannot take place in other circumstances. His commitment to privacy as a way of life and of writing both shapes his poem and provides a good deal of its subject matter.

The special achievement of *The Task* can be cogently defined in terms of the poem's celebration of a precisely located kind of privacy. The long, miscellaneous blank verse poem was not in itself a new idea. Cowper's most illustrious predecessor in the form, James Thomson, who enlarged *The Seasons* over the course of twenty years, dealt with at least as many different subjects, and as wide a range of subjects, as did Cowper. But the poetic effects achieved by *The Seasons* and *The Task* differ enormously, partly because of the different ways in which the two poets insert themselves into their poems.

Cowper describes a country existence rich not only in zephyrs but in such mundane crops as cucumbers, which need to be manured. He speaks of weeds as well as flowers, of harsh weather and balmy. He writes also of the urban life he has abandoned, of its enticements and particularly its corruptions. And he employs himself specifically in the character of someone actively engaged in the process of writing. Although, like Thomson, he allows himself magisterial pronouncements on such matters as slavery, government, religion, and the South Sea Islands, he finds ways to keep reminding his readers that these pronouncements issue from a mind situated in particular ways. *Privacy* is not a term he uses, but the situation he rather elaborately and insistently describes depends on a highly particularized kind of privacy, important not only for what it excludes (although that too) but mainly for what it enables.

In literal terms, the poet's privacy exists quite outside the realm of servants and mostly outside that of architecture. He delineates himself as wanderer, peripatetic inhabitant of the landscape; as contemplator, resident primarily of a mental world that is by its very nature one of privacy; and as suffering soul, primarily concerned with his private relation to God. These aspects of his situation—his freedom to exist in the natural world, his reliance on the vagaries of his inner life, and his commitment to the service of God—enable his creativity. So, too, does what he calls his "domesticity." These comprise dramatically different aspects of privacy.

Earlier poets had on occasion suggested that the state of privacy, largely by virtue of what I have called its negative aspects, what it shuts out, could facilitate mental exploration and thus, by implication, poetic production. So Pope, imitating Horace (Epistle 2.2), could write,

> Soon as I enter at my Country door,
> My Mind resumes the thread it dropt before;
> Thoughts, which at Hyde-Park-Corner I forgot,
> Meet and rejoin me, in the pensive Grott.
> There all alone, and Compliments apart,
> I ask these sober questions of my Heart.
>
> (205–10)

He asks, and he receives answers. The kind of thinking he can do in rural solitude registers as morally superior to that possible in Hyde Park.

Cowper makes larger claims, more complicated and more indirect. He begins with mock-heroic specification of the "task" he has been assigned:

"I sing the Sofa." He writes, he explains, because "the Fair commands the song" (7); he writes on this unlikely subject after having most recently composed verse on the subjects of Truth, Hope, and Charity. This preamble introduces a hundred-odd lines offering a mock-heroic history of the sofa's development, then moving into praise for the sofa as a place for repose. But at line 103, the poet abandons the sofa as subject and diverges into Wordsworthian reminiscence of boyhood rambles. That topic leads to reflection on his present pleasure in the natural world and to invocation of his "dear companion" (144), Mary Unwin. The speaker requests her to serve as witness of his authenticity:

> Thou know'st my praise of nature most sincere,
> And that my raptures are not conjur'd up
> To serve occasions of poetic pomp,
> But genuine, and art partner of them all.
>
> (150–53)

From this point on, *The Task* appears to be organized by a process of free association.

Only in retrospect, after engaging more fully with the consciousness the poet represents, can one realize the full importance of this opening sequence. As a matter of biographical fact, we know that Lady Austin rescued Cowper from a state of intense depression, in which he found poetic composition impossible, by assigning him the arbitrary topic of the sofa. The spirit of the poem, at least at its beginning, though, has no apparent connection with depression. On the contrary, a sense of playful freedom permeates the early part of the first book. Expatiating on the sofa is obviously a joke of sorts. Evoking the natural world is quite the reverse. An atmosphere of excitement hovers around both poetic activities: excitement dependent on the fact that both are possible, that anything is possible, that the poet has found his liberty to say what he will. And that is exactly what he does: he says whatever he will. The moment of doubt that leads him to call on Mary Unwin for corroborating testimony does not linger. Not even the break of a verse paragraph intervenes before Cowper is speaking directly, with no need for corroboration, about the breeze and the view from a hill of which he is fond.

As the poem proceeds, the speaker specifies in various ways the nature of his social and psychological environment. He reports being charmed by a peaceful cottage in an isolated recess, where he could imagine possessing "The poet's treasure, silence" (235), enabled to "indulge / The dreams of fancy, tranquil and secure (235–36). But almost immediately he repudiates the idea of residence there, realizing the physical inconveniences of such life. "If solitude make scant the means of life," he concludes, "Society for me!" (248–49). The cottage may remain material for fantasy, but he will not long to live there. Later in book 1, he glorifies the situation of one "who dwells secure" (593), his admittedly numerous wants readily supplied, given his "temp'rate wishes and industrious hands" (599). He depicts himself consistently as a moderate man of moderate desires, existing in a situation that satisfies him.

The beginning of book 3 brings a few lines of praise for "Domestic happiness," characterized as "thou only bliss / Of Paradise that has surviv'd the fall!" (41–42). The poet does not, however, at this point specify the nature of the happiness he celebrates. Instead, he digresses into a diatribe about one of its alternatives. Those not committed to domesticity, in his account, fall into prostitution. But prostitution itself symbolizes broader forms of corruption, endemic throughout England in crowded social situations. Oddly—or perhaps, in the deep logic of the poem not oddly at all—this subject leads directly to the well-known "stricken deer" passage, in which the speaker characterizes himself as a wounded animal rescued by Christ. Emphasis rests on the contrast between the destructive environment of the "herd" and the relative solitude that succeeds the poet's salvation:

> Since then, with few associates, in remote
> And silent woods I wander, far from these
> My former partners of the peopled scene;
> With few associates, and not wishing more.
> Here much I ruminate, as much I may,
> With other views of men and manners now
> Than once, and others of a life to come.
>
> (117–22)

These lines in effect lay out the rationale for *The Task* as a whole. Authority for the poem's commentary on political, religious, and social actualities inheres in the commentator's comparative isolation, the fact that he resides outside the social scene. His state of privacy is virtually by definition one of insight. Uncompromised by association, far from old alliances, illuminated by clear religious commitment, he can "view" men and manners with the perspective of distance. His wandering in the woods corresponds to his wandering on the page, from topic to topic as his consciousness dictates. He finds himself in a position to "ruminate" and to remark, precisely because he no longer suffers the distractions of society.

Such a formulation of the sources of poetic power recurs in the course of *The Task*. Cowper intermittently reiterates the point that the situation of outsider, the situation of seclusion, constitutes the ideal position from which to observe and criticize. Observation and criticism, as it turns out, define his "task" as it develops. He makes the point especially clear early in book 4, as he specifies more fully the nature of the domesticity he endorses and of its value. The domestic scene includes a glowing fire and an urn of tea, but also shutters fast closed against the world. In such a scene, one can "welcome peaceful ev'ning in" (41). The quality of peace promptly gets defined by its opposite—the crowded theater, or the equally crowded scene of public speaking. In contrast, the shared tea at the fireside in the shuttered room requires no performance, supplies no spectators, and entails no noise.

In this idyllic context, the speaker reads the newspaper. He finds there a record of the chaos implied by what Wordsworth would call the accumulation of men in cities—"Cat'racts of declamation," "forests of no meaning" (73, 74), a confusion of advertisements and of subject matter ("Sermons, and city feasts, and fav'rite airs, / Aethereal journies, submarine exploits" [84–85]) that epitomize the confusion of the social world the poet vigorously rejects. As he formulates his position in relation to this disorder of information, he once more declares the importance of his role as outsider. He feels himself elevated to a "more than mortal height" (96), from which he surveys the tumult and remains still. He gleans information where information is to be had and partakes vicariously of adventure—"While fancy, like the finger of a clock, / Runs the great circuit, and is still at home" (118–19). At this point, the speaker appears altogether identified with his fancy, through which he travels, experiences, and investigates; with which he remains at home. Chaos becomes order in his experience of it. Like the finger of a clock, his fancy records the passage of time (the time of his own domesticity, but also that of the world's excitement) in predictable and regular fashion. No danger threatens the elevated observer, whose position allows him both to know and to judge, even to take pleasure in the knowledge of what he actually condemns.

The poem's incorporation of such passages as this, in which its voice becomes grounded and located, contributes importantly to the intimate sense of personality that *The Task* evokes, a note differentiating it from its poetic predecessors and suggesting the qualities that would make it admired throughout the nineteenth century. Without making his personal feelings part of his poetic subject, Cowper yet consistently meditates on the nature of his immediate project, and the meditations greatly strengthen his poem. The recurrent subject of "the task," in particular, invites the reader to consider how and why the poem works.

The word *task* occurs so frequently in Cowper's poem that mere tabulation would prove a demanding exercise. To look with some closeness at five extended passages concerning tasks, however, may indicate the subtlety and significance of the poem's reflexivity. The specific tasks at issue in these sequences range from raising cucumbers to writing poetry. No matter what the nature of the individual enterprise, every undertaking makes demands on its performer and reveals aspects of that performer's character.

Like the meditations on the poet's immediate situation that we have just considered, the first of the extended reflections on a task comes embedded in a context of commentary on national issues. It follows a sequence about how Britain has lost national purpose, seeking eminence now in jockeyship rather than in war, and precedes one about the proper use of the pulpit. Wedged between these extended discussions are roughly forty lines about the writing of poetry. They begin with reference to pleasure: "There is a pleasure in poetic pains / Which only poets know" (2.285–86). *Pleasure* mutates into *pleasing*, designating the "occupations of the poet's mind" (299); finally *joys* summarizes the experience of him "that sings" (304). Yet three lines later the verse comments on how "arduous" is the "task" of poetic composition.

The initial juxtaposition of the idea of pleasure with that of "poetic pains" prepares for the apparent disjunction between the notions of poetry as self-indulgence and as hard work. The narrative indicates that the pleasure consists in the work, which is carefully described. This work involves constant pursuit (*chase*, Cowper says) of the right word. The terms the poet seeks resemble flirtations women, "coy, and difficult to win" (289). Or they are like passing images in a mirror, which must be "arrest[ed]," held fast, forced to sit still. Pleasure apparently resides in the power involved in winning, capturing, holding, forcing. This is the power of the poet's labor and skill, which make him resemble a painter, offering faithful likenesses and disposing them in the best possible light.

The pleasure consists in the work, I said. One could argue equally well that the work consists in the pleasure, for the pleasure turns out to serve a difficult and serious purpose. The winning, holding, and so on are occupations

So pleasing, and that steal away the thought
With such address from themes of sad import,
That, lost in his own musings, happy man!

He feels th' anxieties of life, denied
Their wonted entertainment, all retire.

(299–303)

Two kinds of entertainment are at issue: that provided by the activity of
poetry denies entertainment to the anxieties that ordinarily pursue their
own activity in the poet's mind. This third-person poet uses his pleasure to
"steal away" his mental processes. The "chase" after the right word functions secondarily as a pursuit of anxieties. Or perhaps the effort to dispel
anxiety is in fact primary, the effort to find exact terms actually a means to
quite another end.

The task, in other words, proves complicated. It includes, the speaker
summarizes, both dangers and escapes. Neither can be known by the audience for poetry, "Aware of nothing arduous in a task / They never un-
dertook" (307–8). They derive little "amusement" from what most amused
the creator. At this point he turns to the first person:

But is amusement all? Studious of song,
And yet ambitious not to sing in vain,
I would not trifle merely, though the world
Be loudest in their praise who do no more.

(311–14)

And he goes on to consider the power of satire, suggesting that although it
may correct minor foibles, it has no force against vice, no capacity to re-
claim the heart. His endeavor, in other words, will end in futility.

The surprising turns in this verse argument call attention to the
speaker's complex attitudes toward himself and the world he inhabits. Crucial to its various shifts are the assumption that the poet—a term designating both the third-person, generic poet and the particular poet-
speaker—lives apart, happiest when "lost in his own musings," happy
precisely because he can lose himself in musings rather than in external
bustle. The search for poetic form provides a vicarious sexual outlet (those
coy, difficult to win words . . .) and an arena for the exercise of power, both
harmless, even therapeutic. The poet's endeavor converts the world's evil
into good, but it depends on separation. The speaker's attitude toward his
audience, representatives of the world he rejects, partakes of hostility. His
acknowledgment of futility in endeavors to reform others expresses even
more hostility. Yet he needs the rejected realm of "society" to provide subject matter ("ambitious not to sing in vain") and the audience that must acknowledge his effort even though it fails to profit from the poet's pains.

The poet's activity, keeping the world at exactly the proper distance, both flourishes on and preserves his privacy.

In his next extended account of his "task" (3.361–87), Cowper abandons his aggressive tone but stresses his separation even more emphatically, dwelling once more on the urgency of the interior life. "The service of mankind" is his goal, he says (372). This announcement leads not to specification of the nature of his service but to an economical and compelling account of his inner experience.

> He that attends to his interior self,
> That has a heart, and keeps it; has a mind
> That hungers, and supplies it; and who seeks
> A social, not a dissipated life;
> Has business; feels himself engag'd t' achieve
> No unimportant, though a silent, task.
>
> (373–78)

What "business," exactly, does this person have? How does it contribute to "the service of mankind"? The text provides answers to neither of these fundamental questions. The actions of keeping, supplying, and seeking that it specifies suffice, it seems, to testify to a man's virtue, and such virtue by its nature will mysteriously exert a public effect. The poem continues to elaborate a metaphor of pearl diving. Wisdom is the pearl, sought successfully only in clear water, beneath clear skies. If one "is ever occupied in storms" (383), he either will not dive or will find "a disgraceful prize" (384) instead of a pearl.

The storms that might distract the pearl fisher could be external, the tumult of a distracting and hostile world, or internal, the disruption of an unquiet mind. In either case, they eliminate the possibility of finding wisdom. And wisdom is an end in itself. Indeed, the "task" appears to be an end in itself. Its nature hardly matters; only the fact of it matters. The next verse paragraph begins with an image of "the self-sequester'd man / Fresh for his task, intend what task he may" (386–87). His self-sequestering automatically testifies to his right thinking. The speaker's task may be the writing of poetry, but he does not say so here. It may be the service of mankind, but he feels no apparent interest in how he might serve. His acceptance of the obligation to perform a task establishes his right relationship with God.

What I have quoted so far gives a misleading impression of the passage as a whole. In their straightforwardness and clarity, the quoted lines diverge sharply from the mode of the sequence that precedes them. The discussion of the unspecified task begins with a first-person pronoun, in the objective rather than subjective case, and proceeds by means of contorted, almost impenetrable syntax.

> Me, therefore, studious of laborious ease,
> Not slothful; happy to deceive the time,
> Not waste it; and aware that human life
> Is but a loan to be repaid with use,
> When he shall call his debtors to account
> From whom are all our blessings; bus'ness finds
> Ev'n here: while sedulous I seek t' improve,
> At least neglect not, or leave unemploy'd,
> The mind he gave me; driving it, though slack
> Too oft, and much impeded in its work
> By causes not to be divulg'd in vain,
> To its just point.
>
> (361–72)

The grammatical subject of the first clause, suspended for six lines, is "bus'ness." Business finds the speaker; he does not find it. In the context of the preceding financial metaphors of loan and debtors, "bus'ness" seems to have commercial meaning. If it signifies merely occupation, it yet suggests that the speaker's occupation, whatever it may be (and of course it will never be specified), partakes of a transaction of exchange with God. But the essence of the exchange remains mysterious. At the point in the poetic text where business finds him, the speaker can become more direct, declaring himself subject rather than object of the action. Yet this sequence as a whole expresses massive uncertainty about the self. The convoluted syntax conveys the difficulty of expression; the series of qualifications ("At least neglect not . . .") discloses doubt; the division between "I" and "The mind he gave me" indicates a sense of fragmentation. And the passage ends by calling attention to what it fails to disclose, those causes of impediment not to be divulged in vain.

From one point of view, the "task" passage as a whole abounds in self-revelation. We learn of the speaker's self-doubt, and something of its nature. He reiterates his religious commitment in rather precise metaphorical terms. He justifies once more, and most emphatically, his privacy. He asserts his involvement in "the service of mankind," and he specifies the nature of his righteousness, reminds us of his internal impediments, and insists on his constant effort, the effort to drive his mind to the proper point. From another point of view, the passage functions as an exercise in self-concealment, behind torturous syntax, lack of specificity on crucial points (what is the task? what the service?), and deliberate obfuscation (about the nature of those fundamental impediments). It simultaneously insists on faith and conveys doubt. Thus it dramatizes both an almost intolerable internal conflict and the means of confronting it, through religious faith.

Among the poem's various efforts to meditate on the idea of the task, this seems to me one of the most important. Powerfully personal in its statement, it yet draws on the force of generalization. The idea of "the service of mankind" in its refusal to specify insists on the significance of the concept rather than its details; so does the unspecified task, not unimportant though silent. The poet's treasured physical privacy finds a textual equivalent as he both confesses to and tantalizes his audience, revealing just enough, not too much, as he surrounds himself with a select company, just enough, not too much. *The Task*, as it goes on to discuss the anonymous self-sequestered man with any task at all, gives that man a set of physical circumstances and a female companion corresponding exactly to the poet's own. The speaker, in other words, has generalized himself, made himself anonymous, even as he reveals the details of his life.

Given the poem's title, such an extended treatment of the task as this must appear to refer to the enterprise of poetry itself. When Cowper considers, a bit later, the highly specific task of raising cucumbers, he still manages to talk about poetry. This georgic interlude begins with an elevated discussion of manure. It soon announces itself as concerned with a task:

> When now November dark
> Checks vegetation in the torpid plant
> Expos'd to his cold breath, the task begins.
> (3.467–69)

That task involves many details of husbandry—spreading mulch, building a cold frame, planting seed in pots, and so on. The tone of the discussion is faintly comic, with occasional mock-heroic overtones. The product produced by much lavishly narrated labor serves the whims of the rich, yet remains a common fruit. Soft in inception, hard in fruition; simple in nature, yet arduously produced; a "tender trust" for the farmer producing it (561), demanding many expedients and shifts, the cucumber becomes finally a metaphoric equivalent for poetry—indeed, for the particular poem in the process of being written:

The learn'd and wise
Sarcastic would exclaim, and judge the song
Cold as its theme, and, like its theme, the fruit
Of too much labour, worthless when produc'd.

(562–65)

The consciousness of possible, even probable, negative judgment reiterates the poet's suspicion of and aggression toward his imagined audience and reminds the reader once more of the urgency of his privacy. But his task inheres in the labor, not the product. As the previous discussions of the task insist, its specific nature does not matter: one can accept the responsibility of writing a poem about a sofa, or of raising a cucumber, and the responsibility automatically declares its own importance. One must reject debilitating self-doubt about the value of what results from it. The acceptance of obligation in itself declares the human being's appropriate relation to God, appropriate acceptance of his own place in the universe.

The Task ends in a flurry of references to the idea of the task. They elaborate and clarify the implications of the previous discussions. First, the poet discusses the notion that "Man praises man" (6.694), pointing out that encomium once was poet's work, but "The task now falls into the public hand" (718). He himself has chosen a different task:

And I, contented with an humble theme,
Have pour'd my stream of panegyric down
The vale of nature, where it creeps, and winds
Among her lovely works with a secure
And unambitious course.

(719–23)

He will consider the labor of poetry worthwhile, he claims, if his verse improves the lot of animals by making even one person aware of the need for pity.

The insistent modesty of these claims creates an effect of disingenuousness. *The Task* has included much more than the praise of nature, and certainly much more than proclamation of the rights of animals. One may even wonder about its "unambitious course." The poem has in fact engaged with large public subjects and intermittently made large claims, as the poet affirms divine authorization for his pursuit of a task he often imagines in grander terms than those proclaimed here. A few lines later, returning to the idea of the task, he acknowledges more presumptuous hopes. He speaks of divine prophecy, its themes too grand for mortals to touch, and confesses the desire to touch on divine subjects. That desire runs so deep that not to attempt the task, "arduous as he deems / The labour, were a task more arduous still" (757–58). Once more he speaks of himself in the third person, filling the generic role of poet, yet he adumbrates a personal sense of conflict between the yearning to testify to the divine dispensation and the sense of inadequacy to the task. This task, however, he goes on to perform, in a splendid outpouring of biblical paraphrase and visionary exaltation.

The poem's peroration moves from the vision of earth-made-heaven to a final summary of earth's existing corruption. Then comes an account of the "happy man," whose situation, we will by now not be surprised to find, involves "an obscure but tranquil state" (908). The world overlooks him, but in quite a different sense he overlooks the world, provided with the special perspective of his exclusion. He claims no public achievements, no trophies. He lives in nature; "His warfare is within" (935). He triumphs over himself, while the world ignores him. Yet perhaps that world depends on him for its very survival. His solitary prayer may generate the sunshine and rain, the spring and harvest. He serves his country by his virtue; his role is important.

> The man, whose virtues are more felt than seen,
> Must drop indeed the hope of public praise;
> But he may boast what few that win it can—
> That if his country stand not by his skill,
> At least his follies have not wrought her fall.
>
> (972–76)

This exemplary man stands alone. If the lack of concrete detail in his evocation makes him appear generic, the insistence of his virtue and the suggestion of his power over weather and seasons establishes him as unique. Nothing in the text explicitly claims identification between this personage and the poet himself, but the emphasis on his separation from the world, the insistence on the humbleness of his station and his lack of ambition, the claim of his position as "author of no mischief and some good" (953)—such elements in the extended account of this figure directly recapitulate aspects of the poet's reiterated self-characterization. For all his determined modesty, the poet finally implies large claims for himself: claims essentially of sainthood.

Of course he does not make such claims explicit. He concludes his poem, though, with a final reference to "the task" that quite openly argues the importance of his accomplishment. The poet first imagines his own death, then comments:

> It shall not grieve me, then, that once, when call'd
> To dress a Sofa with the flow'rs of verse,
> I play'd awhile, obedient to the fair,
> With that light task; but soon, to please her more,
> Whom flow'rs alone I knew would little please,
> Let fall th' unfinish'd wreath, and rov'd for fruit;
> Rov'd far, and gather'd much.
>
> (1006–12)

The fruit he gathers may taste harsh, but those that can taste immortal truth will appreciate it.

> But all is in his hand whose praise I seek.
> In vain the poet sings, and the world hears,
> If he regard not; though divine the theme,
> 'Tis not in artful measures, in the chime
> And idle tinkling of a minstrel's lyre,
> To charm his ear, whose eye is on the heart;
> Whose frown can disappoint the proudest strain,
> Whose approbation—prosper even mine.
>
> (1017–24)

These concluding passages, beginning with the evocation of the saintly solitary man and continuing through the explicit discussion of the writer's poetic task, insist, directly and indirectly, on the poet's right relationship with God. As a matter of biographical fact, we know of Cowper's agonized doubts about his own theological status. *The Task* itself has even alluded to these doubts, and to the pain of the poet's psychotic depression. But the poem concludes in confidence, warranted partly by the speaker's prolonged meditations on the nature of his daily existence: an existence of privacy, separated from worldly corruption, creating a position from which to analyze and criticize that corruption. The task with which the poet began, that of dressing a sofa with flowers of verse, has been transformed. By accepting its obligations, he has learned to discover the "immortal truth" that he now purveys. He can imagine for himself a serious didactic function, not dependent on the praise of an earthly audience but perhaps meriting the approval of a heavenly one. Doubt remains: the *if* of line 1019 ("If he regard not . . .") acknowledges the possibility that God may not accept even his best efforts. But the pervasive tone speaks of hard-won confidence.

Inasmuch as these final lines recapitulate the effort of the poem as a whole, they indicate clearly that Cowper finds three distinct elements in his poetic scheme: himself, the world, and God. The final definition of his task depends on the self-God relation, source of the slightly precarious pride in the last three lines. By comparison with "the proudest strain" that he can imagine, Cowper's own poetry remains humble. He tries to subordinate his own purposes to God's. Yet he can presume the possibility of divine approbation, a source of profound personal satisfaction.

The poem itself has discussed in detail all three components of the project, dwelling on the situation of the speaker himself, recurring to several versions of religious obligation, and insistently delineating and criticizing the world rejected by the solitary man. Its successive discussions of the notion of "the task" reveal the intricate relation among the three in the course of clarifying the importance of privacy to the poetic enterprise. Every task—writing poetry, raising cucumbers, the unspecified "service of mankind"—demands that its performer accept both external discipline, the discipline inherent in the particular charge he has assumed, and internal discipline, the willingness to cleave to immediate obligation. (I have used the masculine pronoun because Cowper mainly does so himself. But in fact he also evokes his female companion embroidering flowers, calling hers a "busy task" [4.150] and pointing out that she, like the poet— who speaks in the final lines of working on his own wreath—produces "A wreath that cannot fade, of flow'rs that blow / With most success when all besides decay" [156–57]. Women too, in other words, have tasks to perform, and partake of the universal order in performing them.) The capacity to focus on external obligation and to use innate capacities to the fullest belongs only to those who exist outside the bustle of a distracting world. These capacities, properly employed, lead the worker to God. The value of privacy is both positive and negative. It excludes interference from conflicting demands, desires, and possibilities presented by a crowded social environment; in this negative sense it facilitates appropriate relationship to the divine. As a positive force, it throws the secluded man back on himself and allows him to discover, as well as to use, his own powers. *The Task* dramatizes precisely this process of discovery and use. It both represents and demonstrates the right performance of responsibility.

More than once in the course of the poem, Cowper expatiates directly on the value of seclusion. Perhaps the most moving and persuasive instance of his meditations on the subject occurs in book 3, in the context of an account of his work as gardener. He imagines the gardener as an imitator of divine creation, producing finally a "bright design" (3.654) that will declare the possibility of order. The work is never done, he explains, describing the garden in quasi-allegorical terms: flowers supported against external evil, flowers "fair, / Like virtue" (663–64), all flowers hating "the rank society of weeds" (670). The occupation of enabling order and beauty makes possible the further discipline of "seclusion": "Oh, blest seclusion from a jarring world, / Which he, thus occupied, enjoys!" (675–76). Such seclusion cannot restore lost innocence, but it can protect against the assaults of evil,

> proving still
> A faithful barrier, not o'erleap'd with ease
> By vicious custom, raging uncontroll'd
> Abroad, and desolating public life.
> (680–83)

The contrast here adumbrated between "public" and private life indicates the poet's sense of the danger he has escaped (as he writes a few lines later, "to fly is safe" [688]) and prepares for the disgust with which he indicates the hopelessness of trying to reform

> Dissipated minds,
> And profligate abusers of a world
> Created fair so much in vain for them.
> (695–97)

The poet, he explains, considers himself "blest" (694) by what he has: everything he could possibly wish—health, leisure, peace, friendship, his muse, and "constant occupation without care" (693). Most important of all, he inhabits "those scenes which God ordain'd / Should best secure" the cause of piety, truth, and virtue (708–9). He describes and attempts to evoke them as part of his divinely ordained responsibility (his "task") to exercise a good effect on the world. But that disgust perceptible in his every account of what he has left behind shades readily into anger, apparent in what can only be called diatribes against universal social corruption.

Repeating the Fall over and over again, in Cowper's view, humankind willingly leaves, actively rejects, the equivalent of paradise,

> Scenes form'd for contemplation, and to nurse
> The growing seeds of wisdom; that suggest,

By ev'ry pleasing image they present,
Reflections such as meliorate the heart,
Compose the passions, and exalt the mind.

(3.301–5)

The accumulation of men in cities is not only regrettable but sinful, implying active choices of the worse life over the better. Those powerful scenes that compose the passions and exalt the mind belong to the poet in his privacy. He tries in vain to call back others, knowing the futility of his effort and necessarily ambivalent about it, since if all men sought the country, his seclusion would vanish.

The choice of that seclusion controls and rationalizes what may appear the random structure of *The Task*. It makes sense of the strange combination of emotions at work in the text, the reiterated alternations of rage, at current political, social, and religious practice, and exaltation, generated by contemplation of nature or of God, timeless facts. Social criticism and exegesis of the natural and the domestic realms belong, in Cowper's figuration, to a single texture. One implies the other: the speaker has left "the world" behind because of its corruption, choosing his rural privacy; his commitment to retreat lends him the appropriate perspective from which to criticize the world; his happiness in relative isolation correlates with his anger at those too blind to elect it. Indeed, his happiness *demands* his anger: in the poetic logic of *The Task*, the peace the speaker has found entails the obligation to preach the values that enable it. One may suspect that psychological logic does not in this instance correspond to poetic logic, that the anger palpable in the passages of social denunciation derives, rather, from the poet's ambivalent response to a world that has rejected him, he may plausibly feel, before he rejected it. But poetic logic is what counts here. Accepting as his obligation the lightly offered task of singing the sofa, Cowper discovers a way to speak of the more serious obligation he feels to praise the God who has rescued him and blame those who do not share his commitment.

Cowper is, so far as I know, unique in his period in his dedication to privacy as opportunity and obligation. Much admired by his contemporaries, the poet became an object of imitation for such poets as Charlotte Smith. But the difference between Smith and Cowper is instructive, exemplifying the pervasive differences between the poetry of sensibility and what I have been calling the poetry of privacy. For Smith, emotions comprise the central subject. She writes of nature in order to write of herself. For Cowper, writing of nature protects him from having to write of himself. The privacy he embodies operates on the page as well as in the life he describes.

Except in the well-known "stricken deer" passage—and there only briefly—he rarely speaks openly of his feelings. He may allude in passing to causes of pain that he will not describe; he may emphasize with an intensity that suggests his fear of its opposite the peace he has attained. But he describes his experience more by its external than its internal facts. I have used terms like *rage* and *exaltation* to render the mood of his utterances, but they are not his subject. He aligns himself with the poets of sensibility in his concern for the rights of animals and his proclamations of feeling for all humankind, but his interior life does not make the center of his interest.

Or at least it does not *openly* comprise the center of his interest. One might argue that the proliferation of external subject matter in *The Task*, both the rural detail and the commentary on public affairs, functions like the blushes of eighteenth-century novelistic heroines, as simultaneous revelation and disguise. If Cowper does not, like Robert Burton, directly report dramatic alternations of mood, he illustrates exactly such sequences in his progressions and shifts of topic. Reading his long poem as a record of his psychic life, one discovers conflict and tension, temporary willed resolution, moments of unexpected ease, hope and despair, desire and fear, religious dedication and secular delight—a large emotional repertoire. The poet proclaims and demonstrates his privacy and its importance, but he undermines it in the act of proclaiming it. Yet the conviction, rhetorical or literal, that privacy enables him animates his long poem.

Cowper's deployment of his subject matter, I have suggested, lends itself to analogy with the blushes of heroines. That analogy serves yet better the techniques of Charlotte Smith, for whom intermingled reticence and display provide a central poetic subject as well as a procedural mode. As we have seen more fully in previous chapters, eighteenth-century women cultivated interior privacy partly because largely deprived of its physical equivalent. (Men, obviously, might cultivate the same state—but perhaps with less urgency.) Unlike Cowper (in many works her poetic model), Smith constructed a perpetual tease about her inner life. In her frequently expanded and republished series *Elegiac Sonnets*, she made her sorrow her subject—without ever specifying its causes or manifestations in more than the vaguest terms. Readers complained of her tonal monotony, although they continued to buy her books. She defended herself, first indirectly, by a familiar appeal to the reader of sensibility ("I can hope for readers only among the few, who, to sensibility of heart, join simplicity of taste" [Charlotte Smith 3]), then, in the 1792 preface to the sixth edition, by autobiographical allusion. A friend, she reports, suggests to her "a more cheerful style of composition." The poet explains that she originally did not intend the notes of her "melancholy lyre" for the public: "It was unaffected sorrows drew them forth: I wrote mournfully because I was unhappy—And I have unfortunately no reason yet, though nine years have since elapsed, to *change my tone*" (6). She elaborates the point in the preface to volume 2 (1797): "That these are gloomy, none will surely have a right to complain; for I never engaged they should be gay. But I am unhappily exempt from the suspicion of *feigning* sorrow for an opportunity of shewing the pathos with which it can be described" (11).

Sorrow is her subject, sorrow her way of life. In prose and in verse, she insists that she can write of nothing else. Yet she writes of this only allusively. As she asserts the dominance of a single emotion, she refuses to share its etiology or (except conventionally) even its symptoms. The more one reads of her misery, the more conscious one becomes of all that the poetic persona conceals. Paradoxically, this woman who proclaims her heartbreak her subject makes her privacy central to her poetic effects.

The first sonnet in the sequence announces a dual subject and exemplifies Smith's method. The writing of poetry and the experience of sorrow merge as topics: the muse has favored the speaker from her earliest hours, but the muse brings no happiness. On the contrary:

> For still she bids soft Pity's melting eye
>   Stream o'er the ills she knows not to remove,
> Points every pang, and deepens every sigh
>   Of mourning Friendship, or unhappy Love.
> Ah! then, how dear the Muse's favours cost,
> *If those paint sorrow best — who feel it most!*
> (Sonnet 1, 9–14)

The speaker's claim, borrowed from Pope, has it that her profound personal knowledge of sorrow enables her to represent it successfully. That knowledge appears to be both vicarious (Pity's eye streaming over other people's irremediable ills) and direct (friendship and love betrayed or frustrated). The sonnet employs a syllogistic structure: it accumulates vague but insistent evidence of suffering and concludes with a *then* that declares a rational sequence. The vagueness carries its own message: the nature of the sorrow endured does not matter; only the fact matters. It is the vagueness—a rhetorical equivalent for privacy—that enables the poem: that enables, in fact, a long series of poems.

Thus Smith begins sonnet 4 with conventional praise of the moon, conventionally invoked as "Queen of the silver bow!" (1). The moon's shadow in the stream, the clouds that surround the planet, the "mild and placid light" that calms the speaker (5–6): all sound familiar. Gradually, though, the sonnet turns from the usual sorts of description to focus on the speaker's thoughts, which direct themselves once more to grief: first that of "the wretched," "The sufferers of the earth," and "the sad children of Despair and Woe" (8, 9, 11), but in the concluding couplet, to her own position. Wishing to "reach thy world serene," she characterizes herself at last as "Poor wearied pilgrim—in this toiling scene!" (13–14). The metaphor has no context except for the preceding third-person consideration of other generalized sufferers. It carries a charge of intense desire, yet it remains mysterious. Once more, self-concealment—the kind of privacy one carries around—energizes the poetic utterance.

An astonishing degree of aggressive force marks some deployments of Smith's technique of vagueness. Her best-known sonnet, "Written in the church-yard at Middleton in Sussex," with its evocation of bones unearthed from their graves by a storm, concludes, characteristically, with a self-referential quatrain:

> But vain to them the winds and waters rave;
> *They* hear the warring elements no more:
> While I am doom'd—by life's long storm opprest,
> To gaze with envy on their gloomy rest.
>
> (11–14)

The announcement of suffering has the force of extreme self-assertion. To resolve the macabre scene of storm-tossed skeletons by the statement that the speaker's doom is worse than theirs—more conscious, more prolonged—insists that the self is more important than any of its imaginings. The self's consciousness of itself marks its specialness and its particularity, known only to its possessor, proudly, deliberately, withheld from the reader. The combination of emotional insistence with premeditated withholding marks much of Smith's verse.

Like Cowper, Smith articulates her awareness of issues beyond herself: the national and international concerns virtually inevitable for any commentator in the period of the French Revolution. Unlike Cowper, she emphasizes imagination more than direct experience as the source of her articulations. The extraordinary vision that inaugurates *Beachy Head* is altogether hypothetical: the speaker does not recline on the rocks, she *would* recline, allowing her fancy to "go forth, / And represent"—represent, specifically, in the first instance, the scene of God's creation (4). She has certainly seen the landscape and seascape she describes in compelling detail, but she does not claim to have seen it; she claims that she *would*—

would wish to—see it. The difference between physical and imaginative vision becomes elided as the speaker moves from the sight of a "ship of commerce richly freighted" (42) to imaginary Asians wearing turbans and Indians diving for pearls. Fancy takes her into the "visionary vales" (86) of the sunset; Contemplation rests on a rock and summons "recording Memory" (119) to recite the history of England. Implicitly she claims imagination and contemplation as sources of knowledge comparable to that gained from life in the world and purportedly factual books.

The persona of *The Task* remembers his own life in the city, from which he has escaped into his rural privacy. The persona of *Beachy Head* remembers an idyllic country childhood. Past and present merge as she evokes its scenes, re-creating for a public audience a private landscape, a landscape of the heart. The private made public self-evidently no longer belongs to the realm of privacy. Yet that realm continues to be important, not only as the source of inspiration but also as the substance of poetic consciousness. Such consciousness provides the deep subject for *Beachy Head*.

Cowper, in *The Task*, wrote of the processes of poetry to exemplify the poet's fulfillment of large responsibilities, even in the act of taking pleasure. Smith manifests no sense of responsibility, not even intermittent awareness of her relationship to any personalized version of the divine. Nor does she evoke the pleasure in poetic pains: the details of the poetic process do not concern her on the page. Rather, she indirectly insists on the importance of a mysterious inner spring of awareness, composed partly of memory, partly of imagination, that generates her creation.

Beachy Head concludes with two extended figures for the poet as separated from the community and mysterious in feeling. The "Shepherd of the Hill" is quite literally a poet, producing "songs" incorporated within the text of the poem. The villagers who see him try to interpret him as he complains of his fate, telling the wind "of cold neglect / And baffled hope" (527–28). He sings of love, imagining reunion with a lost beloved; he dreams of life shared with another in a natural paradise. The larger poem's speaker summarizes:

The visionary, nursing dreams like these,
Is not indeed unhappy. Summer woods
Wave over him, and whisper as they wave,
Some future blessings he may yet enjoy.
And as above him sail the silver clouds,
He follows them in thought to distant climes.

(655–60)

By virtue of being a dreamer, the shepherd retains capacity for happiness—as well as for especially vivid experience of unhappiness. He resembles in this respect the persona of Smith's sonnets, with her reiterated claims of unspecified suffering and her evocations of consolatory beauty and imagination. The exact nature of the shepherd's dreams remains unknown and unknowable; the most that can be said of them is that they are "dreams like these." The mystery of his experience and his feelings fascinates those who see and hear him; the mystery of the poet's experience and feelings lie in the background as comparably fascinating.

The Hermit of the Rocks, whose story comprises the final sequence of Smith's uncompleted poem, emits no poetic utterance. He too resembles the speaker of the sonnets, though, in the nature of his heart:

> his heart
> Was feelingly alive to all that breath'd;
> And outraged as he was, in sanguine youth,
> By human crimes, he still acutely felt
> For human misery.
>
> (687–91)

Not a dreamer but a feeler, the hermit, like the self-portrayed speaker of the sonnets, suffers on behalf of others. His actions substantiate the claim of feeling: he rescues mariners threatened by angry seas and buries those who do not survive. Finally a storm kills him as well, and the villagers bury him, without grieving, since he has died "in the cause of charity" (729).

Where he has come from and why remain unknown. Perceived as a "lonely man" (721), he keeps his own secrets, the secrets of his inward life of consciousness. His most compelling aspect is his inexplicable disgust "with the world / And all its ways," a disgust that makes him appear "to suffer life / Rather than live" (674–76). The history that might account for this feeling remains occluded, to the poem's reader as to the villagers. Smith's narrative reports actions more than emotions, yet calls attention to the unknowable emotions that energize actions. Experience generates feeling, her story of the hermit suggests, but experience can be concealed. It belongs, in that case, only to the person who has undergone it. And feeling generates experience, in the sense illustrated by the hermit's active compassion: his unknown past might explain his generous behavior, but the explanation would presumably depend on emotional structures generated by that past. The hermit's privacy consists less in his relative solitude than in his hidden consciousness.

In *The Emigrants*, her most "public" poem, Smith not only concerns herself with the fate of French exiles, she also modifies her poetic persona. Although she proclaims her private sorrows (at one point comparing herself with Marie Antoinette in her "sad experience" [2.170]), she stresses more insistently than in the sonnets her interest in and care for others. She feels the woes "that injustice, and duplicity / And faithlessness and folly, fix on" her (1.59–60), but she insists that the thought of others' misery troubles her greatly. Indeed, in making her subject the "Poor vagrant wretches! Outcasts of the world!" (1.303) whom France has rejected, she also appropriates the subject of human compassion. The poem's first book ends with a powerful panegyric to the "just compassion" (1.360) that she declares always dominant over English hearts. The "bloodless laurels" attached to "acts of pure humanity," the poem asserts, are "nobler far" than fame acquired by battle, however triumphant (368, 369). Feminine values, in other words, trump their masculine equivalents.

But the subject of compassion does not control *The Emigrants* as a whole. Even in this relatively "public" poem, dedicated to William Cowper, with its program of advocating human sympathy and its familiar eighteenth-century personifications ("Vengeance, seeking blood, / And Avarice; and Envy's harpy fangs" [1.347–48]), Smith's emotional energy intensifies when she turns to her inner life—not the life of pain to which she so often alludes, but that associated with "Memory." Memory can recall her to "hours of simple joy" in which she played on the riverbank (2.331); memory evokes for her the colors and textures of the natural world she then inhabited; memory rescues her not only from suffering but from pressing knowledge of other sufferers with claims on her attention. The poetic tactic that Wordsworth would make familiar works for her as it would for Wordsworth, to restore her to full imaginative vitality.

Such restoration, such commitment to the interior life in its creativity, bear little connection to what we usually think of as "privacy." But Smith's consistent concern for memory and imagination, like her constant awareness of her suffering as poetic subject, calls attention to an end point for eighteenth-century interest in possibilities for psychological privacy. Like Cowper, whom she greatly admired, Charlotte Smith celebrates sympathy, deprecates (though not nearly so extensively as her model) life in cities, and evokes details of the natural world. Unlike Cowper, she—with ten children, an exigent husband, and demanding financial pressures—cannot choose domestic privacy. The retreat inward, not into sensibility but into memory, constitutes her literary equivalent. As a literary and psychological tactic, it would largely dominate the next century.

Afterword

As an imaginative category, privacy carries enormous power, even without being fully articulated as a concept. Few, if any, of the writers and fictional characters treated in this study speak or would have spoken of themselves as seeking or enjoying or suffering privacy, yet many of the works here explored reveal in their renditions of relationship dramatic tensions between needs for separateness and for community: the fundamental conflict of privacy. The imaginative energy of privacy perhaps intensifies when its value has not yet become a matter of common agreement. The novelistic protagonists who, like Juliet in *The Wanderer,* adopt by necessity new forms of protection against intrusion experience their need directly and must devise strategies to meet it. Although they find in various forms of social convention strategies ready to hand, turning such conventions to personal use significantly asserts the claim of the self. Cowper's discovery of privacy as psychological resource, grounding for poetic possibility, possesses extra strength because of the personal nature of that discovery.

Privacy does not provide a "theme" or a "subject" for any of the works I have considered. Its literary functions include evoking an atmosphere (e.g., Cowper), creating plot obstacles (*The Vicar of Wakefield*) or clarifying plot complexities (*Clarissa*), revealing character (*A Sentimental Journey*) and elucidating action (Ryder's diary), providing insight into how social custom affects individual possibility (Burney's novels), helping to generate techniques for erotic promise, revelation, and concealment (*Fanny Hill*), and more. A reader's awareness of it can clarify a text's operations. *Clarissa,* for instance, is not "about" privacy, yet the patterns sketched in my first chapter show that privacy provides, at the very least, a revealing rubric for the novel's central dynamic of advance and retreat, power gained and power lost. The heroine's defense of her right to privacy—her locking of doors, her possessiveness about her correspondence—might be said to epitomize her insistence on her own spiritual integrity, even after the loss of her physical integrity. Conversely, Lovelace's violation of the privacy of her correspondence, to say nothing of the privacy of her person, reveals the harsh intrusiveness implicit in the masculine assertion central to his character. The issue of privacy extends yet farther, suggesting a way to think about the functions of epistolarity in the novel: personal letters at once publicize the personal and internal and claim a privacy of two, the privacy of intimacy. In Richardson's novel, the most important decision to publicize the private, thus abolishing personal privacy, belongs to the heroine who has previously defended her own privacy, who refused to prosecute her rapist partly because of the publicity of the open court. The choice to publicize her history perhaps (among its many other functions) comments on the self-elected doom of privacy suffered by Clarissa's mother, who, like generations of other women, silently endured her husband's oppression. It also declares Clarissa's posthumous transcendence of convention and of concealment.

Cowper's great poem, *The Task*, provides another revealing instance. Like *Clarissa*, it does not focus on privacy; rather, it assumes privacy as the earthly condition of possibility. Privacy makes sense of the poet's textual life, accounting for his outrage at public corruption and helping to justify his often jarring inclusiveness of topics. The position of privacy lends him perspective and authority. His capacity to comment on public evil, in turn, justifies, in the logic of the poem, the choice of privacy itself, which finally allows him to hint his possession of transcendent vision and power.

Frances Burney, who has appeared so often in this book, supplies its best single example of a writer who employs the concept of privacy as a rich fictional and personal resource. In three of her four novels (in *Evelina* less strikingly and more ambiguously), she uncovers complex interplays of social pressure and individual need, relating the nexus of pressure and need to the anguish each of her protagonists endures. Cecilia, Camilla, and Juliet all attempt some measure of self-determination, only to discover the need for deviousness, concealment, and something uncomfortably close to hypocrisy as tactics of self-protection. They also experience the pain of certain kinds of privacy as social imperative, caught in a web of constricting convention.

Margaret Anne Doody has argued strongly for Burney's force as a social critic. Summarizing two of Burney's novels, she comments, "If in *Cecilia* we saw a fully developed society uneasily tottering at the edge of change, perhaps of a crash, in *The Wanderer* we see a static society that has refused to admit any change" (328). The fact that privacy remains an equally urgent impossibility and imposition in both societies underlines its intimate implication with social structures, fully developed, static, or changing. Burney's intense interest in it calls attention to her primary concern: not with "society" as an entity in itself, but with the ways it operates on individuals. To see Burney in her diaries deploying her textual privacy as a form of linguistic authority conveys special satisfaction in the context of her meticulous novelistic renditions of privacy as sign of female desperation or of social imposition.

But I do not propose to recapitulate all my previous literary arguments. Rather, I want to summarize some ways in which contemplation of privacy has provided literary insight. For me, I think, the most surprising revelations of this investigation have been the discoveries about the literature of sensibility. Recent years have provided much fruitful study of both the cult and the literature of sensibility, but it remains difficult to grasp fully the power of the set of assumptions we now associate with sensibility. That power perhaps manifests itself most vividly in sensibility's effect on literary modes quite removed from what we usually consider "sentimental." Examination of erotic and quasi-erotic narratives, for instance, reveals that sensibility can function textually as a defense against uncomfortable personal revelation—a point obscured by critical associations of sensibility and sexuality that concentrate on their shared demand for notation of feeling and on their closely related kinds of feeling. The link between sensibility and rage, which becomes clear in scandalous memoir and in sentimental fiction, has also been neglected. The literature of sensibility and that of satire lie close together at some points; both exploit—for rather different ends—the meanings of privacy. The theatricality of sensibility is manifest in its descriptions. To think about privacy helps expose the social and personal uses of the particular kinds of performance involved in displays of sensibility. Sensibility, as we have seen, can conceal as well as reveal feeling. Itself a social convention like the rules of good manners and good conversation, although in eighteenth-century culture assigned more far-reaching meanings, sensibility, like those other conventions, lends itself to varied personal uses.

We began this study by thinking about the figure of the reader, as imagined by eighteenth-century writers in textual representations as well as in addresses and allusions to readers outside the text. The familiar notion of the private reader, attended with many ambiguities, has recurred throughout the book. Indeed, in this as in other critical works, the private reader functions centrally: all criticism involves the imposition of a private vision on more or less familiar written material. Of course the private reader as professional critic, the reader who reads in order to write and in turn be read, is shaped by more obvious pressures from others than is a reader like

Elizabeth Bennet. Inevitably formed by the traditions of previous criticism and the imagined presence of further readers, the professional critic in her functioning calls attention to the possibility that the notion of a private reader is no more than a comforting fantasy—comforting because it implies the dream of a privacy so complete as to include independence even from the voices in our heads, although life and literature alike reveal the multifarious trammels, internal and external, that we all experience.

If privacy, total privacy, is a wistful dream, it is one that has persisted, perhaps generally with increasing force, over the past two centuries or more. But privacy, like other ideas, has looked different at different times. The issue of masking, the problem of human opacity, for instance, no longer seems for most a troublesome aspect of privacy. Most people now, I fancy, take it for granted that we employ social masks for social occasions. Our eighteenth-century predecessors knew the same fact but apparently accepted it with rather less equanimity. At any rate, this aspect of social intercourse provided a subject for contemplation and on occasion for overt concern in a period when the desirability of community was largely assumed. The well-known eighteenth-century preoccupation with hypocrisy, in its obviously pejorative sense and in its ancient meaning of acting on a stage, becomes more comprehensible when one focuses on privacy. The universality of social masking, for our forebears, raised questions about the fundamental nature of human relations. If the association of men and women in harmonious communities defined the human condition, what could it mean that such association depended on falsification?

The problem of hypocrisy and disguise loomed large for moralists and guides to conduct, who might see the necessity of concealment as a social practice yet deplore its effect on the moral lives of, in particular, young women. Consequently, they devised such tactics as those of Camilla's father, insisting on the distinction between dissimulation and praiseworthy self-discipline without elucidating the difference; or they emphasized the degree to which concealment of, say, one's intellectual superiority constituted an act of consideration for others. They did not dwell on the benefits of social dissimulation for the self.

The novels, in particular, that this study has treated illustrate, however, widespread awareness of just such advantages. Privacy existed as a concept in eighteenth-century England, but those holding it understood that it had a dark side. Cecilia's horror of privacy for a marriage ceremony calls attention to the perceived danger of cutting oneself off from social sanctions and support. The manifest gain inherent in privacy consists in the mental and psychological freedom it provides (sometimes physical freedom as well): the liberty for speculation, meditation, and intimate relationship.

The loss attending such gain involves the absence of consistent extended community, with all that community supplies.

One sees such loss represented in Sterne's novels, with no sense that any alternative could exist. Indeed, the fall into privacy appears not to be reversible. True, one can by an act of choice sometimes—if the separation does not derive from temperament rather than choice in the first place—reject willful separation from the community in favor of a cozier alternative. But once the concept exists that a person can claim time and space for the self, the possibility exists as well; and acknowledged possibilities must be utilized.

The developing novel of the eighteenth century helped to consolidate as well as to explore the notion of an inner life. Belief in that life's reality and importance necessarily led to its cultivation; hence, to a perceived need for privacy, though by no means to extirpation of the troubled sense of privacy's social implications. Diaries and poetry as well as fiction confirm the perception that individuals valued and explored privacy yet treated it warily, that they used the existing resources of their society as means for temporarily absenting themselves from that society, yet recognized, or were reminded of, the dangers of doing so.

Even given the perception of danger, the evidence suggests, the idea of privacy appeared to be associated with at least a vague notion of personal authenticity. Inasmuch as the young women represented in novels seek ways to protect from the attention of others their feelings and desires, to protect their feelings even in the face of widespread social demand for "transparency" in women, they use their modes of withdrawal as opportunities to discover who they are. The comic yet pathetic image of Cecilia in her isolated glade, pouring out her sorrows to a dog, condenses the implications of a frequently rendered plight for the young in particular.

And most especially for young *women*. The issue of psychological privacy, if eighteenth-century literary renditions are to be credited, concerns women in particular, because of the social restrictions and social surveillance they face. Men, too, are supposed to behave by rules in their social lives, but their reputations appear to have been less fragile and general suspicion of them less intense. The well-known fact that chastity was the heart of female virtue implied a general sense of danger surrounding women. The girl who revealed inappropriate emotion risked her reputation for virtue; the girl who flirted, or who showed herself to understand a risqué reference in a stage representation, could be thought to reveal the precariousness of her chastity. Emotional self-concealment thus became less indulgence than necessity. In a situation of little external freedom, women could find a kind of equivalent for liberty in hiding, claiming at least an uncoerced inner realm. The more direct evidence of female diaries confirms the suggestions of novels about the prevalence and importance of hiding as a women's strategy.

What privacy protects, then, printed testimony indicates, is often the life of feeling. What it enables, for writers such as Dudley Ryder and William Cowper, is the exploration of feeling. The freedom of psychological privacy, for men and women alike, is the opportunity for emotional expansiveness and investigation. Privacy may take the form of withholding and concealment, but it provides a steam vent for bottled-up feeling. Hence, perhaps, the persistent and varied associations we have discovered between privacy and sensibility, both dependent on high valuation of feeling, both carefully limiting feeling's purview.

A focus on privacy has called attention to the uses of convention, the ubiquity of performance, and varied utilizations of hypocrisy. We have seen in how many ways the writing of the eighteenth century demonstrates strenuous effort—by writers and by fictional characters—to balance the claims of privacy and society. *Sense and Sensibility* provides perhaps the fullest exploration of the precariousness and difficulty of the balance, and of the urgency both of expressiveness and of reserve, of social responsibility and personal need. The story of privacy in the period offers a case history of the intricate merging of psychological and social change. For our forebears as for us, privacy was a subject fraught with import and with emotion.

Works Cited

Adams, Samuel, and Sarah Adams. *The Complete Servant*. 1825. Ed. Ann Haley. Lewes: Southover Press, 1989.

Allen, Anita L. *Uneasy Access: Privacy for Women in a Free Society*. Totowa, N.J.: Rowman and Littlefield, 1988.

Ancourt, Abbé d'. *The Lady's Preceptor; or, A Letter to a Young Lady of Distinction upon Politeness. Taken from the French of the Abbé d'Ancourt, and Adapted to the Religion, Customs, and Manners of the English Nation, by a gentleman of Cambridge*. 2d ed. London, 1743.

Ariès, Philippe. Introduction to *A History of Private Life*, vol. 3, *Passions of the Renaissance*, ed. Roger Chartier, trans. Arthur Goldhammer. Cambridge, Mass.: Belknap Press of Harvard University Press, 1989.

Austen, Jane. *Pride and Prejudice*. Ed. R. W. Chapman. 3d ed. Oxford: Oxford University Press, 1932.

———. *Sense and Sensibility*. Ed. R. W. Chapman. 3d ed. Oxford: Oxford University Press, 1933.

Barker-Benfield, G. J. *The Culture of Sensibility: Sex and Society in Eighteenth-Century Britain*. Chicago: University of Chicago Press, 1992.

Benedict, Barbara M. *Curiosity: A Cultural History of Early Modern Inquiry*. Chicago: University of Chicago Press, 2001.

———. *Framing Feeling: Sentiment and Style in English Prose Fiction, 1745–1800*. New York: AMS Press, 1994.

Boswell, James. *Boswell on the Grand Tour: Italy, Corsica, and France, 1765–1766*. Ed. Frank Brady and Frederick A. Pottle. London: Heinemann, 1955.

———. *Boswell's London Journal, 1762–1763*. Ed. Frederick A. Pottle. New York: McGraw-Hill, 1950.

———. *Life of Johnson*. 1791. Ed. R. W. Chapman. Oxford: Oxford University Press, 1970.

Brissenden, R. F. *Virtue in Distress: Studies in the Novel of Sentiment from Richardson to Sade*. London: Macmillan, 1974.

Bromwich, David. "A Note on the Romantic Self." *Raritan* 14, no. 4 (1995): 66–74.

Burke, Peter. *The Art of Conversation*. Ithaca, N.Y.: Cornell University Press, 1993.

Burney, Fanny. *Camilla, or, A Picture of Youth*. 1796. Ed. Edward A. Bloom and Lillian D. Bloom. Oxford: Oxford University Press, 1983.

———. *Cecilia, or, Memoirs of an Heiress*. 1782. Ed. Peter Sabor and Margaret Anne Doody. Oxford: Oxford University Press, 1988.

———. *The Early Journals and Letters of Fanny Burney*. Vol. 1, 1768–73, and vol. 2, 1774–77, ed. Lars E. Troide; vol. 3, 1778–79, ed. Lars E. Troide and Stewart J. Cooke. Montreal: McGill–Queen's University Press, 1988–94.

———. *The Wanderer, or, Female Difficulties*. Ed. Margaret Anne Doody, Robert L. Mack, and Peter Sabor. Oxford: Oxford University Press, 1991.

Castan, Yves. "Politics and Private Life." In *A History of Private Life*, vol. 3, *Passions of the Renaissance*, ed. Roger Chartier, trans. Arthur Goldhammer. Cambridge, Mass.: Belknap Press of Harvard University Press, 1989.

Chapone, Hester. *Letters on the Improvement of the Mind*. 1773. Female Education in the Age of Enlightenment 2. London: Pickering, 1996.

Chartier, Roger. "The Practical Impact of Writing." In *A History of Private Life*, vol. 3, *Passions of the Renaissance*, ed. Roger Chartier, trans. Arthur Goldhammer. Cambridge, Mass.: Belknap Press of Harvard University Press, 1989.

Cleland, John. *Fanny Hill, or, Memoirs of a Woman of Pleasure*. 1748–49. Ed. Peter Wagner. Harmondsworth: Penguin, 1985.

[Constable, John.] *The Conversation of Gentlemen Considered, In most of the Ways, that make their mutual Company Agreeable, or Disagreeable*. London, 1738.

Cowper, William. *The Poetical Works of William Cowper*. Ed. H. S. Milford. 4th ed. London: Oxford University Press, 1934.

Cox, Stephen. "Sensibility as Argument." In *Sensibility in Transformation: Creative Resistance to Sentiment from the Augustans to the Romantics*, ed. Syndy McMillen Conger. Rutherford, N.J.: Fairleigh Dickinson University Press, 1990.

Defoe, Daniel. *The Fortunes and Misfortunes of the Famous Moll Flanders*. Ed. Juliet Mitchell. Harmondsworth: Penguin, 1978.

The Diaries of a Duchess. Extracts from the Diaries of the First Duchess of Northumberland (1716–1776). Ed. James Greig. London: Hodder and Stoughton, 1926.

The Dimensions of Privacy: A National Opinion Research Survey of Attitudes toward Privacy. Conducted by Louis Harris and Associates and Dr. Alan F. Westin. New York: Garland, 1981.

Doody, Margaret Anne. *Frances Burney: The Life in the Works*. New Brunswick, N.J.: Rutgers University Press, 1988.

Edgeworth, Maria. *Letters for Literary Ladies*. 1795. Ed. Claire Connolly. London: Dent, 1993.

Elias, Norbert. *Power and Civility*. Vol. 2 of *The Civilizing Process*. New York: Pantheon, 1982.

Ellis, Markman. *The Politics of Sensibility: Race, Gender, and Commerce in the Sentimental Novel*. Cambridge: Cambridge University Press, 1996.

Ernst, Morris L., and Alan U. Schwartz. *Privacy: The Right to Be Let Alone*. New York: Macmillan, 1962.

Etzioni, Amitai. *The Limits of Privacy*. New York: Basic, 1999.

Fielding, Henry. *Amelia*. Ed. Martin C. Battestin. Middletown, Conn.: Wesleyan University Press, 1983.

———. *The History of Tom Jones, A Foundling*. Ed. Fredson Bowers. Middletown, Conn.: Wesleyan University Press, 1975.

Fielding, Sarah. *The Adventures of David Simple, Containing an Account of His Travels through the Cities of London and Westminster in the Search of a Real Friend*. Ed. Malcolm Kelsall. Oxford: Oxford University Press, 1987.

Flaherty, David H. *Privacy in Colonial New England*. Charlottesville: University Press of Virginia, 1972.

Fordyce, James. *Sermons to Young Women*. 3d ed. 2 vols. London, 1766.

Fowler, Alastair, ed. *The New Oxford Book of Seventeenth Century Verse*. Oxford: Oxford University Press, 1991.

Fried, Charles. "Privacy." In *Philosophical Dimensions of Privacy: An Anthology*, ed. Ferdinand David Schoeman. Cambridge: Cambridge University Press, 1984.

Gaskell, Elizabeth. *The Life of Charlotte Brontë*. 1857. Ed. Angus Easson. Oxford: Oxford University Press, 1996.

Gavison, Ruth. "Privacy and the Limits of Law." In *Philosophical Dimensions of Privacy: An Anthology*, ed. Ferdinand David Schoeman. Cambridge: Cambridge University Press, 1984.

Genuine Memoirs of the Celebrated Miss Maria Brown. Exhibiting the Life of a Courtezan in the Most Fashionable Scenes of Dissipation. 1766. 2 vols. in 1. New York: Garland, 1975.

Gerstein, Robert S. "Intimacy and Privacy." In *Philosophical Dimensions of Privacy: An Anthology*, ed. Ferdinand David Schoeman. Cambridge: Cambridge University Press, 1984.

Gillis, Christina Marsden. *The Paradox of Privacy: Epistolary Form in "Clarissa."* Gainesville: University Presses of Florida, 1984.

[Gilman], Charlotte Perkins Stetson. *Women and Economics: A Study of the Economic Relation Between Men and Women as a Factor in Social Evolution*. Boston, 1898.

Girouard, Mark. *Life in the English Country House: A Social and Architectural History*. New Haven, Conn.: Yale University Press, 1978.

Gisborne, Thomas. *An Enquiry into the Duties of the Female Sex*. 1797. Female Education in the Age of Enlightenment 2. London: Pickering, 1996.

Goldsmith, Oliver. *The Vicar of Wakefield*. 1766. Ed. Stephen Coote. Harmondsworth: Penguin, 1982.

Goulemot, Jean Marie. "Literary Practices: Publicizing the Private." In *A History of Private Life*, vol. 3, *Passions of the Renaissance*, ed. Roger Chartier, trans. Arthur Goldhammer. Cambridge, Mass.: Belknap Press of Harvard University Press, 1989.

Gregory, John. *A Father's Legacy to His Daughters*. 1774. In *The Young Lady's Pocket Library, or Parental Monitor*. Bristol: Thoemmes Press, 1995.

Gross, Hyman. "Privacy and Autonomy." In *Privacy*, ed. J. Roland Pennock and John W. Chapman. Nomos 13. New York: Atherton, 1971.

Guazzo, Stephen. *The civile Conversation*. Trans. George Pettie. London, 1586.

Habermas, Jürgen. *The Structural Transformation of the Public Sphere: An Inquiry into a Category of Bourgeois Society*. Trans. Thomas Burger with the assistance of Frederick Lawrence. Cambridge, Mass.: MIT Press, 1989.

Hagstrum, Jean H. *Sex and Sensibility: Ideal and Erotic Love from Milton to Mozart.*
Chicago: University of Chicago Press, 1980.

Harvey, A. D. *Sex in Georgian England: Attitudes and Prejudices from the 1720s to the 1820s.* London: Duckworth, 1994.

Haywood, Eliza. *A Present for a Servant-Maid. Or, The Sure Means of Gaining Love and Esteem.* Facsimile of Dublin edition, 1743. New York: Garland, 1985.

Hecht, J. Jean. *The Domestic Servant Class in Eighteenth-Century England.* London: Routledge, 1956.

Hudson, Nicholas. "Fielding's Hierarchy of Dialogue: 'Meta-Response' and the Reader of *Tom Jones.*" *Philological Quarterly* 68, no. 2 (1989): 177–94.

Hunter, J. Paul. *Before Novels: The Cultural Contexts of Eighteenth-Century English Fiction.* New York: Norton, 1990.

———. "Henry Fielding and the Modern Reader: The Problem of Temporal Translation." In *Henry Fielding in His Time and Ours: Papers Presented at a Clark Library Seminar.* Los Angeles: Clark Library, University of California, 1987.

Hussey, Christopher. *English Country Houses: Early Georgian, 1715–1760.* London: Country Life, 1965.

Imbarrato, Susan Clair. *Declarations of Independency in Eighteenth-Century American Autobiography.* Knoxville: University of Tennessee Press, 1998.

Inchbald, Elizabeth. *A Simple Story.* 1791. Ed. J. M. S. Tompkins. Oxford: Oxford University Press, 1967.

Ingham, Roger. "Privacy and Psychology." In *Privacy,* ed. John B. Young. New York: John Wiley, 1978.

Inness, Julie C. *Privacy, Intimacy, and Isolation.* New York: Oxford University Press, 1992.

Iser, Wolfgang. *The Implied Reader: Patterns of Communication in Prose Fiction from Bunyan to Beckett.* Baltimore: Johns Hopkins University Press, 1974.

Jackson, H. J. *Marginalia: Readers Writing in Books.* New Haven, Conn.: Yale University Press, 2001.

Jagodzinski, Cecile M. *Privacy and Print: Reading and Writing in Seventeenth-Century England.* Charlottesville: University Press of Virginia, 1999.

Johnson, Claudia L. *Equivocal Beings: Politics, Gender, and Sentimentality in the 1790s. Wollstonecraft, Radcliffe, Burney, Austen.* Chicago: University of Chicago Press, 1995.

Johnstone, Charles. *Chrysal: or, The Adventures of a Guinea.* 1764. 2 vols. in 1. New York: Arno, 1976.

Kilgour, Maggie. *The Rise of the Gothic Novel.* London: Routledge, 1995.

Klein, Lawrence. "Gender, Conversation, and the Public Sphere in Early Eighteenth-Century England." In *Textuality and Sexuality: Reading Theories and Practices,* ed. Judith Still and Michael Worton. Manchester: Manchester University Press, 1993.

Lambert, Anne-Thérèse, Marchioness de. *Advice of a Mother to her Daughter.* 1727. In *The Young Lady's Pocket Library, or Parental Monitor.* 1790. Bristol: Thoemmes Press, 1995.

Langbauer, Laurie. "Romance Revised: Charlotte Lennox's *The Female Quixote.*" *Novel* 18 (1984): 29–49.

Langford, Paul. *A Polite and Commercial People: England, 1727–1783*. The New Oxford History of England. Oxford: Clarendon, 1989.

Laslett, Peter. "Mean Household Size in England since the Sixteenth Century." In *Household and Family in Past Time: Comparative Studies in the Size and Structure of the Domestic Group over the Last Three Centuries*, ed. Peter Laslett, with the assistance of Richard Wall. Cambridge: Cambridge University Press, 1972.

Lennox, Charlotte. *The Female Quixote, or, The Adventures of Arabella*. Ed. Margaret Dalziel. Oxford: Oxford University Press, 1989.

Locke, John. *Some Thoughts concerning Education*. Ed. John W. Yolton and Jean S. Yolton. Oxford: Clarendon, 1989.

Lynch, Deidre Shauna. *The Economy of Character: Novels, Market Culture, and the Business of Inner Meaning*. Chicago: University of Chicago Press, 1998.

Mackenzie, Henry. *The Lounger* 20 (18 June 1785). In *Novel and Romance 1700–1800: A Documentary Record*, ed. Ioan Williams. London: Routledge and Kegan Paul, 1970.

———. *The Man of Feeling*. 1771. New York: Norton, 1958.

The Man of Manners; or, Plebeian Polish'd: Being Plain and Familiar Rules for a modest and Genteel Behaviour, on most of the ordinary Occasions of Life. 3d ed. London, 1735.

Marcus, Steven. *The Other Victorians: A Study of Sexuality and Pornography in Mid-Nineteenth-Century England*. New York: Basic, 1966.

Markley, Robert. "Sentimentality as Performance: Shaftesbury, Sterne, and the Theatrics of Virtue." In *The New Eighteenth Century: Theory, Politics, English Literature*, ed. Felicity Nussbaum and Laura Brown. New York: Methuen, 1987.

Marshall, David. *The Figure of Theater: Shaftesbury, Defoe, Adam Smith, and George Eliot*. New York: Columbia University Press, 1986.

McKendrick, Neil. "George Packwood and the Commercialization of Shaving: The Art of Eighteenth-Century Advertising; or, 'The Way to Get Money and Be Happy.'" In *The Birth of a Consumer Society: The Commercialization of Eighteenth-Century England*, ed. Neil McKendrick, John Brewer, and J. H. Plumb. Bloomington: Indiana University Press, 1982.

Moore, Barrington, Jr. *Privacy: Studies in Social and Cultural History*. Armonk, N.Y.: M. E. Sharpe, 1984.

Mullan, John. *Sentiment and Sociability: The Language of Feeling in the Eighteenth Century*. Oxford: Clarendon, 1988.

Neill, Elizabeth. *Rites of Privacy and the Privacy Trade: On the Limits of Protection for the Self*. Montreal: McGill–Queen's University Press, 2001.

Novak, Maximillian E., ed. *English Literature in the Age of Disguise*. Berkeley and Los Angeles: University of California Press, 1977.

Nussbaum, Felicity. *The Autobiographical Subject: Gender and Ideology in Eighteenth-Century England*. Baltimore: Johns Hopkins University Press, 1989.

Pearson, Jacqueline. *Women's Reading in Britain, 1750–1835: A Dangerous Recreation*. Cambridge: Cambridge University Press, 1999.

Pennington, Lady [Sophia]. *An Unfortunate Mother's Advice to her Absent Daughters*. 1761. In *The Young Lady's Pocket Library, or Parental Monitor*. 1790. Bristol: Thoemmes Press, 1995.

Pilkington, Laetitia. *Memoirs of Laetitia Pilkington.* 1748, 1754. Ed. A. C. Elias Jr. 2 vols. Athens: University of Georgia Press, 1997.

Pope, Alexander. *The Poems of Alexander Pope.* Ed. John Butt. New Haven, Conn.: Yale University Press, 1963.

Porter, Roy. "Mixed Feelings: The Enlightenment and Sexuality in Eighteenth-Century Britain." In *Sexuality in Eighteenth-Century Britain,* ed. Paul-Gabriel Boucé. Totowa, N.J.: Barnes and Noble, 1982.

Pratt, Walter F. *Privacy in Britain.* Lewisburg, Pa.: Bucknell University Press, 1979.

Radway, Janice A. *Reading the Romance: Women, Patriarchy, and Popular Literature.* Chapel Hill: University of North Carolina Press, 1991.

Reiman, Jeffrey H. "Privacy, Intimacy, and Personhood." In *Philosophical Dimensions of Privacy: An Anthology,* ed. Ferdinand David Schoeman. Cambridge: Cambridge University Press, 1984.

Richardson, Samuel. *Clarissa.* 1748. 4 vols. London: Dent, 1932.

Richetti, John. "The Public Sphere and the Eighteenth-Century Novel: Social Criticism and Narrative Enactment." In "Manners of Reading: Essays in Honor of Thomas R. Edwards," ed. Adam Potkay and Robert Maccubbin. Special issue of *Eighteenth Century Life* 16, n.s. 3 (1992): 114–29.

Rosen, Jeffrey. *The Unwanted Gaze: The Destruction of Privacy in America.* New York: Random House, 2000.

Ross, Deborah. "Mirror, Mirror: The Didactic Dilemma of *The Female Quixote.*" *Studies in English Literature* 27 (1987): 455–73.

Rousseau, Jean-Jacques. *Julie, or, The New Heloise: Letters of Two Lovers Who Live in a Small Town at the Foot of the Alps.* 1758. Trans. and annotated by Philip Stewart and Jean Vaché. Hanover, N.H.: University Press of New England, 1997.

Rybczynski, Witold. *Home: A Short History of an Idea.* New York: Viking, 1986.

Ryder, Dudley. *The Diary of Dudley Ryder, 1715–1716.* Ed. William Matthews. London: Methuen, 1939.

Schoeman, Ferdinand David. *Privacy and Social Freedom.* Cambridge: Cambridge University Press, 1992.

Scott, Sarah. *Millenium Hall.* 1762. Ed. Gary Kelly. Peterborough, Ontario: Broadview, 1995.

Sennett, Richard. *The Fall of Public Man: On the Social Psychology of Capitalism.* New York: Vintage, 1978.

Shaftesbury, Anthony Ashley Cooper, Third Earl of. *An Inquiry Concerning Virtue, or Merit.* 1699. Ed. David Walford. Manchester: Manchester University Press, 1977.

Sheridan, Frances. *Memoirs of Miss Sidney Bidulph.* 1761. Ed. Patricia Köster and Jean Coates Cleary. Oxford: Oxford University Press, 1995.

Sherman, Stuart. *Telling Time: Clocks, Diaries, and English Diurnal Form, 1660–1785.* Chicago: University of Chicago Press, 1996.

Silber, John R. "Masks and Fig Leaves." In *Privacy,* ed. J. Roland Pennock and John W. Chapman. *Nomos* 13. New York: Atherton, 1971.

Simmel, Arnold. "Privacy Is Not an Isolated Freedom." In *Privacy,* ed. J. Roland Pennock and John W. Chapman. *Nomos* 13. New York: Atherton, 1971.

Smith, Adam. *The Theory of Moral Sentiments.* Ed. D. D. Raphael and A. L. Macfie. Oxford: Clarendon, 1976.

Smith, Charlotte. *The Poems of Charlotte Smith.* Ed. Stuart Curran. New York: Oxford University Press, 1993.

Smith, Janna Malamud. *Private Matters: In Defense of the Personal Life.* Reading, Mass.: Addison-Wesley, 1997.

Smollett, Tobias. *Peregrine Pickle.* 1751. 4 vols. Oxford: Blackwell, 1925.

Spacks, Patricia Meyer. *Desire and Truth: Functions of Plot in Eighteenth-Century English Novels.* Chicago: University of Chicago Press, 1990.

Sterne, Laurence. *The Life and Opinions of Tristram Shandy, Gentleman.* 1759–67. Ed. James Aiken Work. New York: Odyssey, 1940.

———. *A Sentimental Journey through France and Italy.* 1768. Ed. Graham Petrie. London: Penguin, 1967.

[Stillingfleet, Benjamin.] *An Essay on Conversation.* Dublin, 1737.

Stone, Lawrence. *Road to Divorce: England, 1530–1987.* Oxford: Oxford University Press, 1990.

Swift, Jonathan. *Swift's Polite Conversation.* Ed. Eric Partridge. London: André Deutsch, 1963.

Thompson, Lynda M. *The "Scandalous Memoirists": Constantia Phillips, Laetitia Pilkington, and the Shame of "Publick Fame."* Manchester: Manchester University Press, 2000.

Tomalin, Claire. *Jane Austen: A Life.* New York: Knopf, 1998.

Van Den Haag, Ernest. "On Privacy." In *Privacy,* ed. J. Roland Pennock and John W. Chapman. *Nomos* 13. New York: Atherton, 1971.

Van Sant, Ann. *Eighteenth-Century Sensibility and the Novel: The Senses in a Social Context.* Cambridge: Cambridge University Press, 1993.

Velecky, Lubor C. "The Concept of Privacy." In *Privacy,* ed. John B. Young. New York: John Wiley, 1978.

Wagner, Peter. *Eros Revived: Erotica of the Enlightenment in England and America.* London: Secker and Warburg, 1988.

———. "The Pornographer in the Courtroom: Trial Reports about Cases of Sexual Crimes and Delinquencies as a Genre of Eighteenth-Century Erotica." In *Sexuality in Eighteenth-Century Britain,* ed. Paul-Gabriel Boucé. Totowa, N.J.: Barnes and Noble, 1982.

Wardhaugh, Ronald. *How Conversation Works.* Oxford: Blackwell, 1985.

Warren, Samuel D., and Louis D. Brandeis. "The Right to Privacy." 1890. In *Philosophical Dimensions of Privacy: An Anthology,* ed. Ferdinand David Schoeman. Cambridge: Cambridge University Press, 1984.

Weinstein, Michael A. "The Uses of Privacy in the Good Life." In *Privacy,* ed. J. Roland Pennock and John W. Chapman. *Nomos* 13. New York: Atherton, 1971.

Wesley, John. *The Journal of the Rev. John Wesley, A.M.* 4 vols. London: Dent, 1906.

Westin, Alan F. *Privacy and Freedom.* New York: Atheneum, 1967.

Wollstonecraft, Mary. *Mary* and *The Wrongs of Woman.* 1788, 1798. Ed. Gary Kelly. Oxford: Oxford University Press, 1976.

Woodforde, James. *The Diary of a Country Parson, 1758–1802*. Ed. John Beresford. London: Oxford University Press, 1935.

Wright, Lawrence. *Clean and Decent: The Fascinating History of the Bathroom and the Water Closet and of Sundry Habits, Fashions, and Accessories of the Toilet Principally in Great Britain, France, and America*. London: Routledge and Kegan Paul, 1960.

Young, John B. "Introduction: A Look at Privacy." In *Privacy*, ed. John B. Young. New York: Wiley, 1978.

Index

Adams, Samuel and Sarah, 197–98
affectation. *See* self-display
Allen, Anita L., 23
ambiguity, 56–57, 63, 79, 82
Ancourt, Abbé d', 111
anxiety, 27, 29, 55, 63, 78, 82–83, 90, 95, 116
appearances, 90, 119, 154, 187, 189–90, 192.
    See also performance, social
Ariès, Philippe, 3
Austen, Jane, 10–12, 30–35, 40–41, 44, 87,
    109–13, 141, 184. Works: *Mansfield Park*,
    11, 31, 113; *Northanger Abbey*, 10; *Pride
    and Prejudice*, 30, 32, 34, 40–41; *Sense
    and Sensibility*, 11, 31, 109–10, 112–13,
    197, 228
autobiography: scandalous, 147, 150; versus
    memoir, 146–47, 190
autonomy, and concept of privacy, 3, 9,
    24–25, 195

Barker-Benfield, G. J., 58
Benedict, Barbara M., 5, 50, 80
Beresford, John Baldwyn, 170
Blackburn, J., 22
book clubs, 30
Boswell, James, 13, 115, 120, 141–47, 149,
    151–53, 155–57, 160, 169–70, 182, 185.
    Works: *Life of Johnson*, 143; *London Jour-
    nal*, 142–46, 152, 185
Brandeis, Louis D., 19, 29
Brissenden, R. F., 58
Bromwich, David, 34
Brontë, Charlotte, 29, 41, 115–16, 125

Brooke, Henry, 126
Burke, Peter, 116
Burney, Frances (Fanny), 11–12, 25, 58, 63–
    64, 67–68, 71–73, 79, 85, 87–88, 92, 94,
    97–99, 101–4, 107–9, 111–12, 114, 166,
    169, 190–95, 223–25. Works: *Camilla, or,
    A Picture of Youth*, 58, 63, 72, 74, 84, 94,
    104; *Cecilia, or, Memoirs of an Heiress*, 87,
    98–99, 101–4, 224; *Evelina*, 194–95, 224;
    The Wanderer, or, Female Difficulties, 92–
    93, 97, 99, 102, 107, 223–24
Burton, Robert, 200–201, 217

Carr, Peter, 79
Castan, Yves, 149
Chapone, Hester, 113
Chartier, Roger, 28
Cleland, John, 154, 156–58, 161; *Fanny Hill,
    or, Memoirs of a Woman of Pleasure*, 154,
    156–58, 161, 223
clothing, women's, eighteenth-century, 145
community: of feeling, 38, 53, 55–56; and
    reading, 34–35, 39–49, 52, 128–29; versus
    self (individual), 21, 115, 201, 223, 226–27
compliance, 111
concealment, as form of privacy, 11–12,
    77–80, 87–88, 92, 96, 101, 107–8, 116,
    119, 146, 224, 226. *See also* self-
    concealment
conduct books (manuals), 91–92, 98, 103,
    110–11, 122, 124
Constable, John, 118–20, 129, 131
convention. *See* rules, social

237

conversation: and good breeding, 122–23; and personal relationship, 121–22, 139; persuasive power of, 133; with the reader, 131–32; social, 12, 14, 115, 155, 186, 225; and social roles, 122, 134; as sexual congress, 129

conversation manuals, 116–17, 119–20, 123, 129–31, 139

countenance, 187. See also masks, social

country house, and physical privacy, 6–7, 197, 199

courtship, 188, 192–93

Cowper, William, 6, 8, 10, 14–15, 25, 201–17, 219–20, 222, 223–24, 228

Cox, Stephen, 128

curiosity, in eighteenth-century Britain, 5

D'Arblay, Frances Burney. See Burney, Frances (Fanny)

decorum, social, 11–13, 97, 101, 103, 105, 107, 109–10, 136, 194

Defoe, Daniel, 25, 60, 129. Works: The Fortunes and Misfortunes of the Famous Moll Flanders, 129, 131–32, 134; Roxana, 9

delicacy, 95–98, 103, 107, 111

depression, and poetry, 203

diaries, 167–69, 171, 173, 177, 179, 184–90, 195, 225, 227–28; as artificial memory, 178; in cipher, 182, 185; eighteenth-century, 13–15, 24, 26, 181–82, 195; published, 168

Dickinson, Emily, 28

didacticism, 39, 73, 137, 139

discourse, formal, and conversation, 122

discretion, 67–68, 70

dissimulation, 98, 101, 103, 109–10

divorce, and women, in the eighteenth century, 149–50, 159

domesticity, and privacy, 202, 204–5. See also privacy, domestic

Doody, Margaret Anne, 224

Drummond, William, of Hawthornden, 199–201

Dyer, John, 198

Edgeworth, Maria, 61

Elias, A. C., Jr., 151

Elias, Norbert, 116

Elizabeth, first duchess of Northumberland, 177–81, 184, 191, 195

Ellis, Markman, 58

emotion(s), 32, 38–39, 41, 47–49, 51, 56, 63, 74, 82, 90, 100, 120, 126, 187–88, 193, 216, 218, 221, 227

epistolary narrative/novel, 59–60, 105, 190, 224

Ernst, Morris, 23

erotica, 158, 225. See also pornography

eroticism, and privacy, 13

Eskimo culture, 89, 196

etiquette, as a device for self-concealment, 12, 89

Etzioni, Amitai, 23

fantasy, resulting from reading, 27–29, 44, 48

feminism, nascent, 163

Fielding, Henry, 15, 25, 35–36, 38–42, 44, 48–49, 52–53, 55, 99, 129, 156. Works: Amelia, 37; The History of Tom Jones, A Foundling, 15, 36–37, 39–40, 131; Joseph Andrews, 99

Fielding, Sarah, 44–49, 53, 85, 126. Works: The Adventures of David Simple, 44–45, 48, 85, 126, 133, 135; Volume the Last, 48

Flaherty, David H., 20

food (menus), in diaries, 170–71, 177

Fordyce, James, 29

Foucault, Michel, 5

Freud, Sigmund, 168

Fried, Charles, 21–22

Gaskell, Elizabeth, 115–16, 125

Gavison, Ruth, 21

gender, and notions of privacy, 25, 95–96, 149. See also privacy, female

generalization, as a narrative mode, 137

Genuine Memoirs of the Celebrated Miss Maria Brown, 158, 161–65

Gerstein, Robert S., 21

Gillis, Christina Marsden, 19

Gilman, Charlotte Perkins, 4

Girouard, Mark, 6, 197

Gisborne, Thomas, 96

Goldsmith, Oliver, 25, 120–21, 123–26,

128–29; *The Vicar of Wakefield*, 120, 124–25, 127, 223
Goulemot, Jean Marie, 147
Gregory, John, 124
Gross, Hyman, 153–54
Guazzo, Stephen, 117–18, 120, 127

Habermas, Jürgen, 4, 6, 8–9, 142
Hagstrum, Jean H., 141
Harvey, A. D., 147
Haywood, Eliza, 55, 198
Heasel, Anthony, 198
Hecht, J. Jean, 197–98
heteroclite, 151, 156
Horace, 199, 202
Hudson, Nicholas, 36, 38
Hume, David, 61
Hunter, J. Paul, 27, 39–40
Hussey, Christopher, 6
hypocrisy, and privacy, 5, 12–13, 15, 17, 24, 55–56, 67–68, 70, 87, 89, 92, 95, 98, 101–3, 107, 113, 116, 118–19, 151, 154–56, 164, 224, 226, 228
hysteria, nineteenth-century, 11–12

imagination, 69, 71, 82–83. *See also* reading, and imagination
Imbarrato, Susan Clair, 79
impotence (sexual inadequacy), 159–61, 166
Inchbald, Elizabeth, 72, 74, 77–79, 84–85
individualism, and privacy, 15, 23–24, 85, 137
industrialization, and privacy, 153
Ingham, Roger, 23
Inness, Julie C., 20–21
innocence, 69–70
integrity, and concept of privacy, 3, 92, 97, 156
interpretation, 31–33, 46, 49, 71–72, 81
intimacy, 21–22, 24, 129, 167, 172, 177, 224
introspection, versus objectivity, in diaries, 181
irony, 32, 36, 79, 131, 165
Iser, Wolfgang, 36, 38

Jackson, H. J., 30
Jagodzinski, Cecile M., 27
Jefferson, Thomas, 79

Johnson, Claudia L., 68
Johnson, Samuel, 16–17, 42, 88, 115–16, 118, 122
Johnstone, Charles, 158, 165–66
journal-writing, 142–43, 169, 190–95. *See also* diaries

Kilgour, Maggie, 34
Kinkead-Weekes, Mark, 38
Klein, Lawrence, 25, 120

Lambert, Anne-Thérèse, Marchioness de, 90
Langbauer, Laurie, 42
Langford, Paul, 88
Laslett, Peter, 197
lechery, 151
legal discourse, and the notion of privacy, 19. *See also* privacy, as a right
Lennox, Charlotte, 42–44, 53–54, 85; *The Female Quixote*, 43, 85, 139, 196, 199
letter-writing (letters), 142, 169, 190–93
literacy, spread of, in the eighteenth century, 9
Locke, John, 51, 122–23, 125
love, 10, 103, 125, 144–45, 155, 193–94
Lynch, Deidre Shauna, 30–31, 34–35

Mackenzie, Henry, 125–28, 157; *The Man of Feeling*, 125, 127–28, 133, 135
Man of Manners, The, 91
manners, 12, 85–86, 87–88, 91, 94–95, 97–98, 100, 102, 105, 109–11, 113, 155, 225
Marcus, Steven, 153, 157, 163
Markley, Robert, 126
marriage, 103–4, 137–38, 182–83, 188
Marshall, David, 57, 60
masks, social (persona), 89, 226
McKendrick, Neil, 144
memoirs, 147–48, 151, 159, 161
memory, 222
Milton, John, 198
moderation, in privacy, 65
money: in diaries, 171; need for, by women, 161, 164–66
Moore, Barrington, Jr., 89, 167, 196
morality, 117, 123
Mullan, John, 58

Neill, Elizabeth, 20, 56, 67
Nin, Anaïs, 169
Novak, Maximillian E., 55
novel, of manners, 25, 87, 92
novels, and novelists, eighteenth-century
English, 8–11, 14–19, 146, 157,
159, 177
Nussbaum, Felicity, 152

Partridge, Eric, 119
Pearson, Jacqueline, 30, 34
Pennington, Lady [Sophia], 89
Pepys, Samuel, 7, 169, 182
performance: conversation as, 125; social,
and privacy, 5, 12, 57, 90, 98, 143, 186,
192, 228
Pilkington, Laetitia, 147–57, 160–61,
162, 166
poetry, 198–200, 202–13, 220, 222, 227;
of privacy, 201, 214, 216; of sensibility,
216–17; and sorrow, 218
Pope, Alexander, 38, 117, 169, 198, 202, 218;
"Ode on Solitude," 198
pornography, 13, 26, 29, 153–54, 157–60, 163
Porter, Roy, 144, 147
power, social, 75, 77, 79, 84–85, 105, 164
Pratt, Walter F., 22
privacy: as authenticity, 8; and choice, 3, 7,
13, 21, 24, 68, 71, 85; and community,
34, 103, 128; as a danger, 104; definitions,
1–2, 19–20, 23–24, 103; domestic, 149–
50, 222; in eighteenth-century Britain, 5;
emotional, 68, 74–75, 77–78, 96, 98; failure of, 105; female, 95–97, 99, 217, 225;
as a form of enablement, 14; of the heart,
66, 96–97; imaginative, 29; individual
versus family, 4, 5; and isolation, 89–90
(see also seclusion; solitude; privacy, physical); as limitation, 128; and love, 124–25,
127; and melancholy, 200; narrative, 105;
personal, 94, 109–10, 112, 224; physical,
5–7, 16, 30, 88, 90, 98, 196, 198, 210, 217;
physical, and architecture, 6, 140, 202;
politics of, 92–93; and power, 73, 79, 195;
psychological, 5–8, 11, 67, 91, 96–97,
120, 140, 222, 223, 228; as a right or
privilege, 2, 3, 19–22, 94, 104, 223;
rural, 216; and self-exposure, 60, 151

(see also concealment; self-concealment);
sexual, 158; and social class, 1, 3, 7, 10,
87–88, 92–94, 99, 127, 197–98; of the
soul, 17, 157; treatment by women writers,
85; twentieth-century theory of, 167;
in twenty-first century, 1–3, 8; as a value,
23; and values (family/community/
societal), 3, 7–8
private reading/private readers, 41–44,
48–49, 53–54, 226
propriety, 12, 14, 95–98, 100, 107, 110
prostitution, 142, 158, 162–165, 204
public oratory, 121
public, versus private, 1, 3–5, 8–9, 25, 62,
115–16, 152, 159, 168, 179, 215

Radcliffe, Ann, 58, 64
Radway, Janice A., 28
rage (anger), and sensibility, 149–51, 161,
163–65, 225
rape, 157, 162
readers: implied (imagined), 35–38, 40–41,
43, 47–52, 61–62, 79, 81, 109; real,
61–62, 79, 83–84; role in eighteenth-
century writing, 17–18, 26
reading: by characters in novels, 30, 42–43;
female, 45; and imagination, 28, 51; novel,
27–32; and privacy, 6, 9–10, 13–14, 28, 30,
62, 225–26; studies of, 35
reading aloud, 30
reading groups. See book clubs
Redford, Bruce, 52
Reiman, Jeffery H., 21
reserve, psychological, 21, 66, 228. See also
decorum, social; privacy, psychological
responsibility, social, 14, 112, 214, 228
Richardson, Samuel, 6–7, 16–19, 25, 61, 146,
157–58, 224. Works: Clarissa, 15, 17–19,
137, 146, 156, 223–24; Pamela, 137, 148,
154, 156
Richetti, John, 8–9
romances (subgenre of novel), 10, 28,
42–43, 45
romanticism, 29
Rosen, Jeffrey, 89
Ross, Deborah, 42
Rousseau, Jean-Jacques, 55–63, 74, 81,
83–84, 143

rules: for conversation, 116–18; social, 111, 123, 223–24, 227–28
Rybczynski, Witold, 140
Ryder, Dudley, 182–83, 185–89, 195, 223, 228

satire, 225
scandal (scandalous narrative), and privacy, 14, 141, 152–53, 159, 161, 164, 169–70, 225
Schoeman, Ferdinand David, 23–25, 93
Schwartz, Alan U., 23
Scott, Sarah, 133–39
seclusion, and privacy, 5, 14, 197, 200, 205, 214, 216
secrecy (secrets), and privacy, 5, 15, 124, 141, 197
self-concealment, 56, 67, 70, 77, 91, 133, 141, 184, 195, 210, 219, 227. *See also* concealment
self-disguise, 117–18
self-display, and conversation, 118, 121, 123
self-doubt, 189–90, 209, 211
self-protection: and conversation, 115, 120, 132; and gender, 74; privacy as a mode of, 13, 111, 113, 141, 194, 224
Sennett, Richard, 8
sensibility, 10–14, 56–58, 61, 63–64, 69, 71–73, 75, 77–78, 82–84, 87, 97, 128, 143–45, 151, 155–57, 160, 165, 217, 222; novels of, 38, 63, 158, 225; and privacy, 11, 56, 61, 85, 228; and sexuality, 141, 146, 225; synonyms for, 76
sentiment (sentimentalism), 62, 80, 126
sentimental fiction (novel), 120, 125, 128–29, 133, 225
servants, and privacy, 197–99, 201–2
sex: and money, 158; and publicity, in eighteenth-century England, 140, 144, 166
sexual activity, of the upper class, 144
sexuality, female, in eighteenth-century Britain, 147
Shaftesbury, Anthony Ashley Cooper, Third Earl of, 196–97
Sheridan, Frances, 105–9, 114
Sherman, Stuart, 176, 195

Silber, John R., 70
Simmel, Arnold, 23, 140
Smith, Adam, 39, 41, 61, 90, 169
Smith, Charlotte, 25–26, 216–22. Works: *Beachy Head*, 219–20; *Elegiac Sonnets*, 217; *The Emigrants*, 222
Smith, Janna Malamud, 124, 149
Smollett, Tobias, 151, 158–60. Works: *Humphry Clinker*, 9, 151; *Peregrine Pickle*, 158–59
society, and privacy, 5, 196, 204, 225, 228
solitude: physical, 21, 24, 149, 167, 198–99, 202, 204, 221 (*see also* privacy, physical; seclusion, and privacy); versus company, 117
Spacks, Patricia Meyer, 42
Sterne, Laurence, 11, 25, 35, 49–54, 79–80, 82–84, 157, 227. Works: *A Sentimental Journey*, 79–80, 82–84, 137, 151, 223; *Tristram Shandy*, 49–52, 131, 137
Stillingfleet, Benjamin, 117–18
Stone, Lawrence, 149
Swift, Jonathan, 12, 39–40, 53, 119–20, 122, 147–48, 152, 166
sympathy, capacity for, 55, 57

theatricality, 57, 60
Thompson, Lynda M., 152, 161
Thomson, James, 201–2
Tomalin, Claire, 184
trivial, as subject matter of diaries, 167–68, 172–73, 176, 182–84
Troide, Lars, 190, 192

Van Den Haag, Ernest, 153–54, 156, 167
Vane, Lady Frances, 161
Van Sant, Ann, 58
Velecky, Lubor C., 20
venereal disease, 141–44
violence, 29
virginity (chastity), 156, 161–62; psychological, 155–56
virtue, 90, 98–99, 101
voyeurism, 152, 166, 168

Wagner, Peter, 158
Wardhaugh, Ronald, 168

Warren, Samuel D., 19, 29
weeping, and privacy, 128
Weinstein, Michael A., 2, 20, 167
Wesley, John, 182
Westin, Alan F., 21, 24, 66
Wollstonecraft, Mary, 58, 64, 78, 92
women writers, on sexuality versus victim-
    ization, 147, 150, 160

Woodforde, James, 170–77, 179–81,
    184–85, 195
Woolf, Virginia, 88, 167, 169
Wordsworth, William, 205, 222
Wright, Lawrence, 7
writing, and privacy, 6, 24, 225

Young, John B., 19